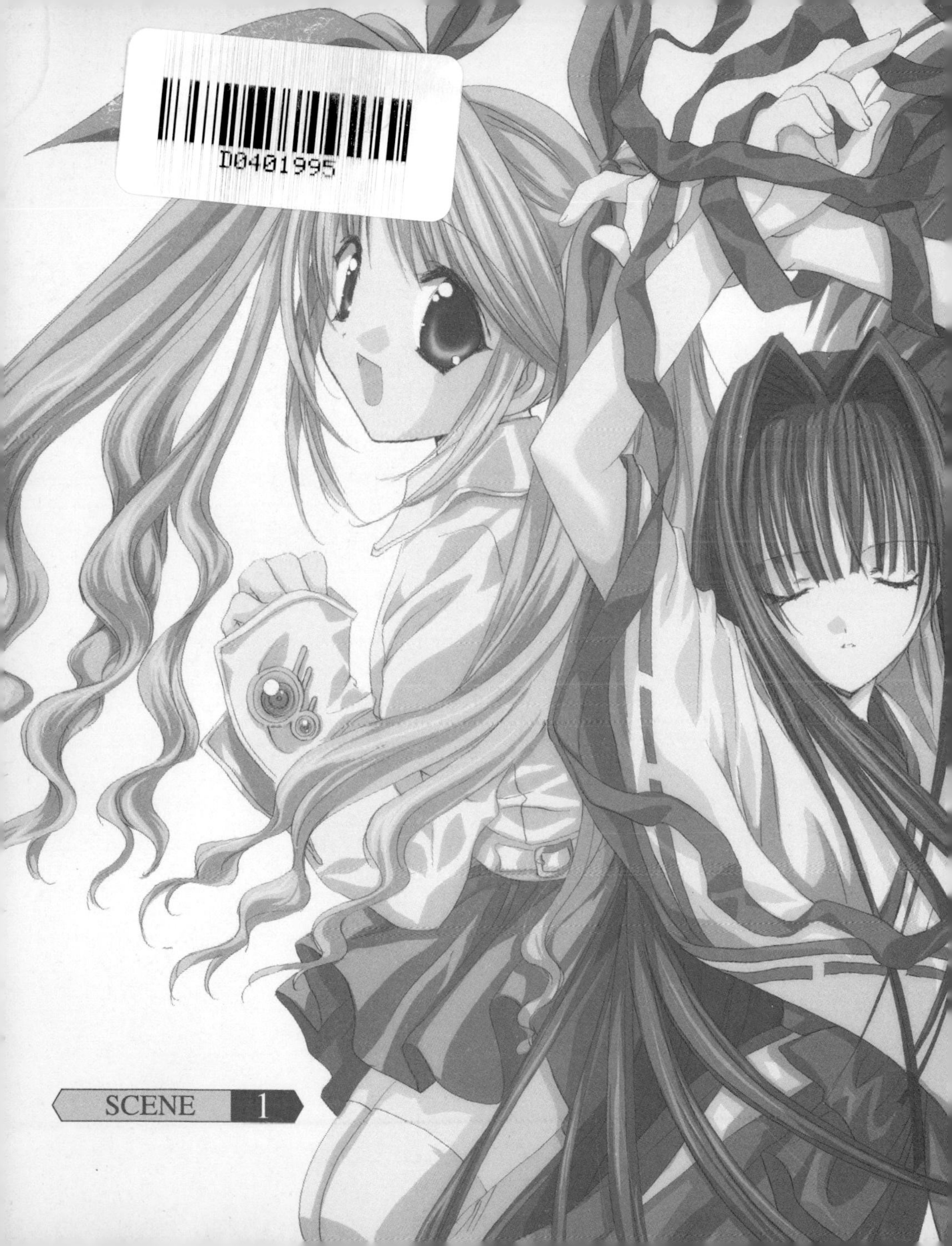

SCENE 1

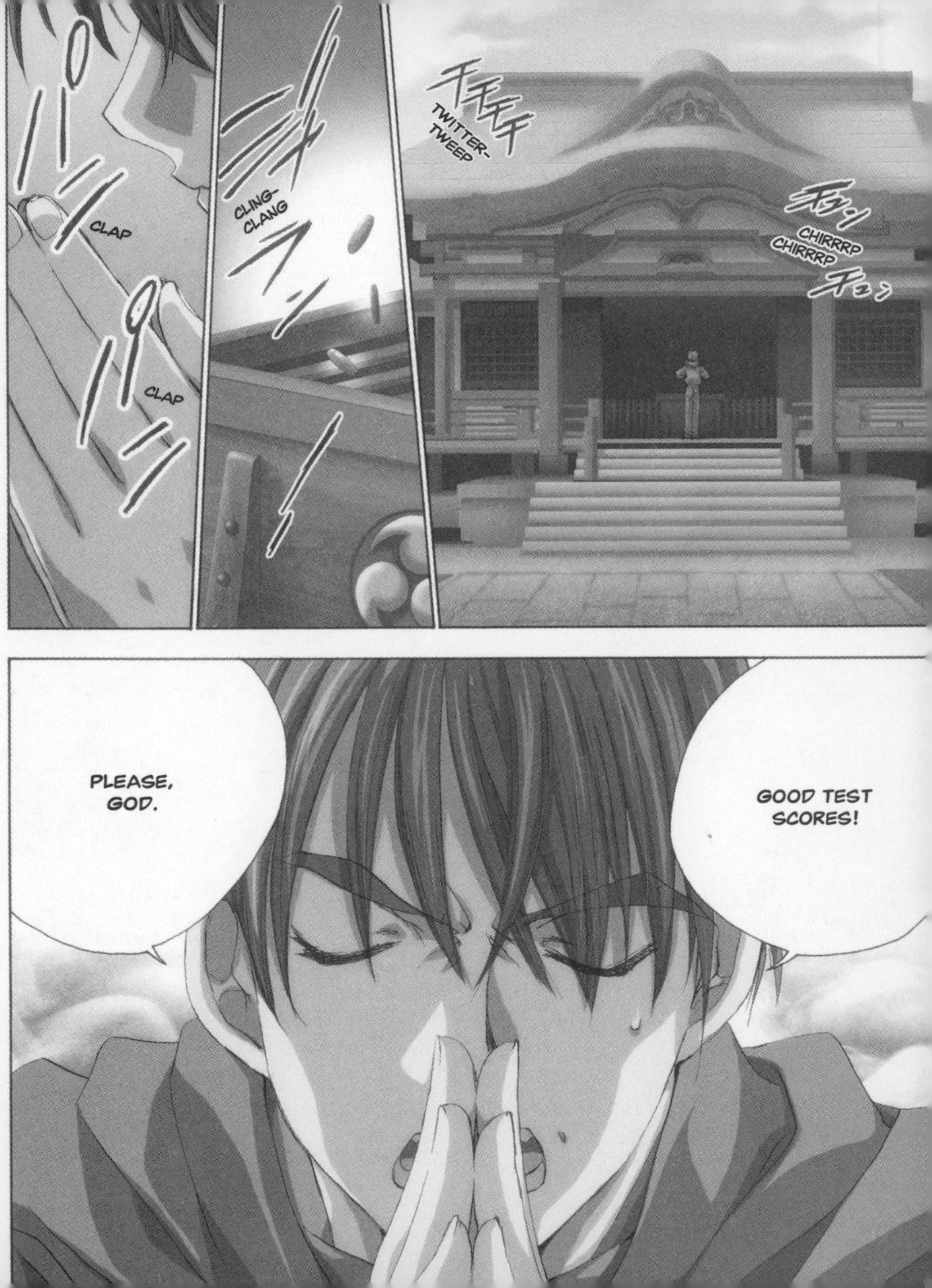
TWITTER-TWEEP
CHIRRRP CHIRRRP
CLING-CLANG
CLAP
CLAP
PLEASE, GOD.
GOOD TEST SCORES!

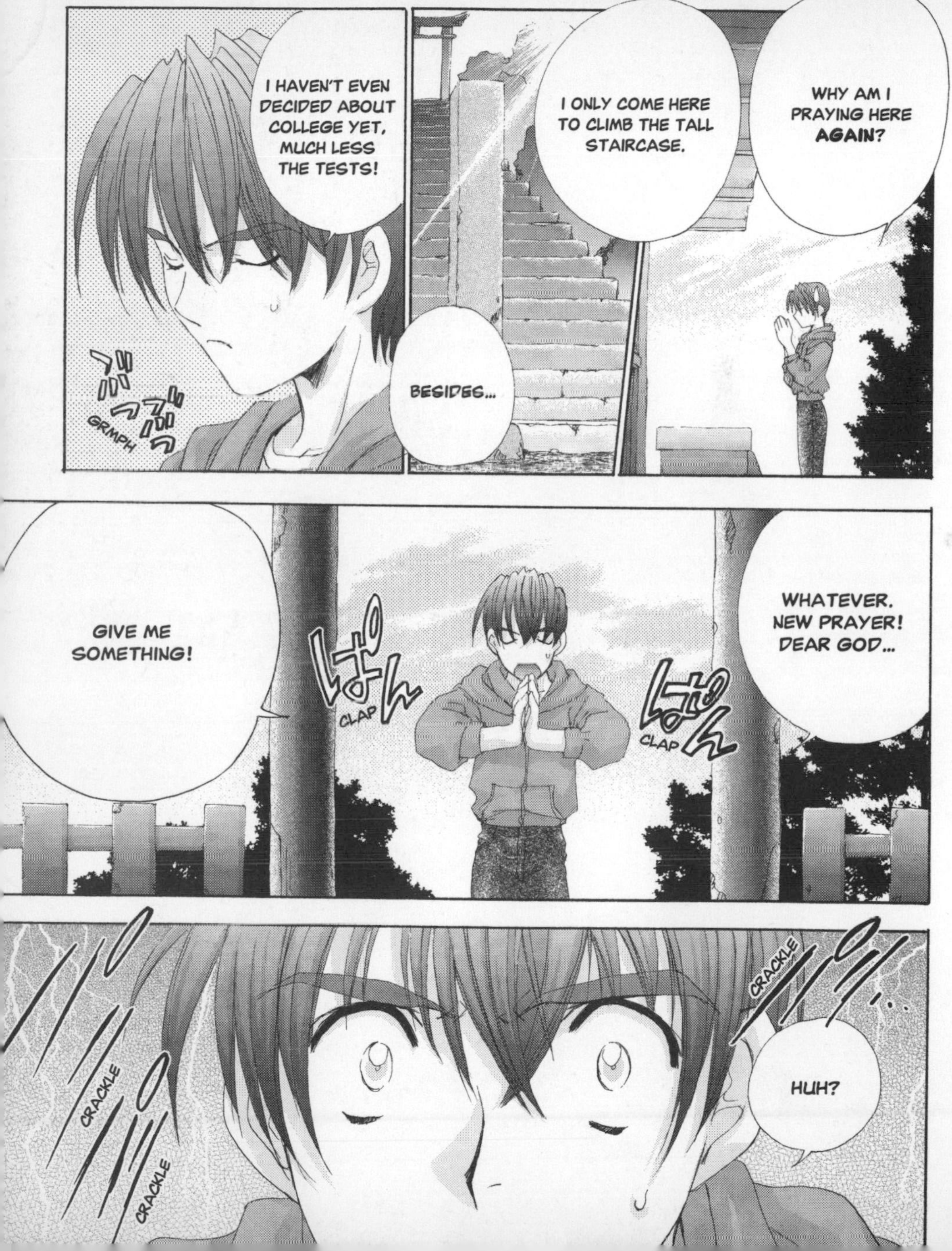
WHY AM I PRAYING HERE AGAIN?
I ONLY COME HERE TO CLIMB THE TALL STAIRCASE.
BESIDES...
I HAVEN'T EVEN DECIDED ABOUT COLLEGE YET, MUCH LESS THE TESTS!
GRMPH
WHATEVER. NEW PRAYER! DEAR GOD...
CLAP
CLAP
GIVE ME SOMETHING!
CRACKLE
HUH?
CRACKLE
CRACKLE

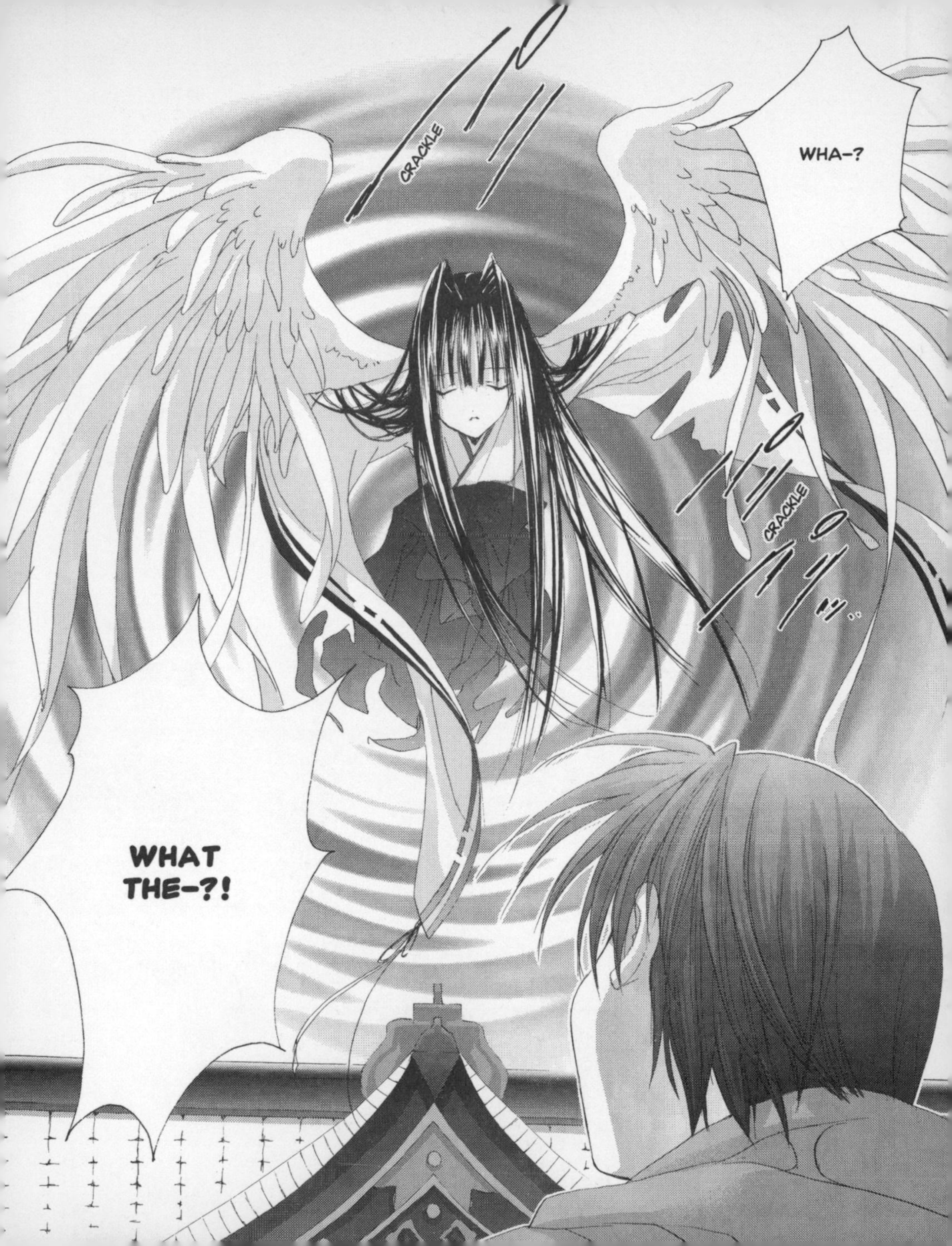
WHA-?
CRACKLE
CRACKLE
WHAT THE-?!

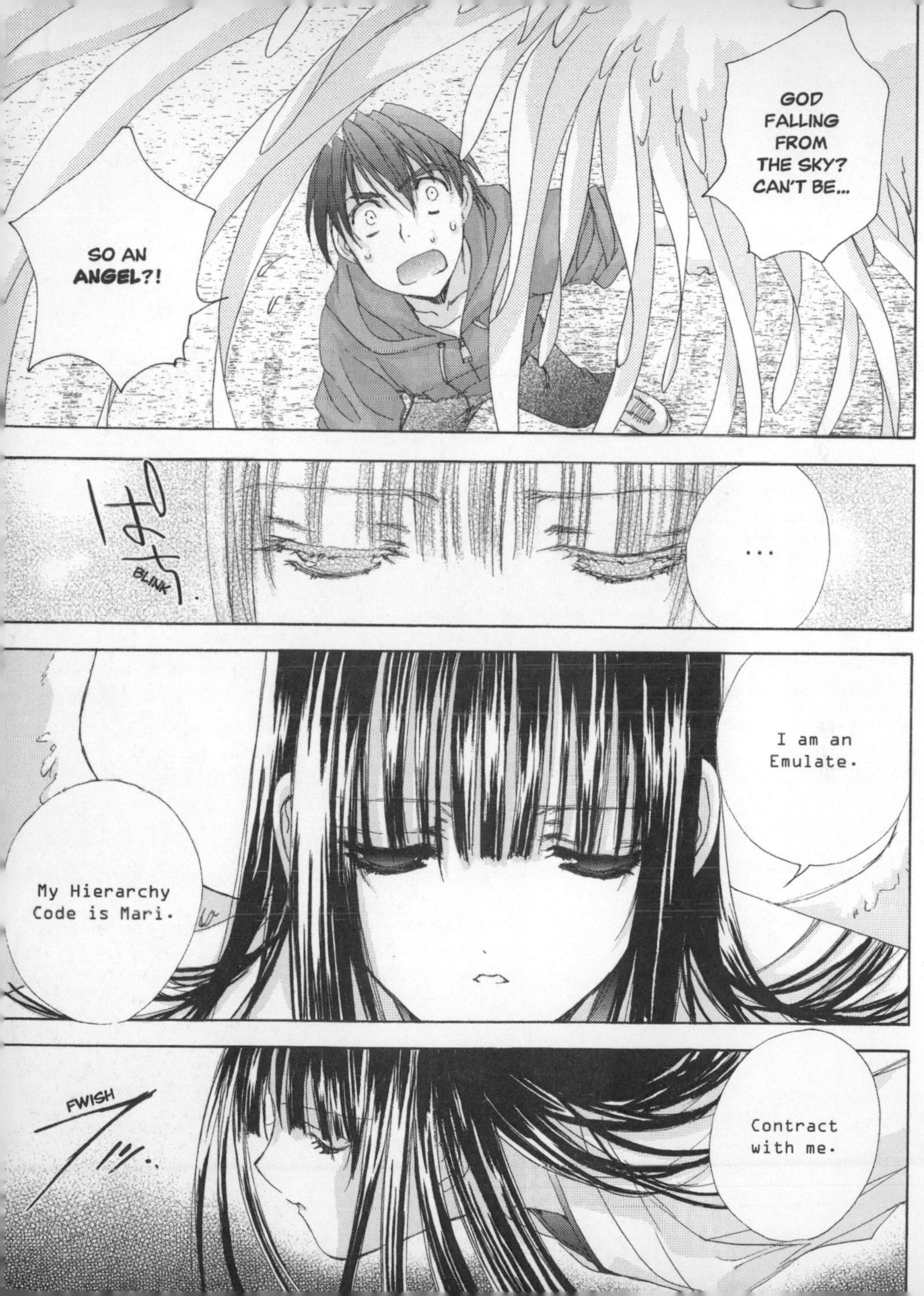
GOD FALLING FROM THE SKY? CAN'T BE...
SO AN ANGEL?!
...
BLINK
I am an Emulate.
My Hierarchy Code is Mari.
Contract with me.
FWISH

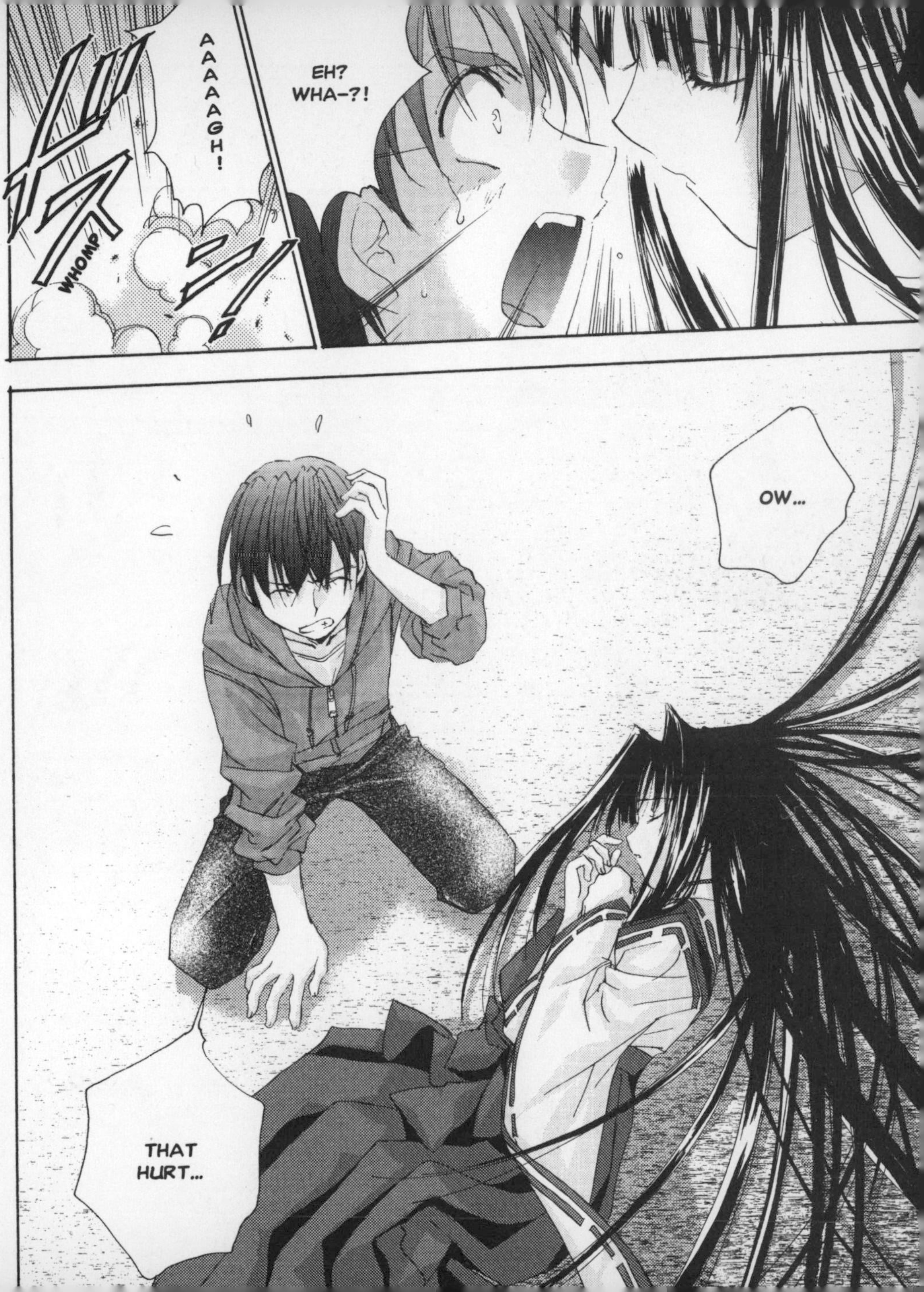

EH? WHA-?!
AAAAAAGH!
WHOMP
OW...
THAT HURT...

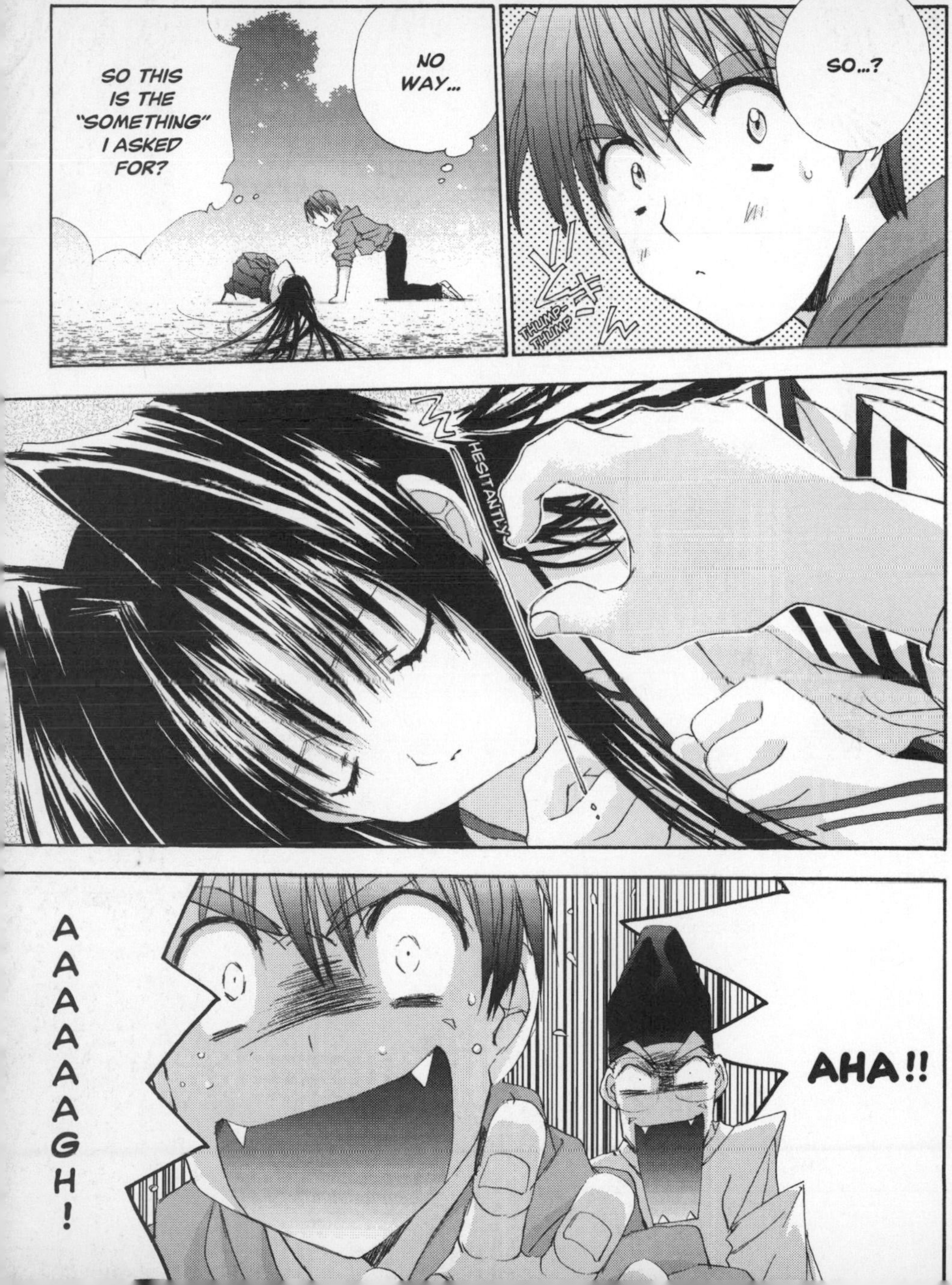
SO...?
THUMP-THUMP
NO WAY...
SO THIS IS THE "SOMETHING" I ASKED FOR?
HESITANTLY
AHA!!
AAAAAAAAGH!

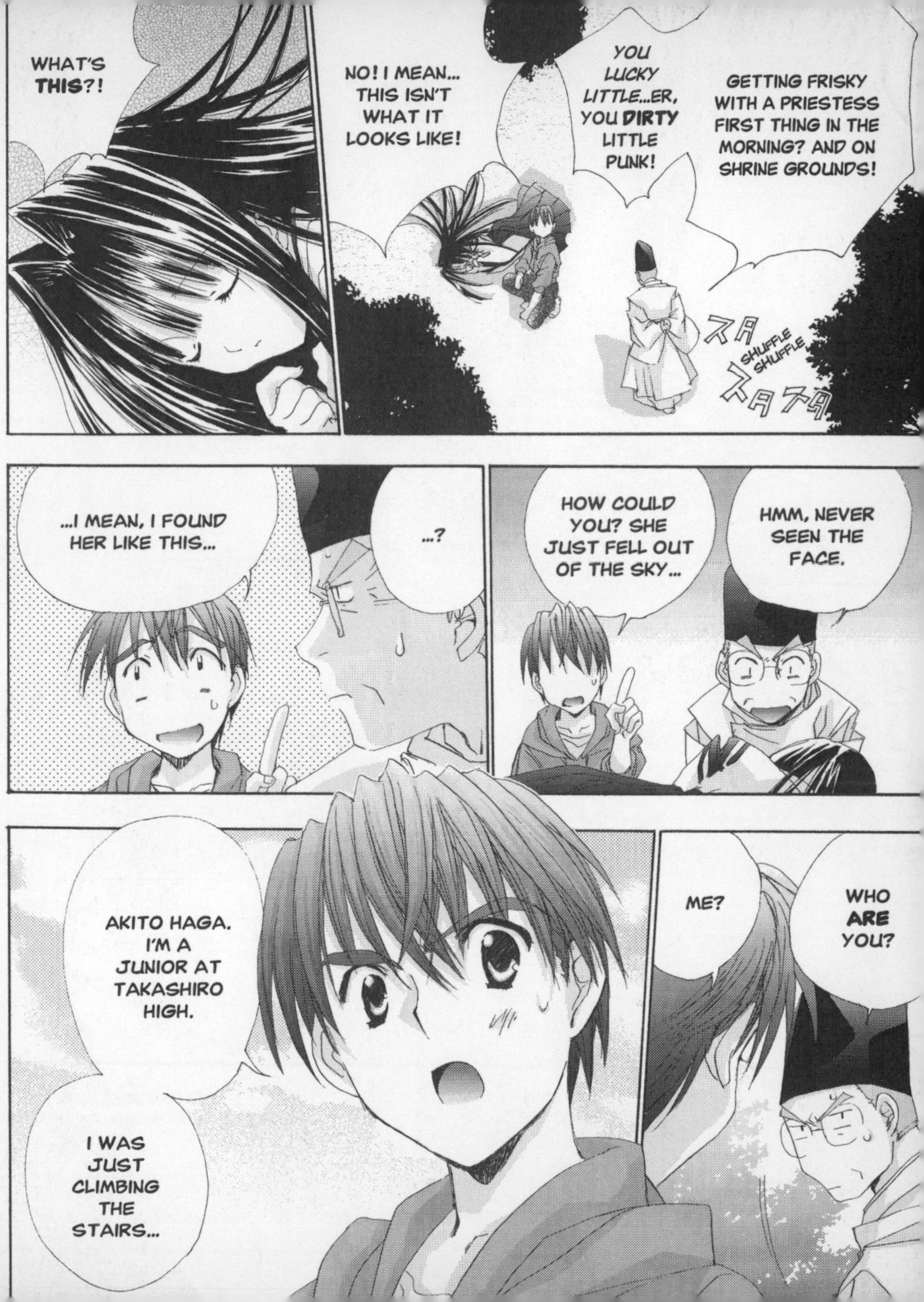
GETTING FRISKY WITH A PRIESTESS FIRST THING IN THE MORNING? AND ON SHRINE GROUNDS!
YOU LUCKY LITTLE...ER, YOU DIRTY LITTLE PUNK!
NO! I MEAN... THIS ISN'T WHAT IT LOOKS LIKE!
SHUFFLE SHUFFLE
WHAT'S THIS?!
HMM, NEVER SEEN THE FACE.
HOW COULD YOU? SHE JUST FELL OUT OF THE SKY...
...?
...I MEAN, I FOUND HER LIKE THIS...
WHO ARE YOU?
ME?
AKITO HAGA. I'M A JUNIOR AT TAKASHIRO HIGH.
I WAS JUST CLIMBING THE STAIRS...

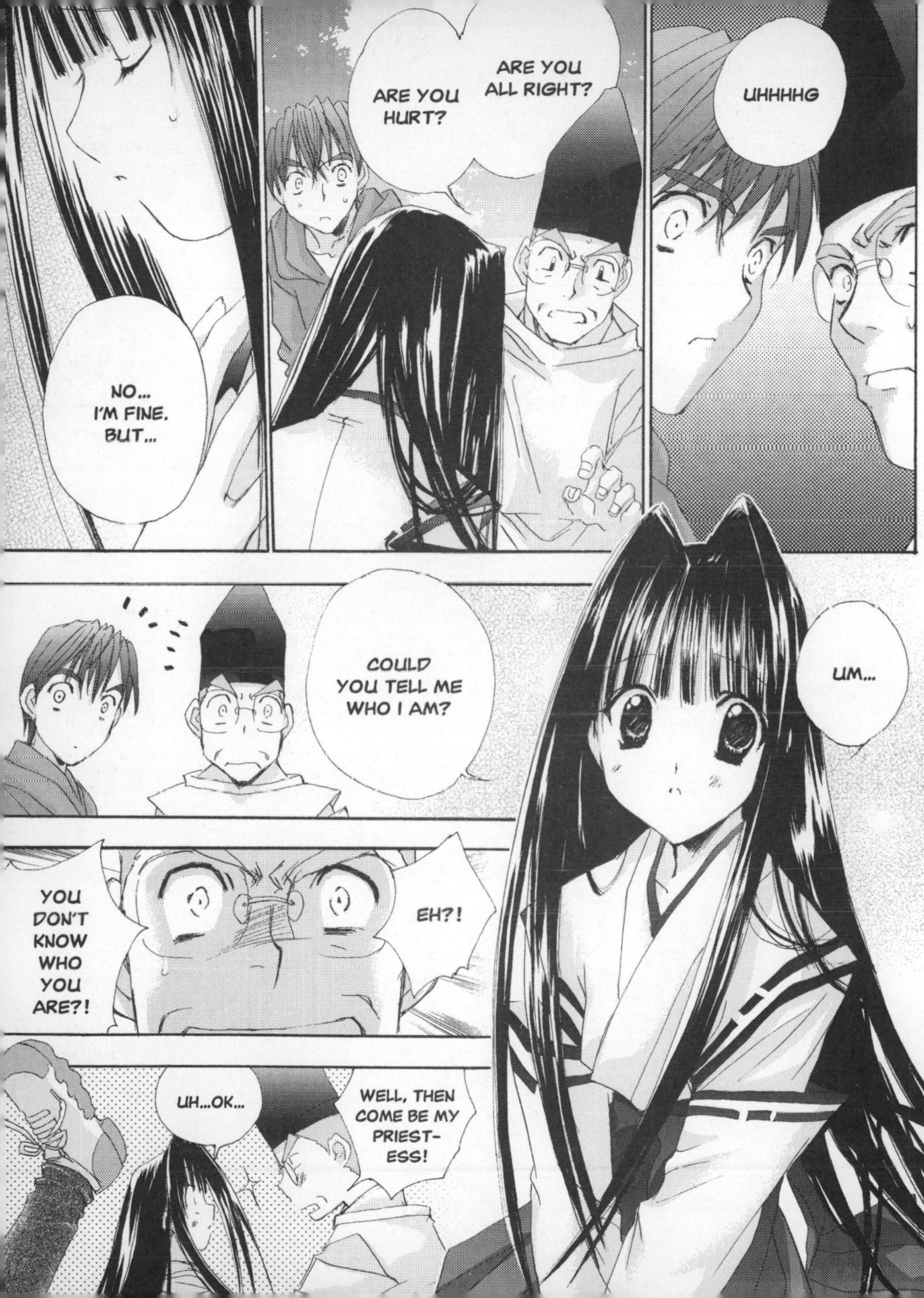
UHHHHG
ARE YOU ALL RIGHT?
ARE YOU HURT?
NO... I'M FINE. BUT...
UM...
COULD YOU TELL ME WHO I AM?
EH?!
YOU DON'T KNOW WHO YOU ARE?!
WELL, THEN COME BE MY PRIEST- ESS!
UH...OK...

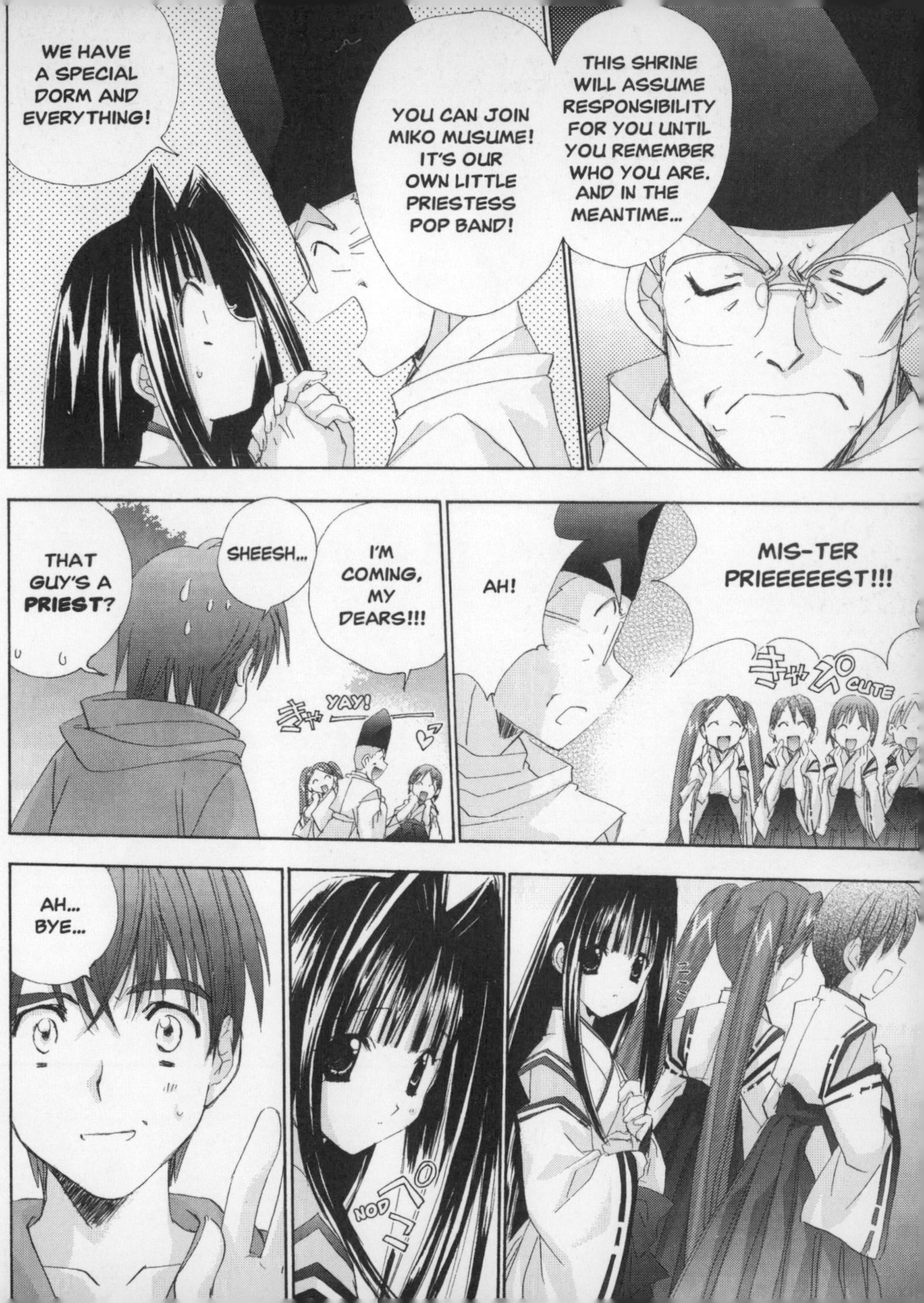
THIS SHRINE WILL ASSUME RESPONSIBILITY FOR YOU UNTIL YOU REMEMBER WHO YOU ARE. AND IN THE MEANTIME...
YOU CAN JOIN MIKO MUSUME! IT'S OUR OWN LITTLE PRIESTESS POP BAND!
WE HAVE A SPECIAL DORM AND EVERYTHING!
MIS-TER PRIEEEEEEST!!!
きゃぴ CUTE
AH!
I'M COMING, MY DEARS!!!
きゃー YAY!
SHEESH...
THAT GUY'S A **PRIEST**?
NOD
AH... BYE...

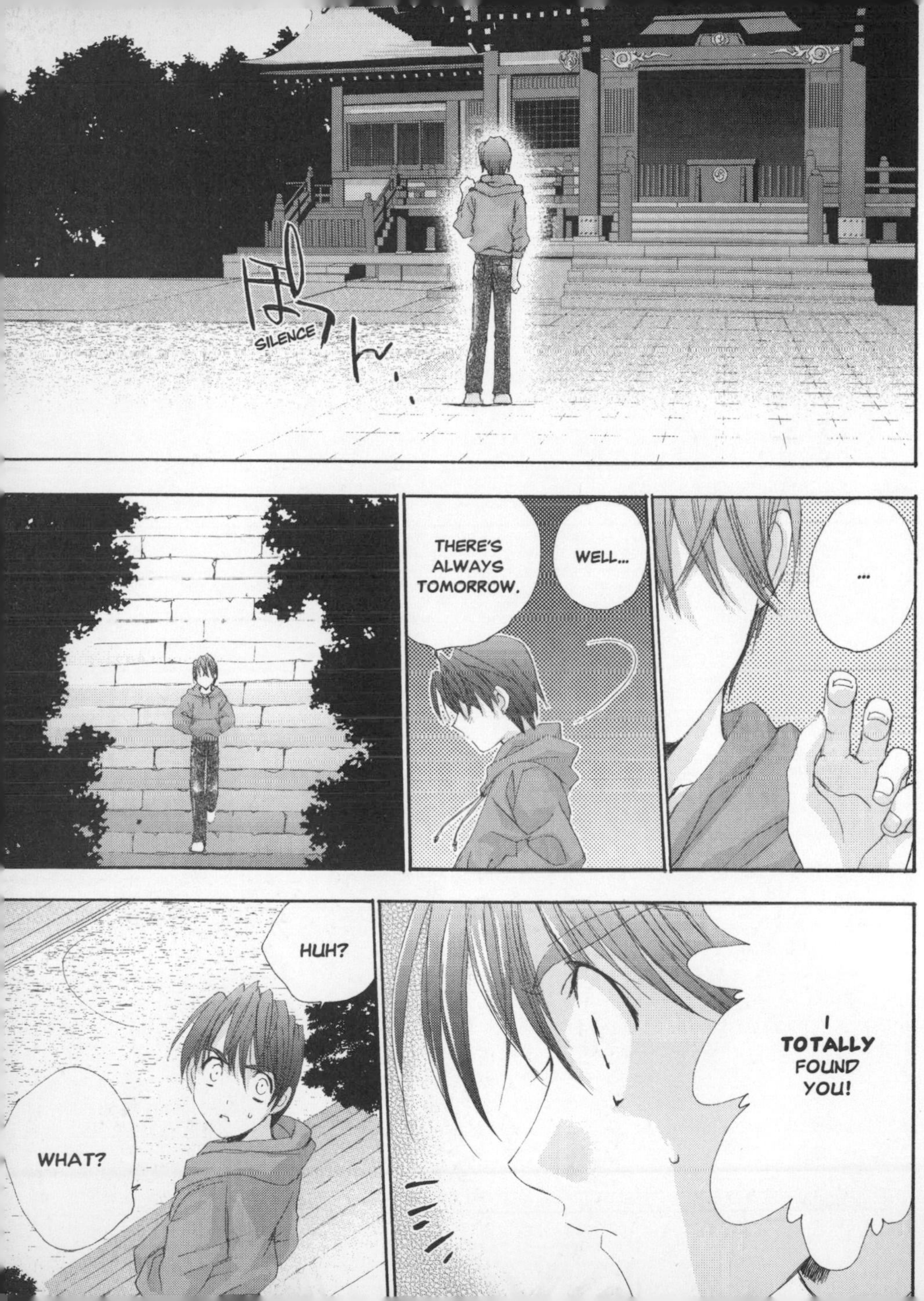
SILENCE
...
WELL...
THERE'S ALWAYS TOMORROW.
I TOTALLY FOUND YOU!
HUH?
WHAT?

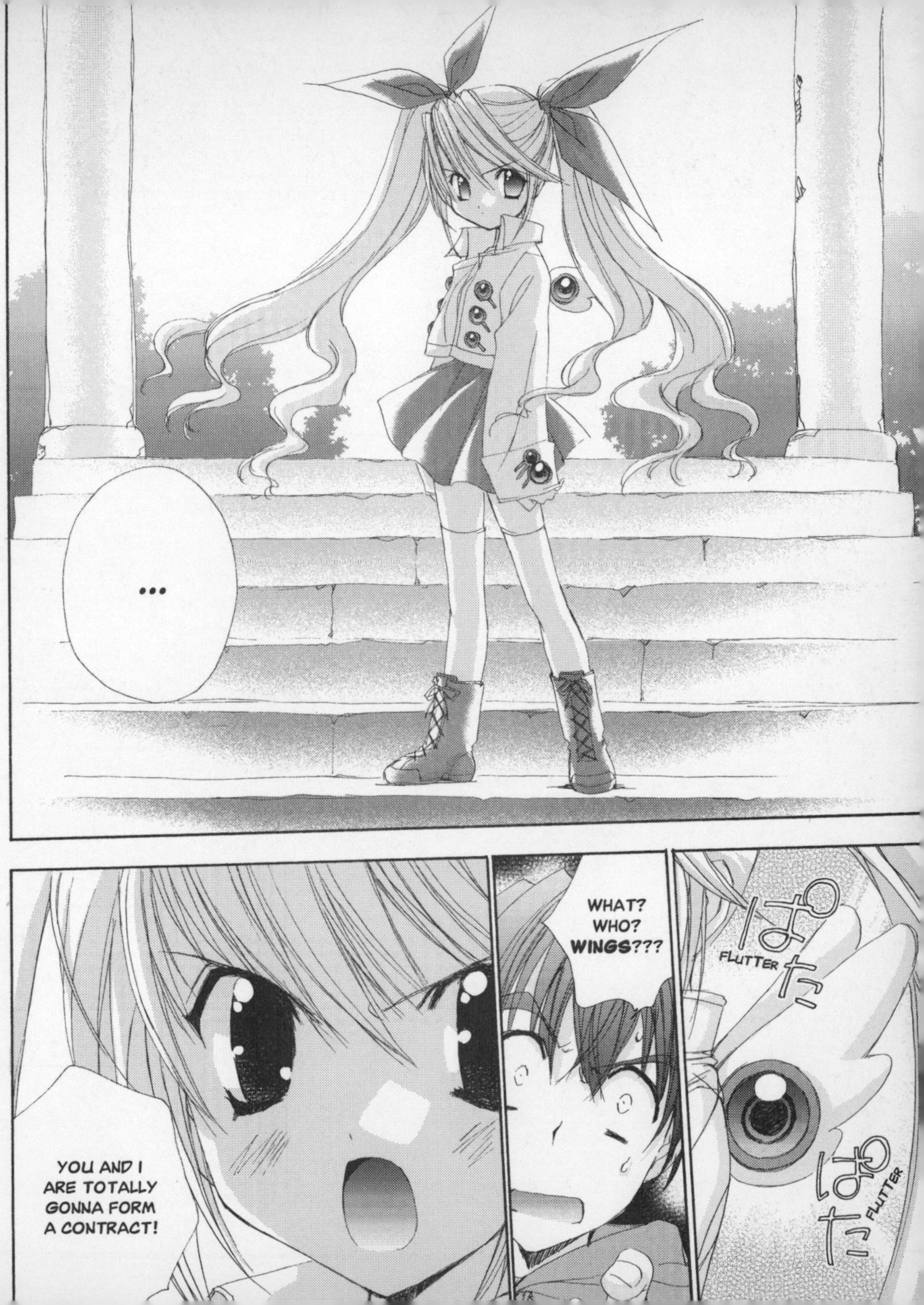
...
ぱた
FLUTTER
ぱたっ
FLUTTER
WHAT? WHO? WINGS???
YOU AND I ARE TOTALLY GONNA FORM A CONTRACT!

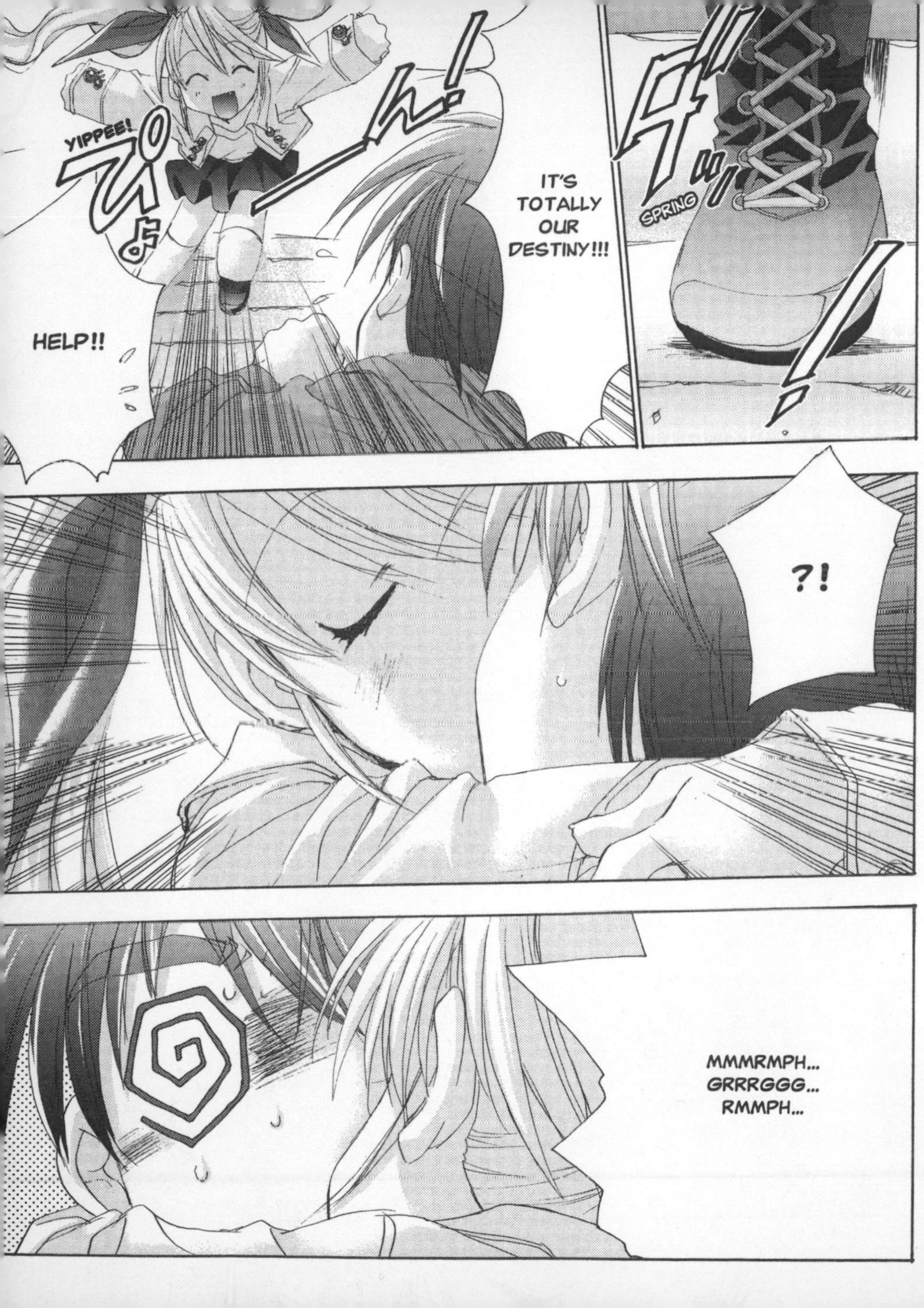
SPRING
YIPPEE!
IT'S TOTALLY OUR DESTINY!!!
HELP!!
?!
MMMRMPH... GRRRGGG... RMMPH...

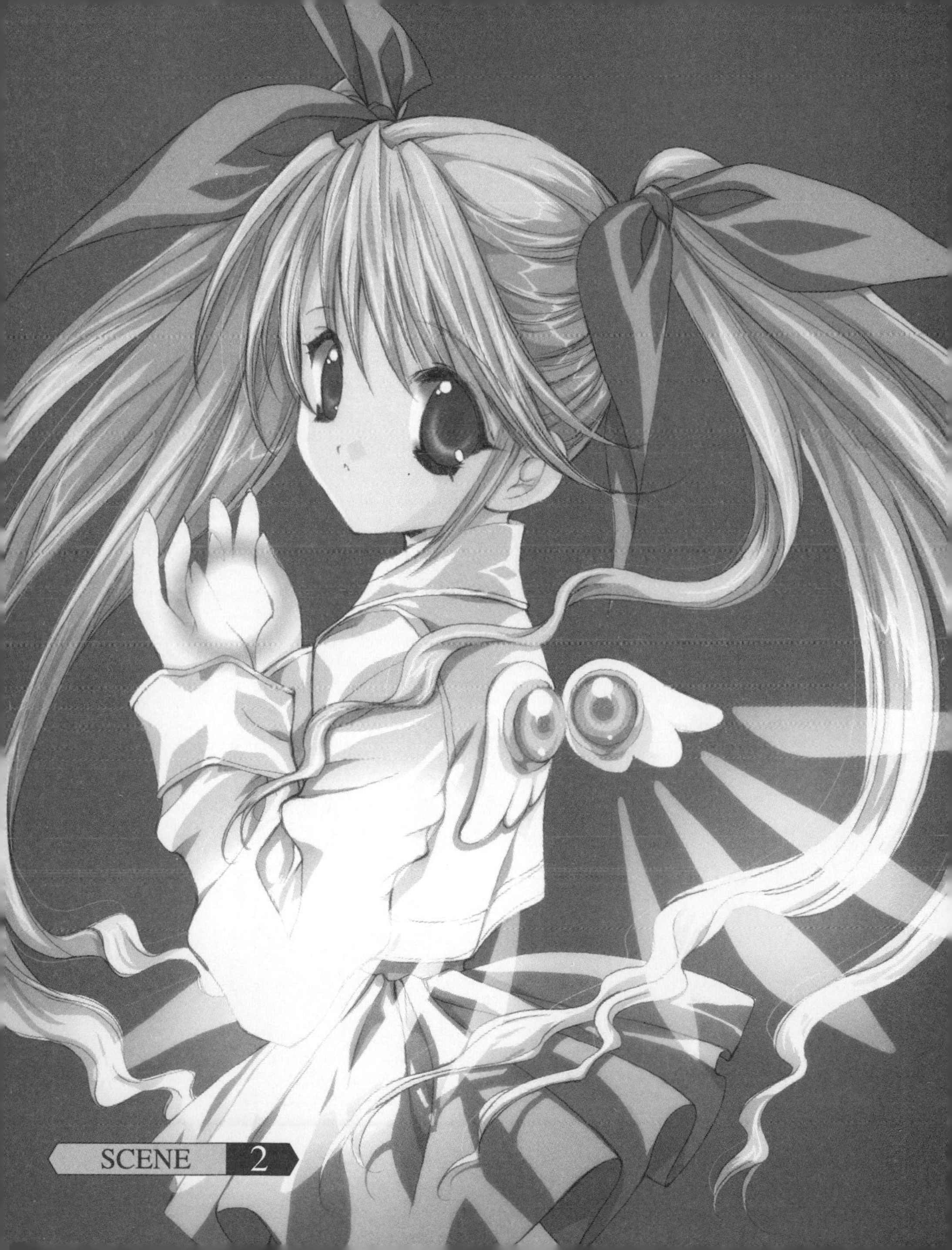

SCENE 2

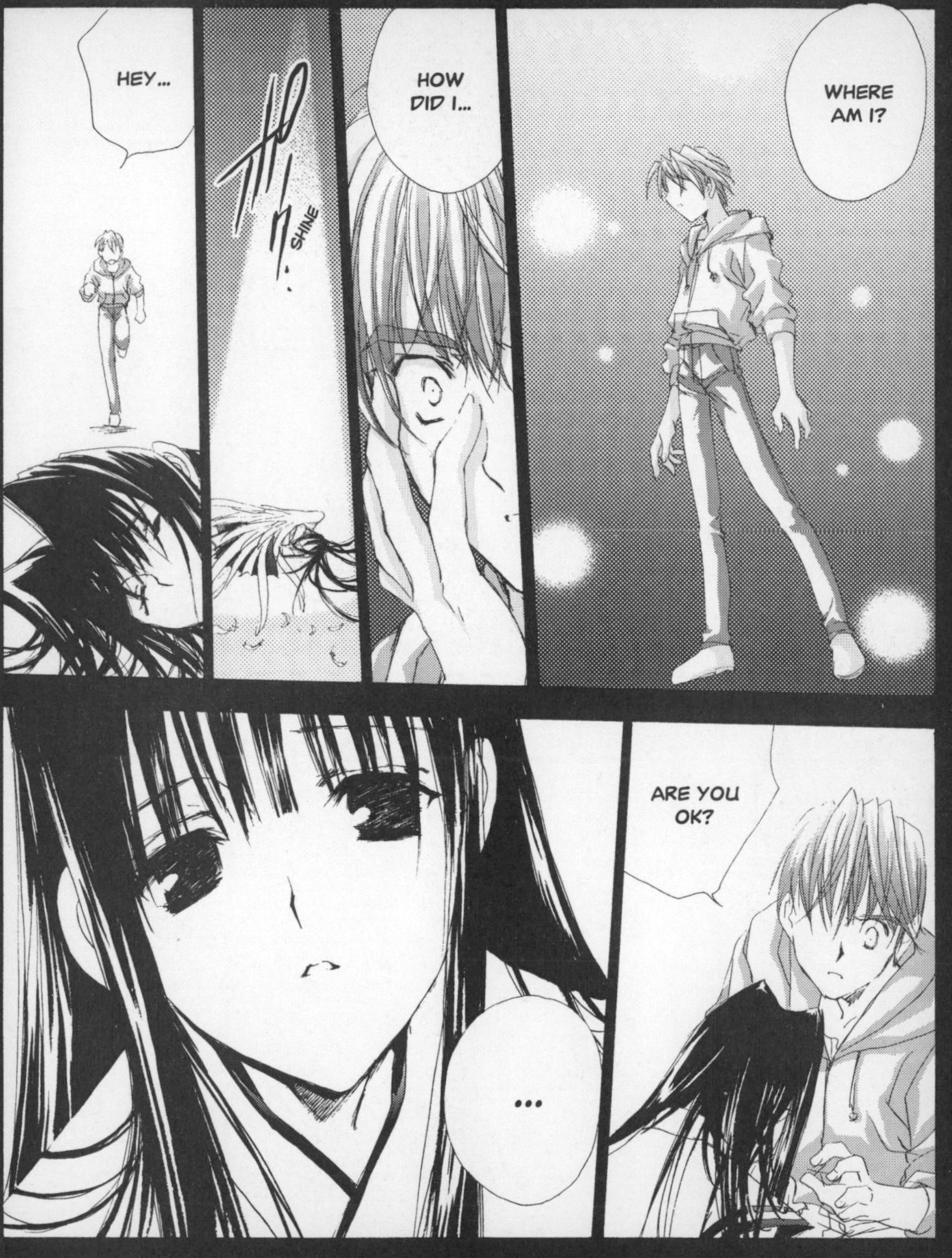
WHERE AM I?
HOW DID I...
SHINE
HEY...
ARE YOU OK?
...

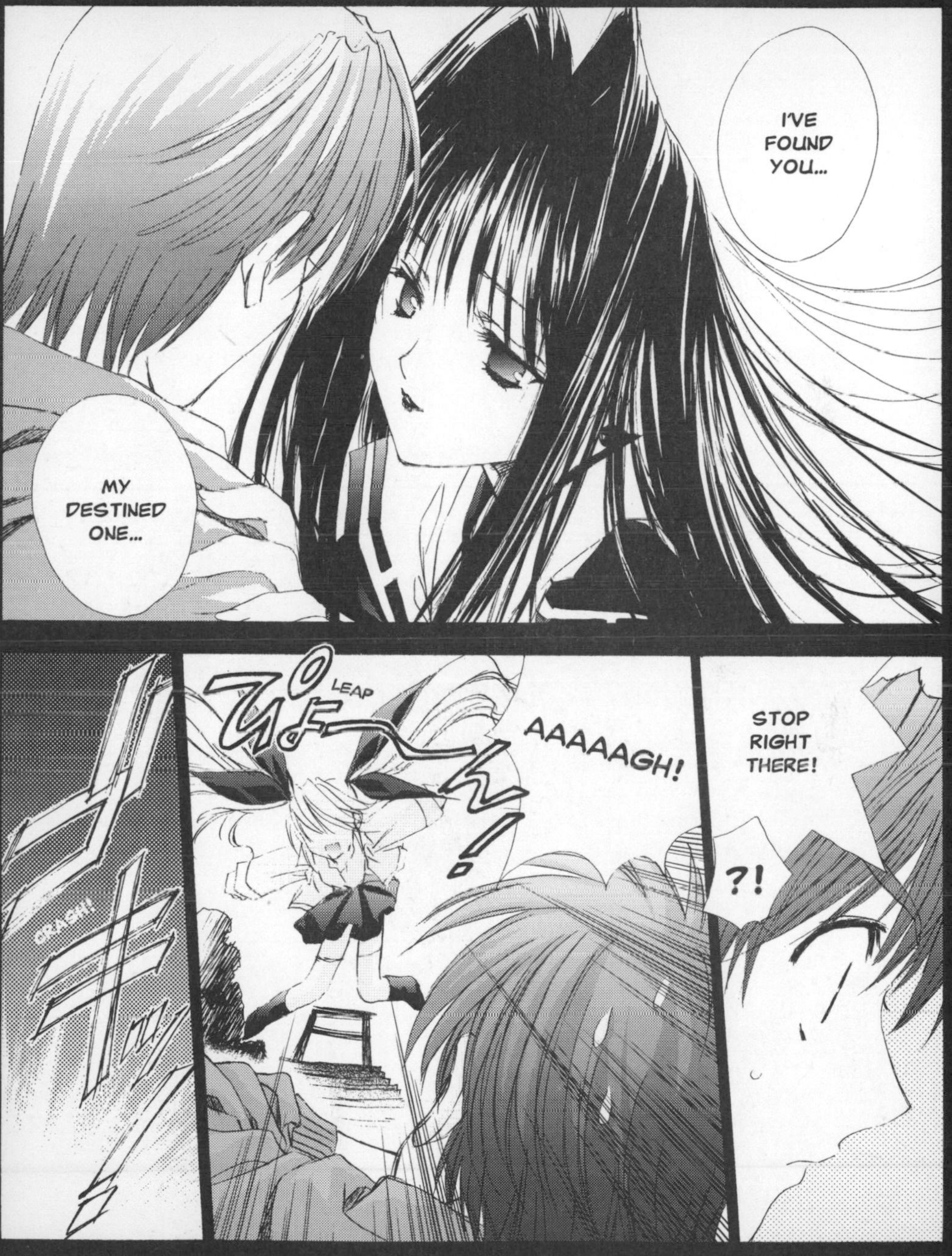
I'VE FOUND YOU...
MY DESTINED ONE...
STOP RIGHT THERE!
?!
LEAP
AAAAAGH!
CRASH!

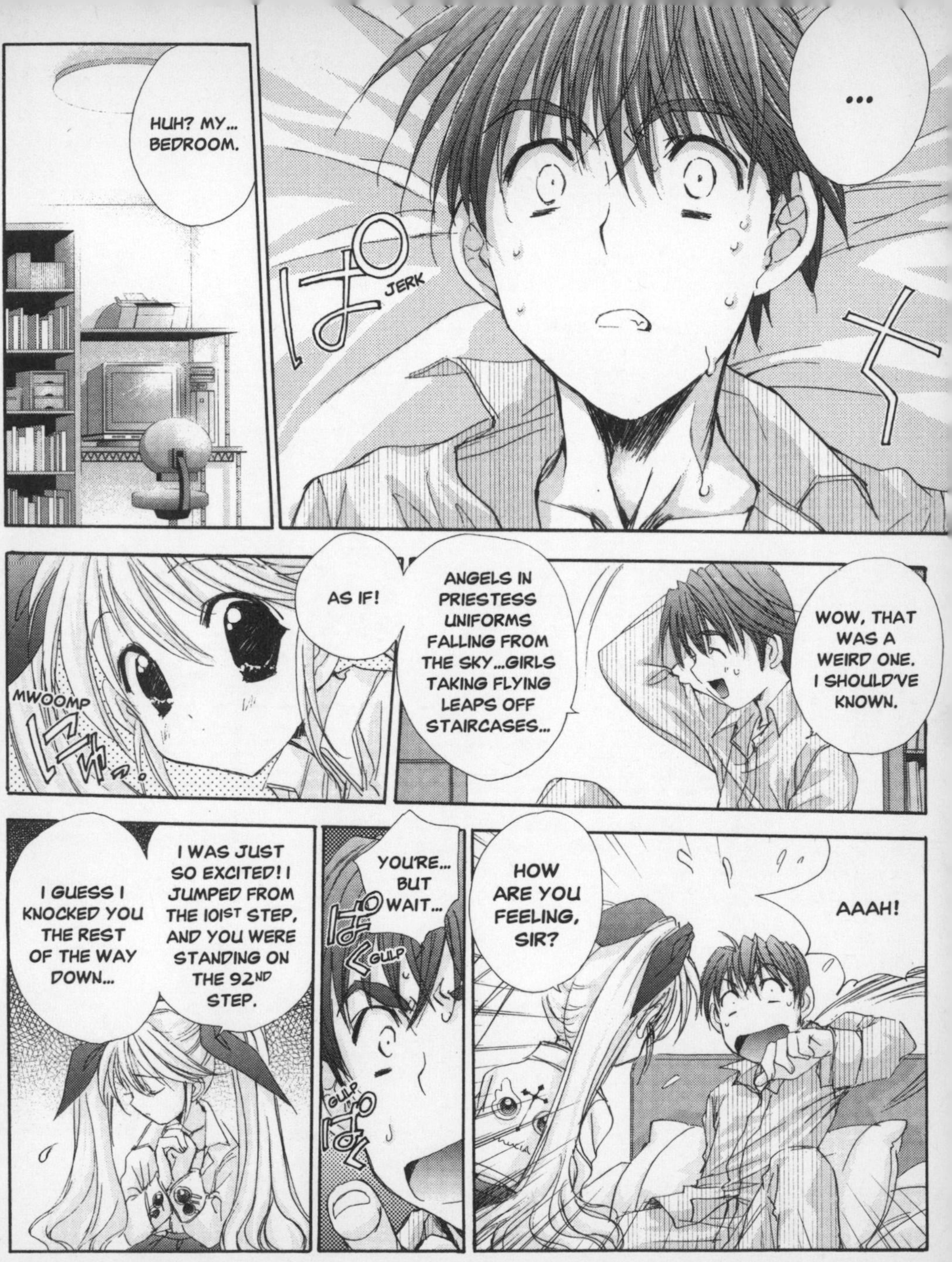
...
JERK
HUH? MY... BEDROOM.
WOW, THAT WAS A WEIRD ONE. I SHOULD'VE KNOWN.
ANGELS IN PRIESTESS UNIFORMS FALLING FROM THE SKY...GIRLS TAKING FLYING LEAPS OFF STAIRCASES...
AS IF!
MWOOMP
AAAH!
HOW ARE YOU FEELING, SIR?
YOU'RE... BUT WAIT...
GULP
GULP
I WAS JUST SO EXCITED! I JUMPED FROM THE 101ST STEP, AND YOU WERE STANDING ON THE 92ND STEP.
I GUESS I KNOCKED YOU THE REST OF THE WAY DOWN...

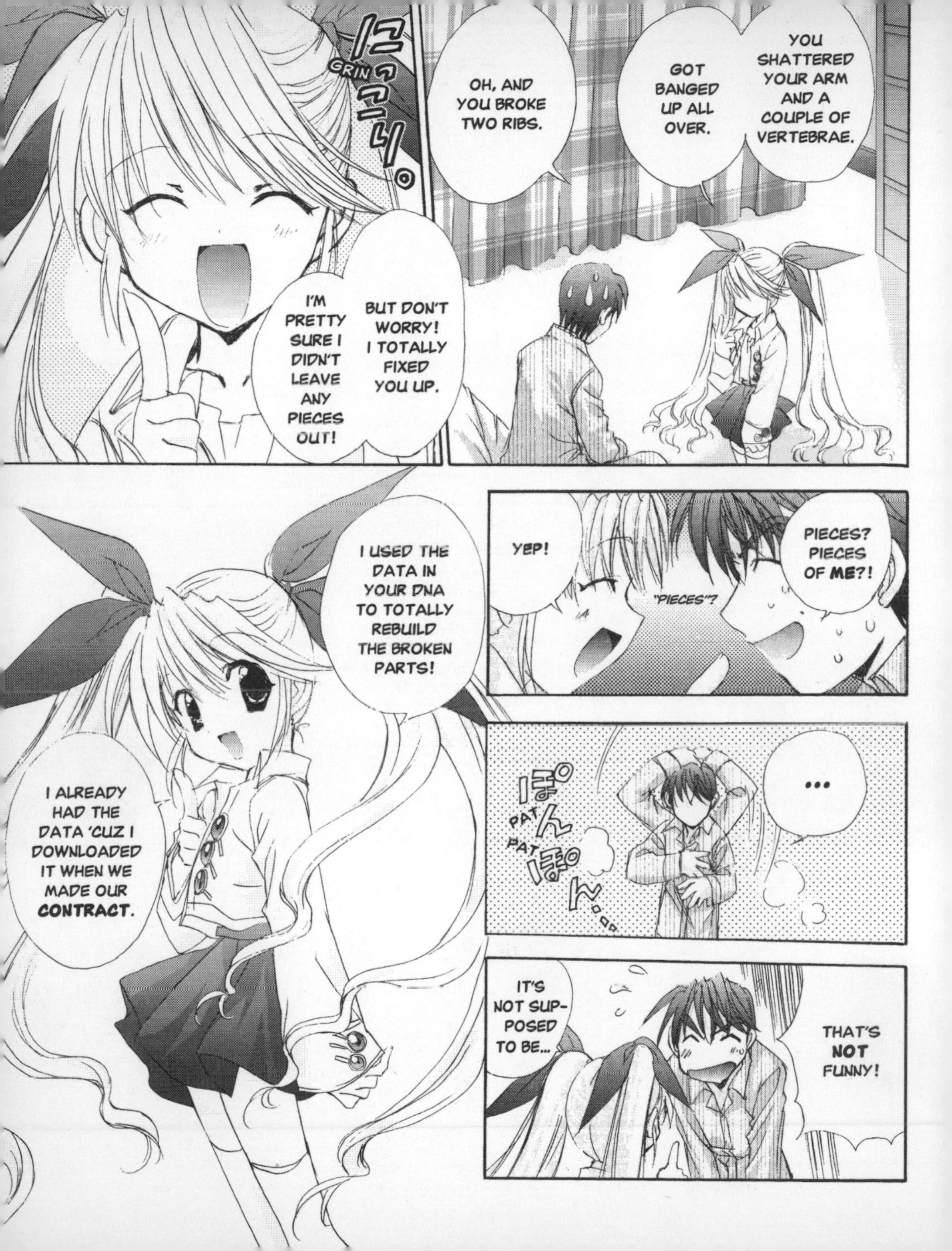
YOU SHATTERED YOUR ARM AND A COUPLE OF VERTEBRAE.
GOT BANGED UP ALL OVER.
OH, AND YOU BROKE TWO RIBS.
GRIN
BUT DON'T WORRY! I TOTALLY FIXED YOU UP.
I'M PRETTY SURE I DIDN'T LEAVE ANY PIECES OUT!
PIECES? PIECES OF ME?!
"PIECES"?
YEP!
I USED THE DATA IN YOUR DNA TO TOTALLY REBUILD THE BROKEN PARTS!
I ALREADY HAD THE DATA 'CUZ I DOWNLOADED IT WHEN WE MADE OUR **CONTRACT**.
...
PAT
PAT
THAT'S **NOT** FUNNY!
IT'S NOT SUP-POSED TO BE...

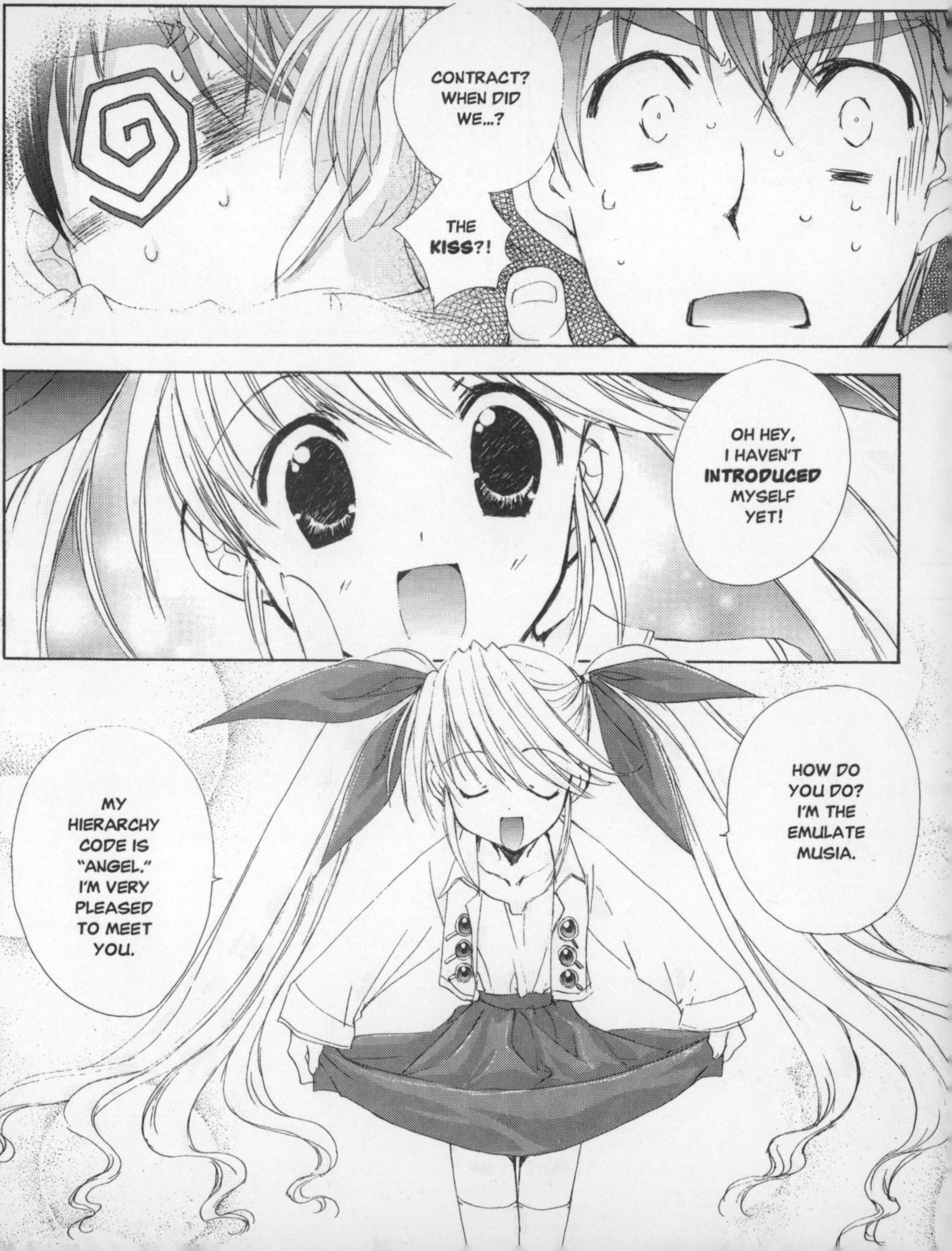
CONTRACT? WHEN DID WE...?
THE **KISS**?!
OH HEY, I HAVEN'T **INTRODUCED** MYSELF YET!
HOW DO YOU DO? I'M THE EMULATE MUSIA.
MY HIERARCHY CODE IS "ANGEL." I'M VERY PLEASED TO MEET YOU.

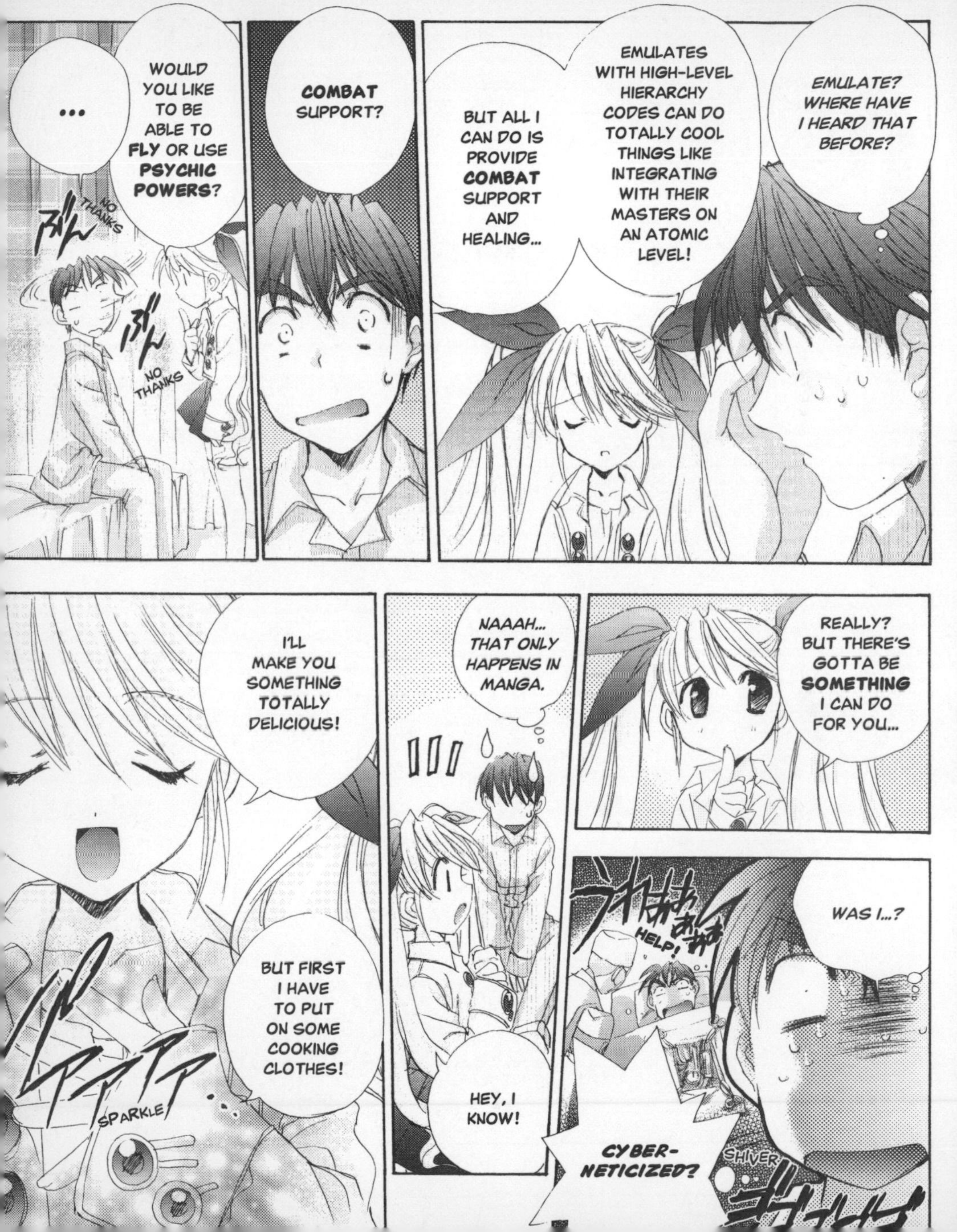
EMULATE? WHERE HAVE I HEARD THAT BEFORE?
EMULATES WITH HIGH-LEVEL HIERARCHY CODES CAN DO TOTALLY COOL THINGS LIKE INTEGRATING WITH THEIR MASTERS ON AN ATOMIC LEVEL!
BUT ALL I CAN DO IS PROVIDE COMBAT SUPPORT AND HEALING...
COMBAT SUPPORT?
WOULD YOU LIKE TO BE ABLE TO FLY OR USE PSYCHIC POWERS?
...
NO THANKS
NO THANKS
REALLY? BUT THERE'S GOTTA BE SOMETHING I CAN DO FOR YOU...
WAS I...?
HELP!
SHIVER
CYBER-NETICIZED?
NAAAH... THAT ONLY HAPPENS IN MANGA.
HEY, I KNOW!
I'LL MAKE YOU SOMETHING TOTALLY DELICIOUS!
BUT FIRST I HAVE TO PUT ON SOME COOKING CLOTHES!
SPARKLE

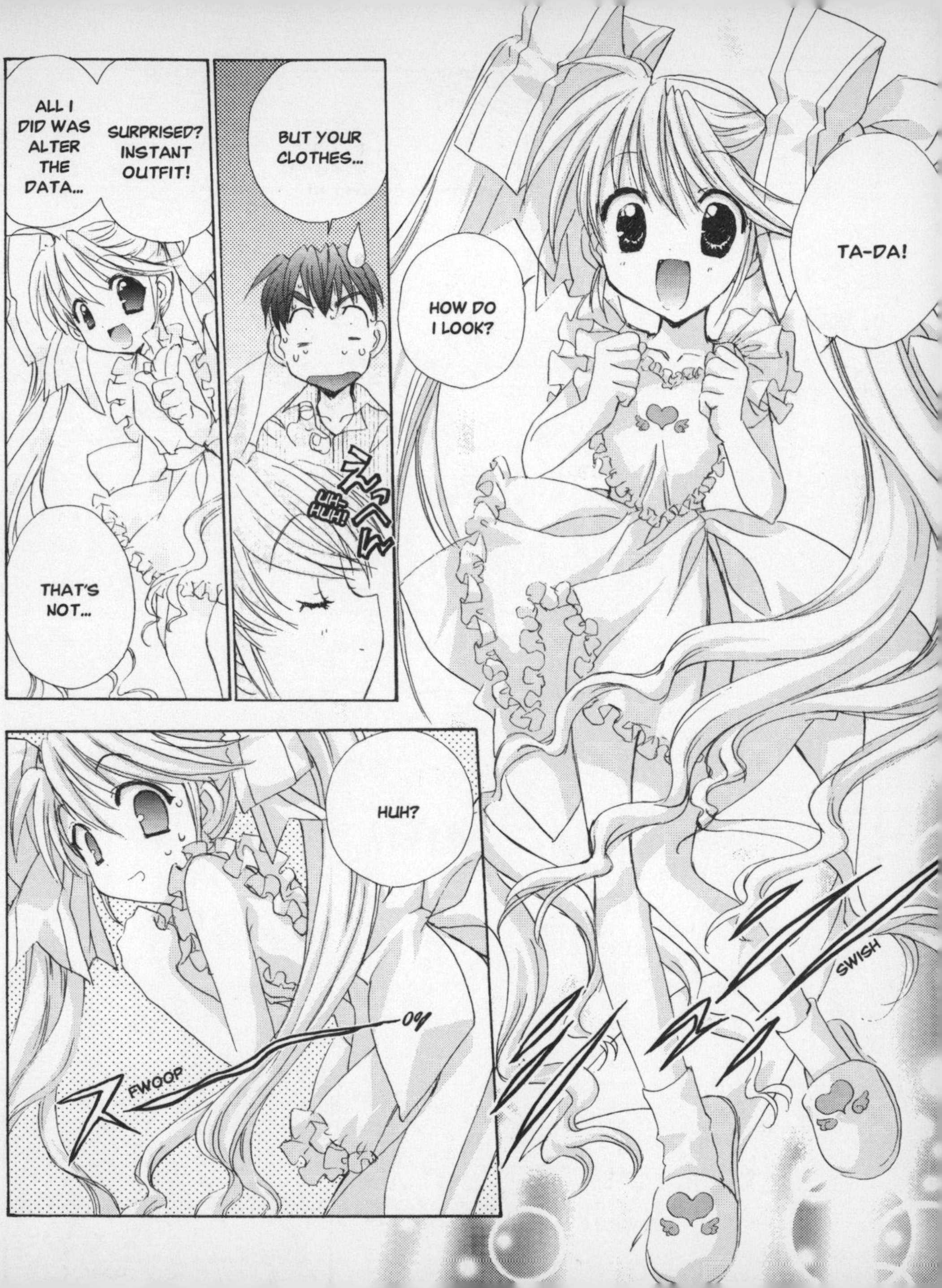
TA-DA!
HOW DO I LOOK?
SWISH
BUT YOUR CLOTHES...
UH-HUH!
SURPRISED? INSTANT OUTFIT!
ALL I DID WAS ALTER THE DATA...
THAT'S NOT...
HUH?
FWOOP

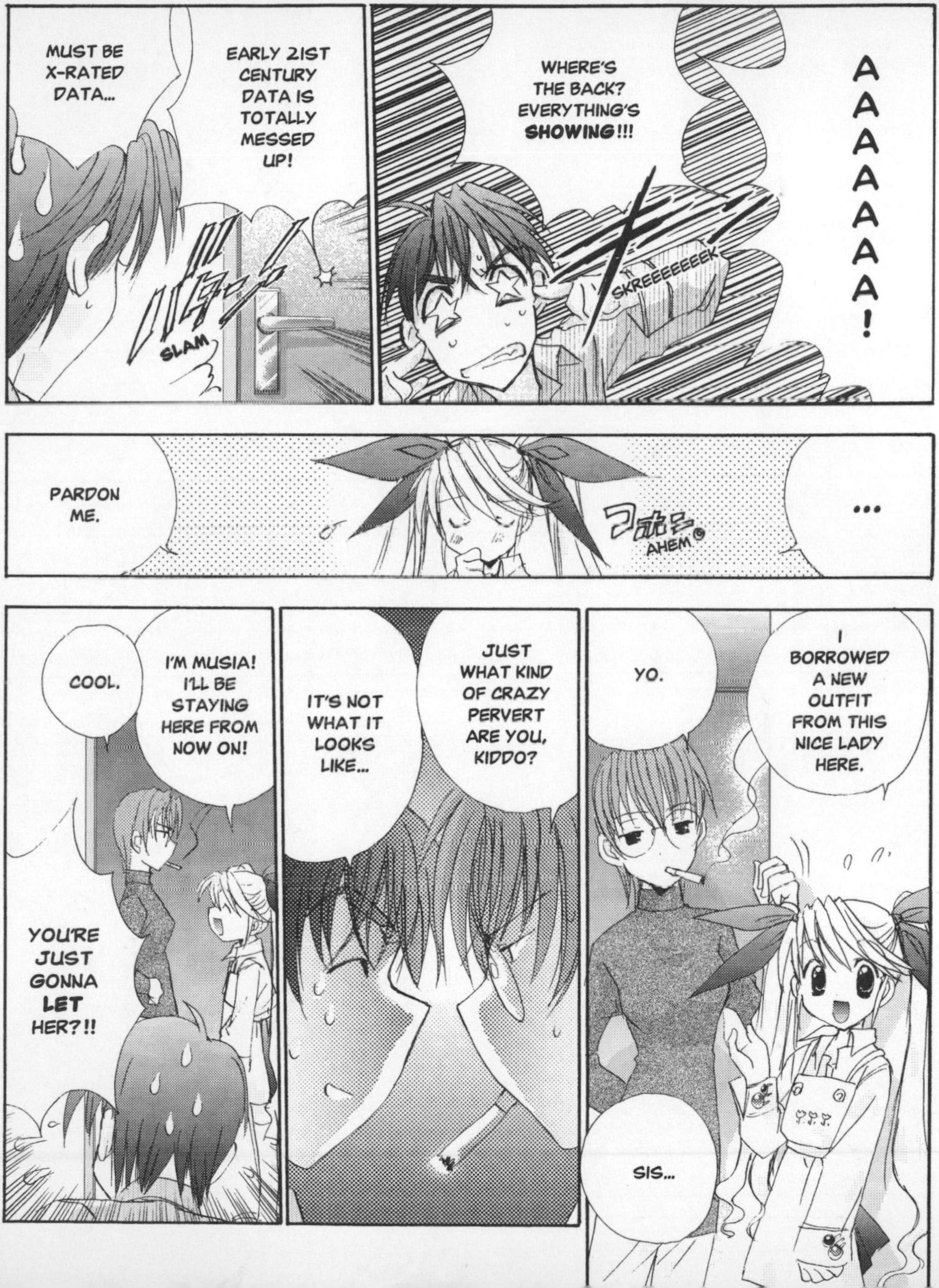
AAAAAAA!
WHERE'S THE BACK? EVERYTHING'S **SHOWING**!!!
SKREEEEEEEK
EARLY 21ST CENTURY DATA IS TOTALLY MESSED UP!
MUST BE X-RATED DATA...
SLAM
...
AHEM
PARDON ME.
I BORROWED A NEW OUTFIT FROM THIS NICE LADY HERE.
YO.
SIS...
JUST WHAT KIND OF CRAZY PERVERT ARE YOU, KIDDO?
IT'S NOT WHAT IT LOOKS LIKE...
I'M MUSIA! I'LL BE STAYING HERE FROM NOW ON!
COOL.
YOU'RE JUST GONNA **LET** HER?!!

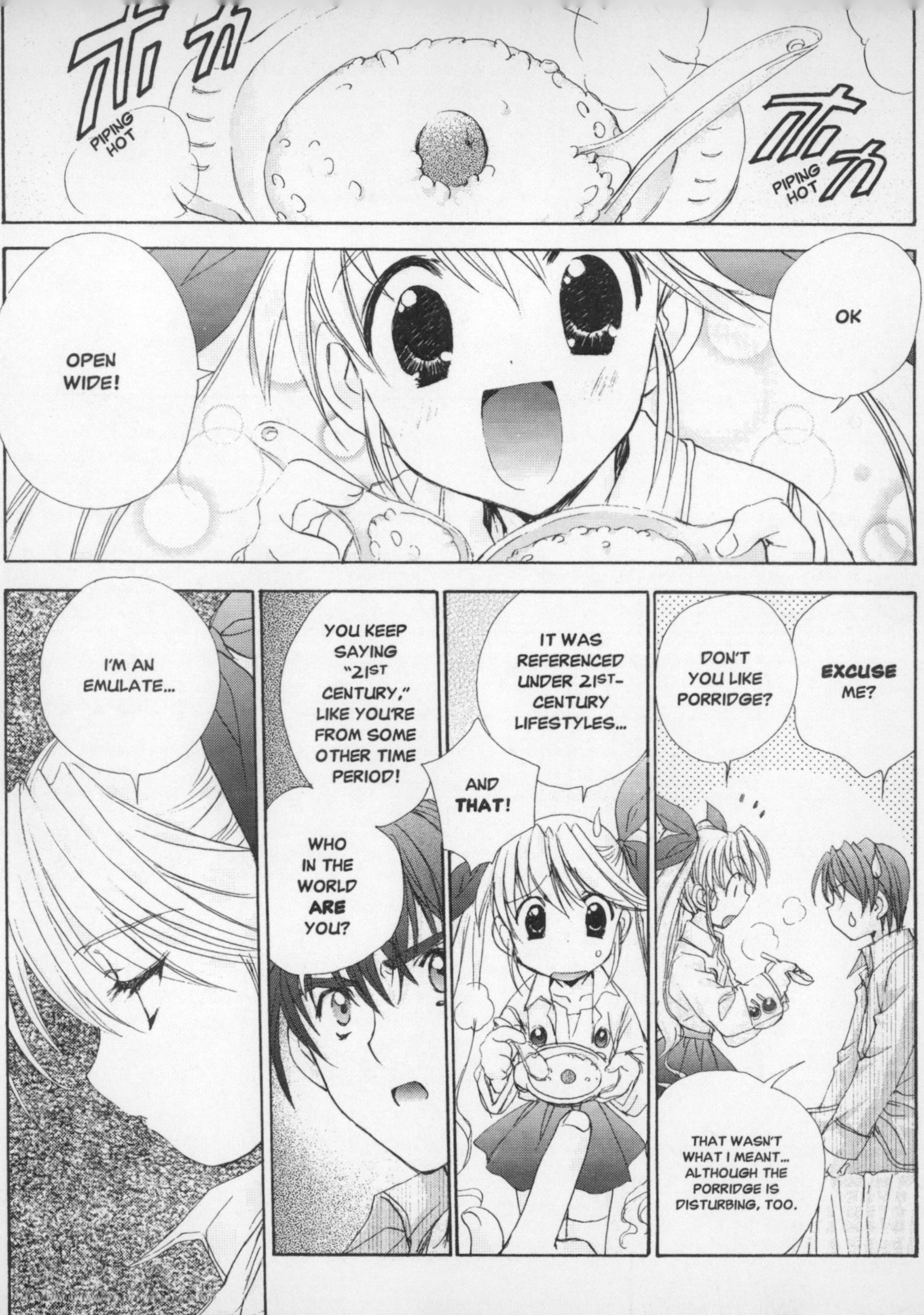
PIPING HOT
PIPING HOT
OK
OPEN WIDE!
EXCUSE ME?
DON'T YOU LIKE PORRIDGE?
THAT WASN'T WHAT I MEANT... ALTHOUGH THE PORRIDGE IS DISTURBING, TOO.
IT WAS REFERENCED UNDER 21ST-CENTURY LIFESTYLES...
AND THAT!
YOU KEEP SAYING "21ST CENTURY," LIKE YOU'RE FROM SOME OTHER TIME PERIOD!
WHO IN THE WORLD ARE YOU?
I'M AN EMULATE...

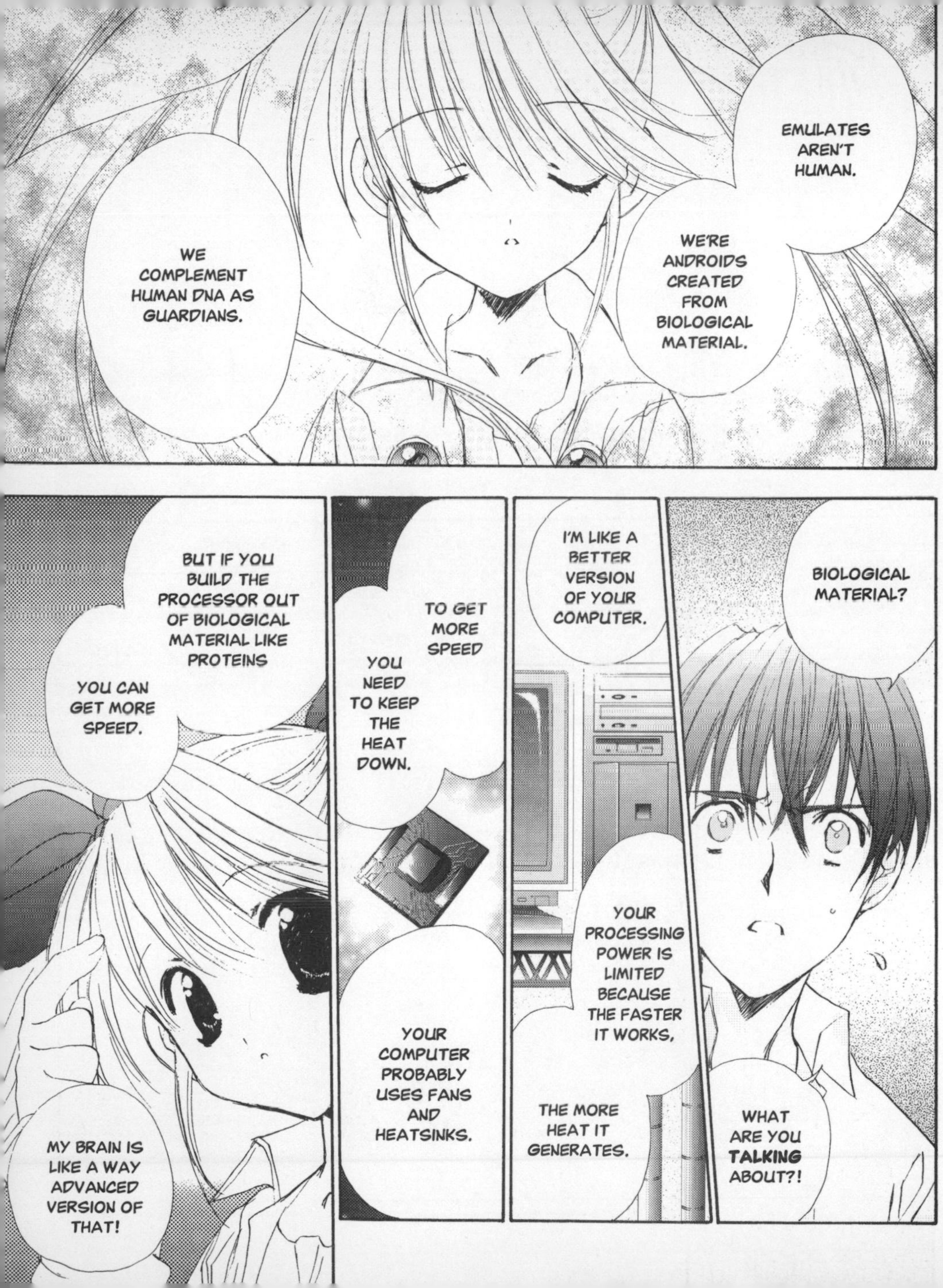

EMULATES AREN'T HUMAN.
WE'RE ANDROIDS CREATED FROM BIOLOGICAL MATERIAL.
WE COMPLEMENT HUMAN DNA AS GUARDIANS.
BIOLOGICAL MATERIAL?
I'M LIKE A BETTER VERSION OF YOUR COMPUTER.
WHAT ARE YOU **TALKING** ABOUT?!
YOUR PROCESSING POWER IS LIMITED BECAUSE THE FASTER IT WORKS,
THE MORE HEAT IT GENERATES.
TO GET MORE SPEED
YOU NEED TO KEEP THE HEAT DOWN.
YOUR COMPUTER PROBABLY USES FANS AND HEATSINKS.
BUT IF YOU BUILD THE PROCESSOR OUT OF BIOLOGICAL MATERIAL LIKE PROTEINS
YOU CAN GET MORE SPEED.
MY BRAIN IS LIKE A WAY ADVANCED VERSION OF THAT!

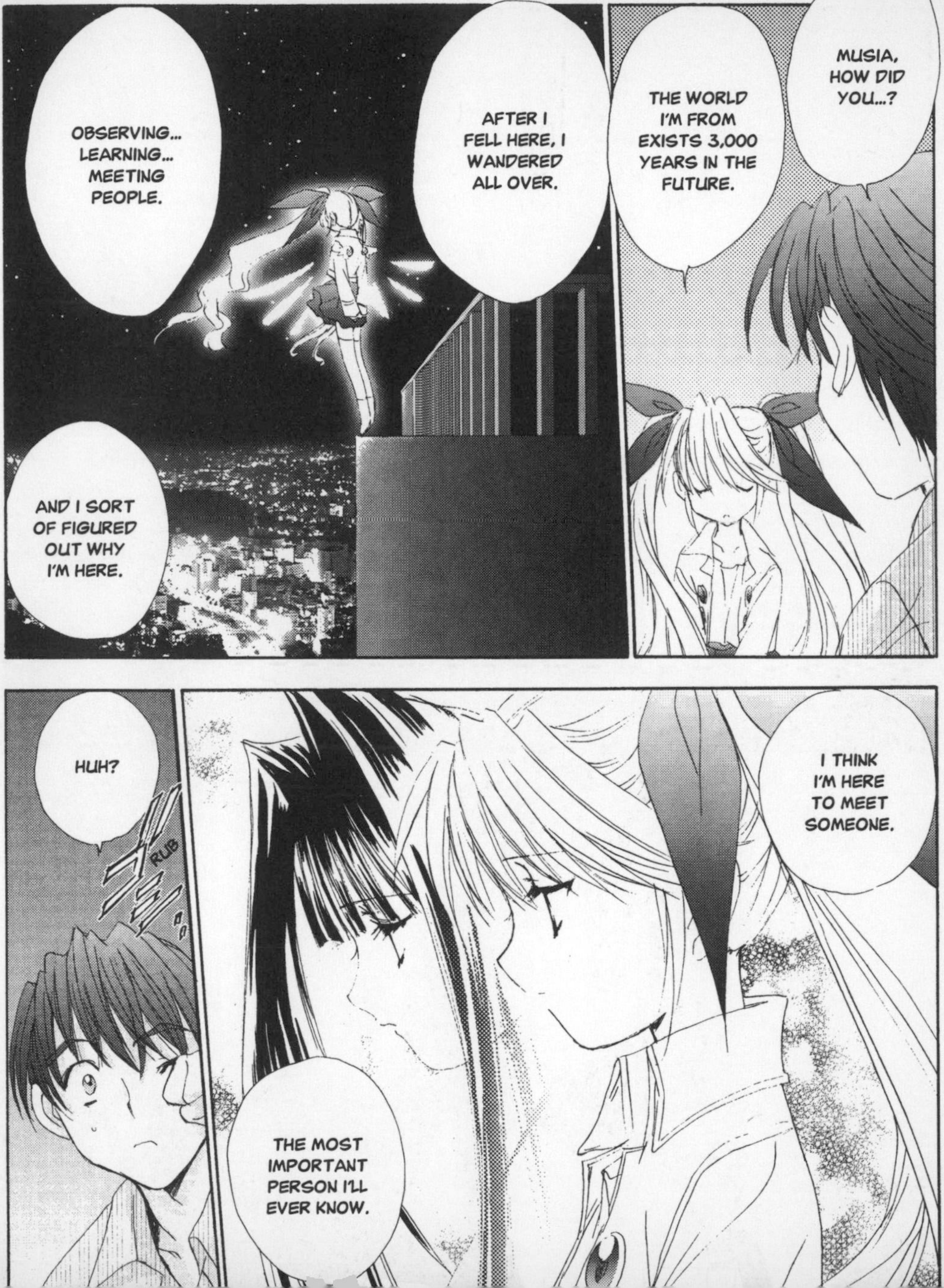

MUSIA, HOW DID YOU...?
THE WORLD I'M FROM EXISTS 3,000 YEARS IN THE FUTURE.
AFTER I FELL HERE, I WANDERED ALL OVER.
OBSERVING... LEARNING... MEETING PEOPLE.
AND I SORT OF FIGURED OUT WHY I'M HERE.
I THINK I'M HERE TO MEET SOMEONE.
THE MOST IMPORTANT PERSON I'LL EVER KNOW.
HUH?
RUB

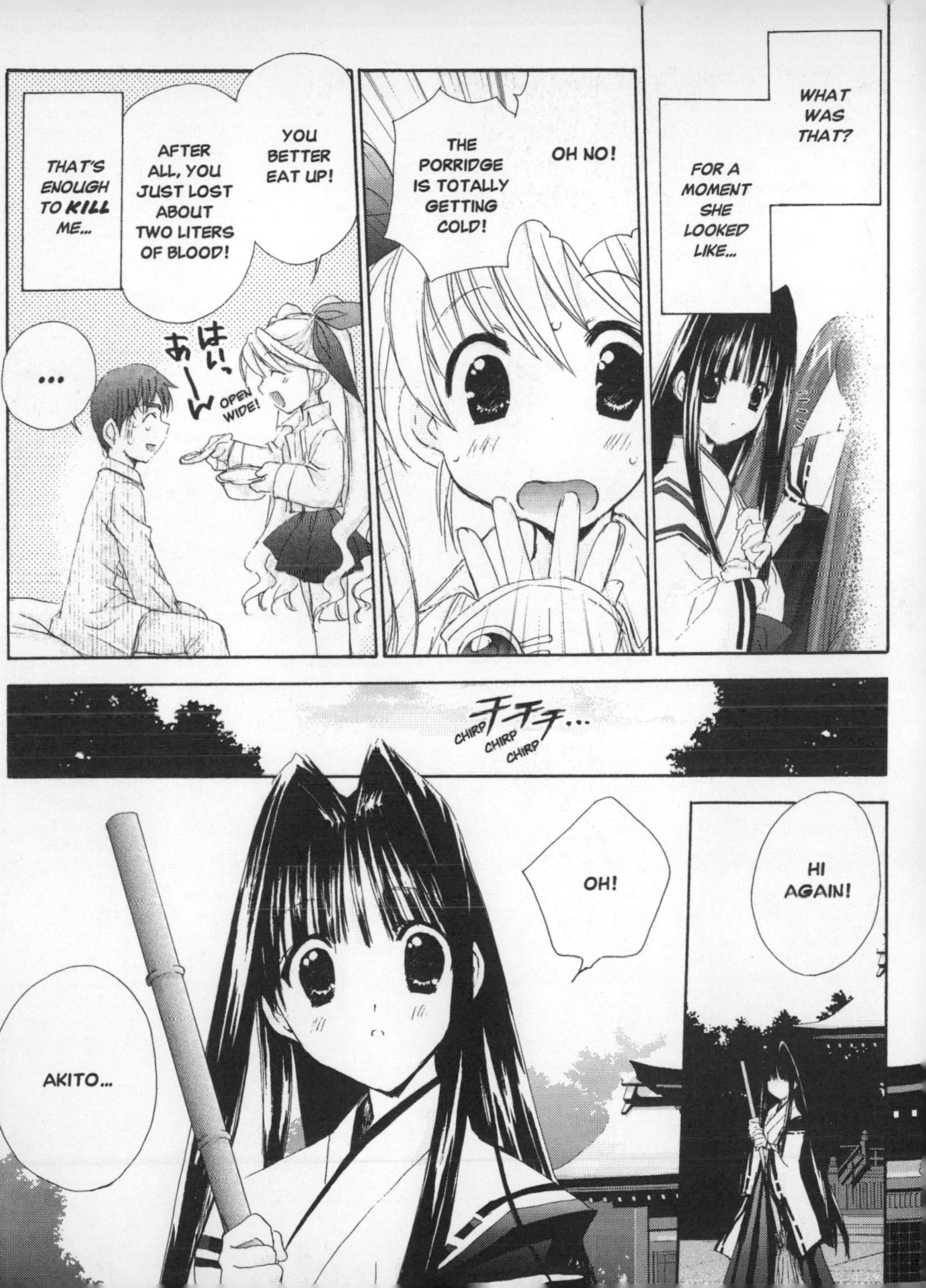
WHAT WAS THAT?
FOR A MOMENT SHE LOOKED LIKE...
OH NO!
THE PORRIDGE IS TOTALLY GETTING COLD!
YOU BETTER EAT UP!
AFTER ALL, YOU JUST LOST ABOUT TWO LITERS OF BLOOD!
THAT'S ENOUGH TO KILL ME...
はい、あ～ん
OPEN WIDE!
...
チチチ…
CHIRP CHIRP CHIRP
HI AGAIN!
OH!
AKITO...

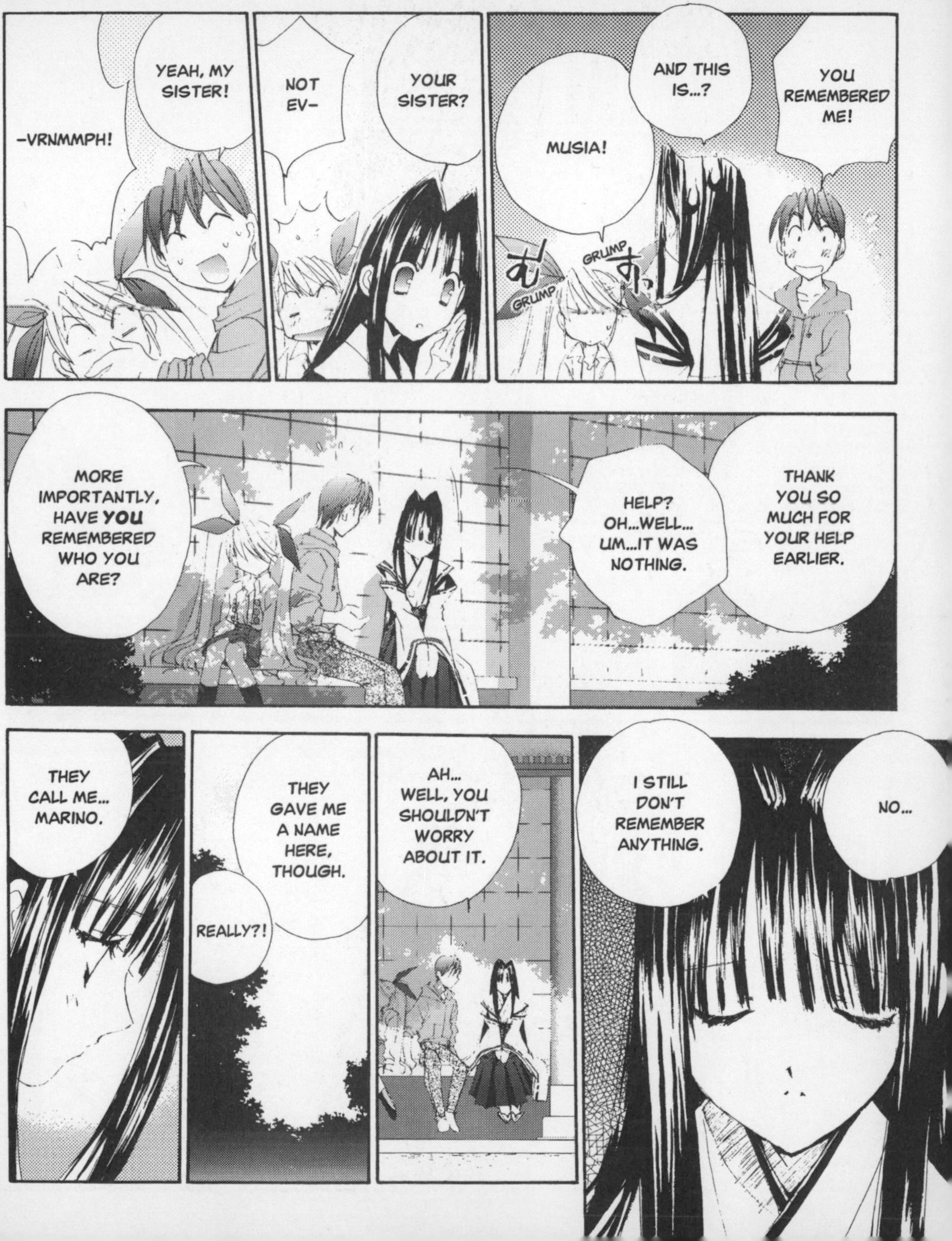
YOU REMEMBERED ME!
AND THIS IS...?
MUSIA!
GRUMP
GRUMP
GRUMP
YOUR SISTER?
NOT EV-
YEAH, MY SISTER!
-VRNMMPH!
THANK YOU SO MUCH FOR YOUR HELP EARLIER.
HELP? OH...WELL... UM...IT WAS NOTHING.
MORE IMPORTANTLY, HAVE YOU REMEMBERED WHO YOU ARE?
NO...
I STILL DON'T REMEMBER ANYTHING.
AH... WELL, YOU SHOULDN'T WORRY ABOUT IT.
THEY GAVE ME A NAME HERE, THOUGH.
REALLY?!
THEY CALL ME... MARINO.

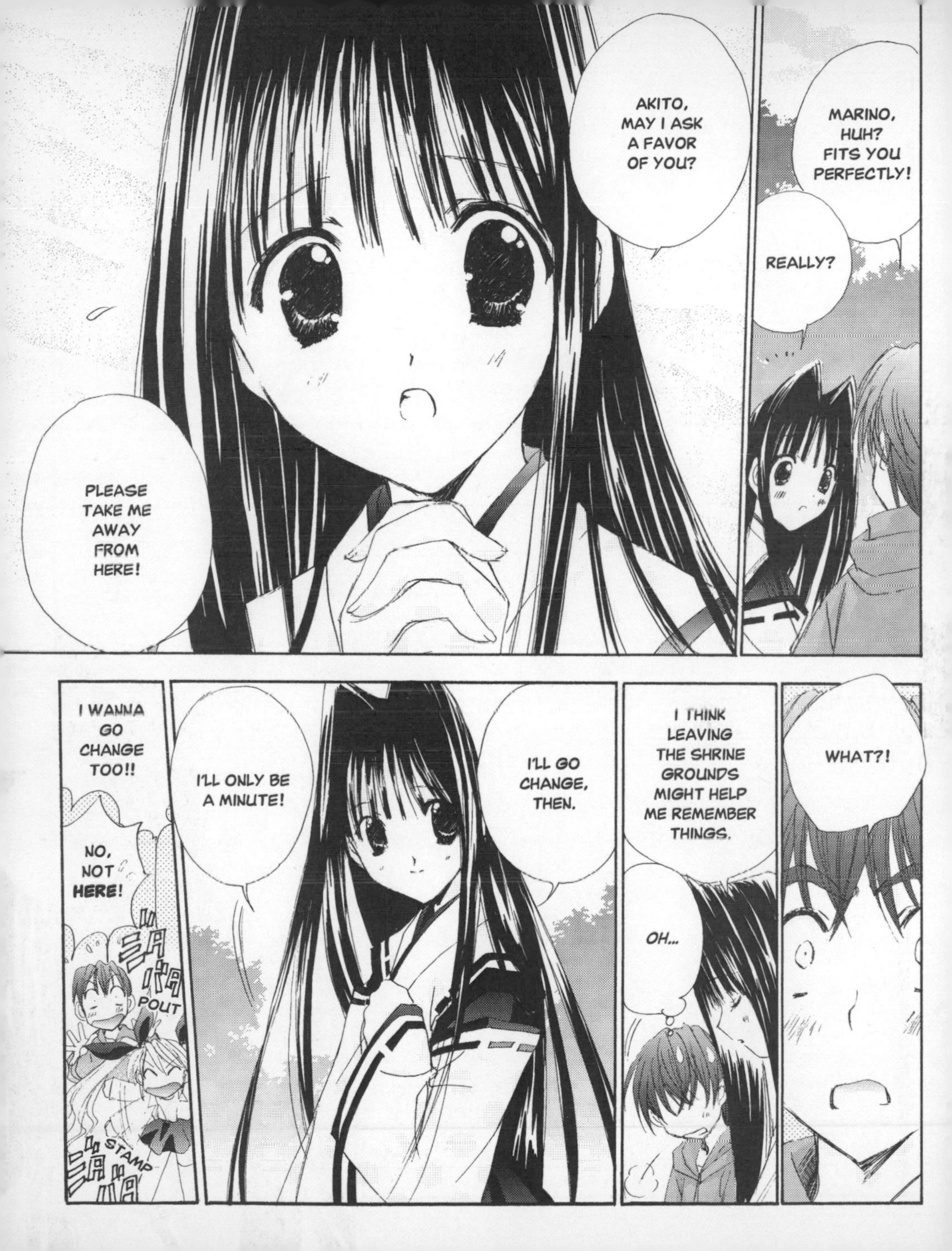
MARINO, HUH? FITS YOU PERFECTLY!
REALLY?
AKITO, MAY I ASK A FAVOR OF YOU?
PLEASE TAKE ME AWAY FROM HERE!
WHAT?!
I THINK LEAVING THE SHRINE GROUNDS MIGHT HELP ME REMEMBER THINGS.
OH...
I'LL GO CHANGE, THEN.
I'LL ONLY BE A MINUTE!
I WANNA GO CHANGE TOO!!
NO, NOT HERE!
POUT
STAMP

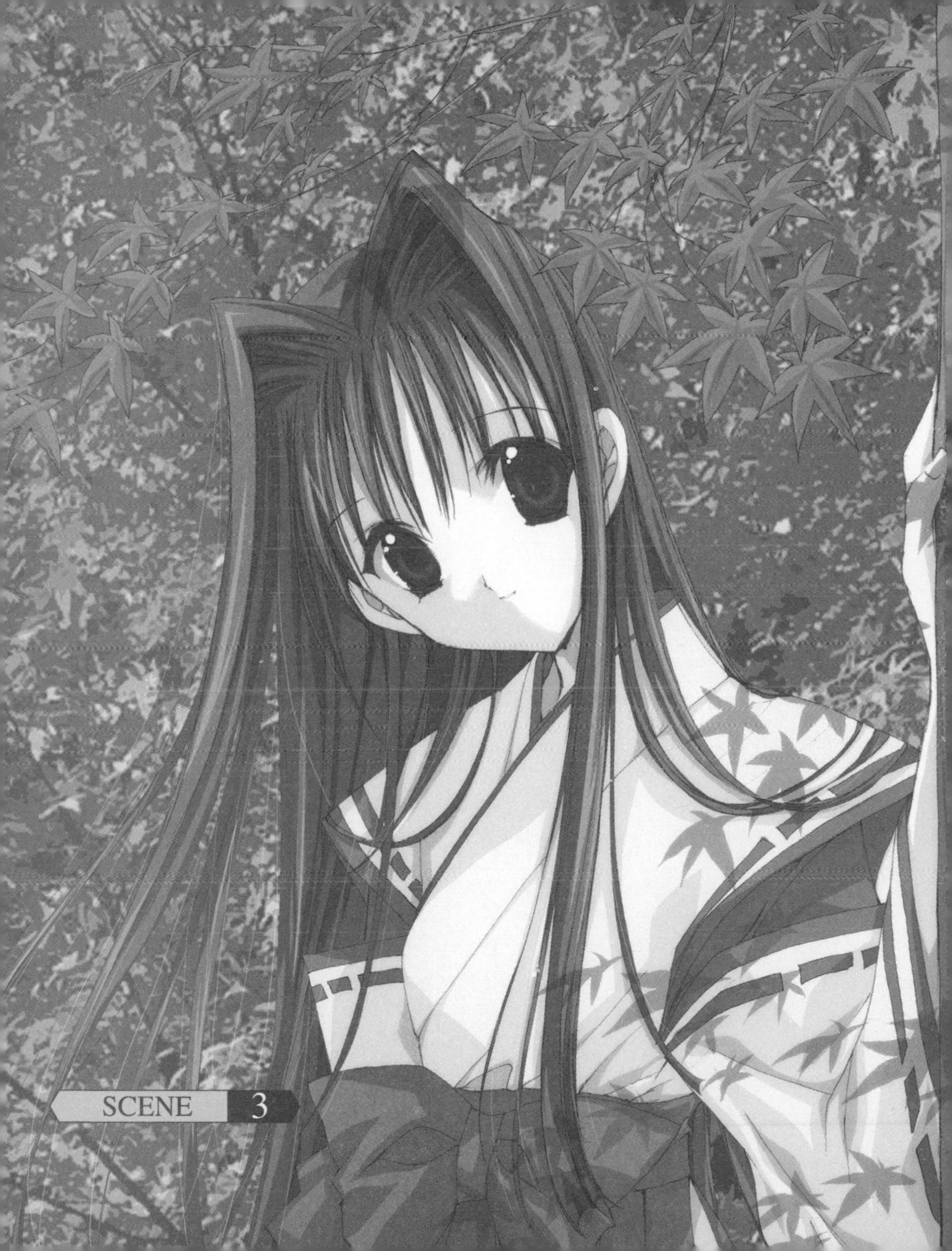
SCENE 3

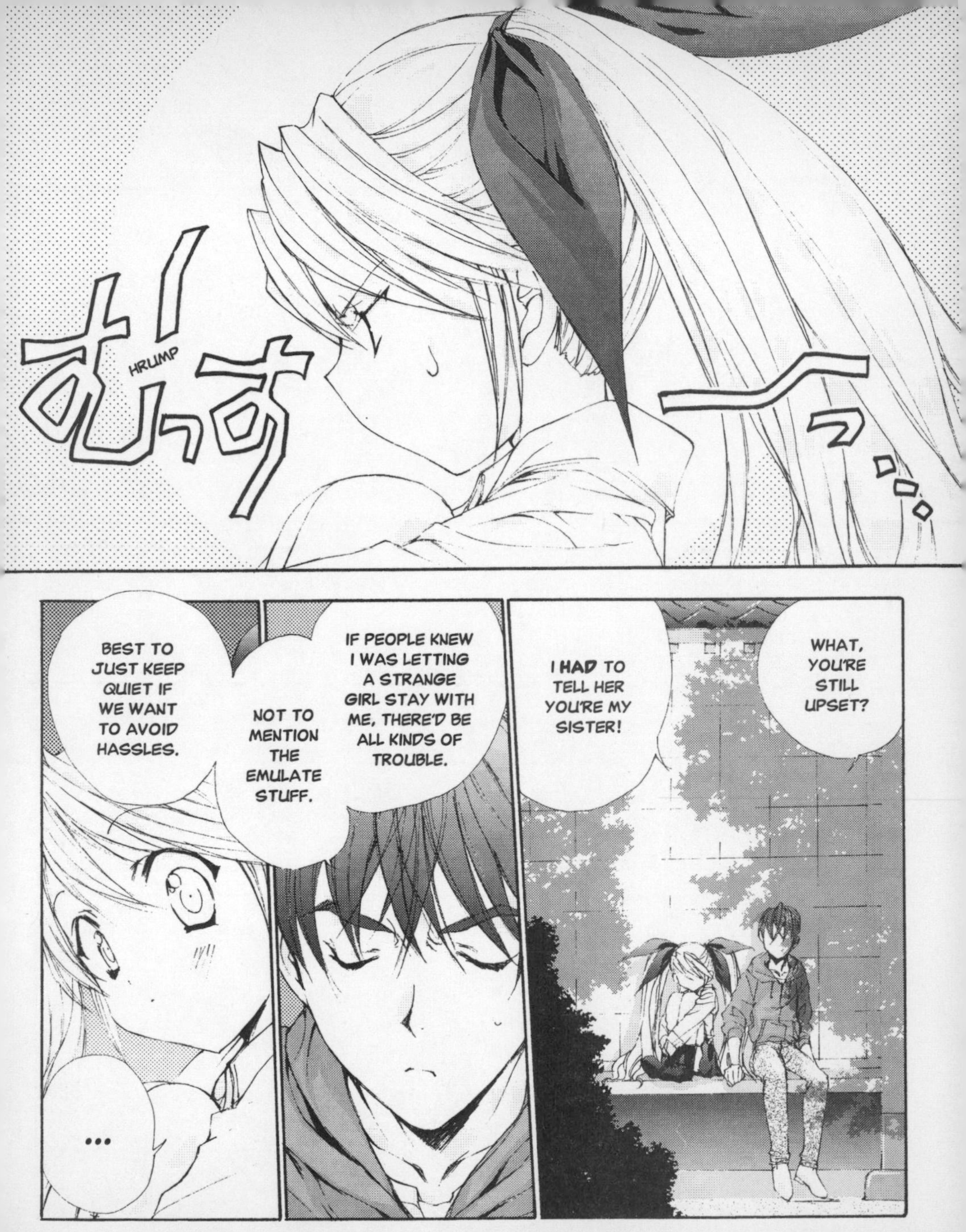
HRUMP
WHAT, YOU'RE STILL UPSET?
I HAD TO TELL HER YOU'RE MY SISTER!
IF PEOPLE KNEW I WAS LETTING A STRANGE GIRL STAY WITH ME, THERE'D BE ALL KINDS OF TROUBLE.
NOT TO MENTION THE EMULATE STUFF.
BEST TO JUST KEEP QUIET IF WE WANT TO AVOID HASSLES.
...

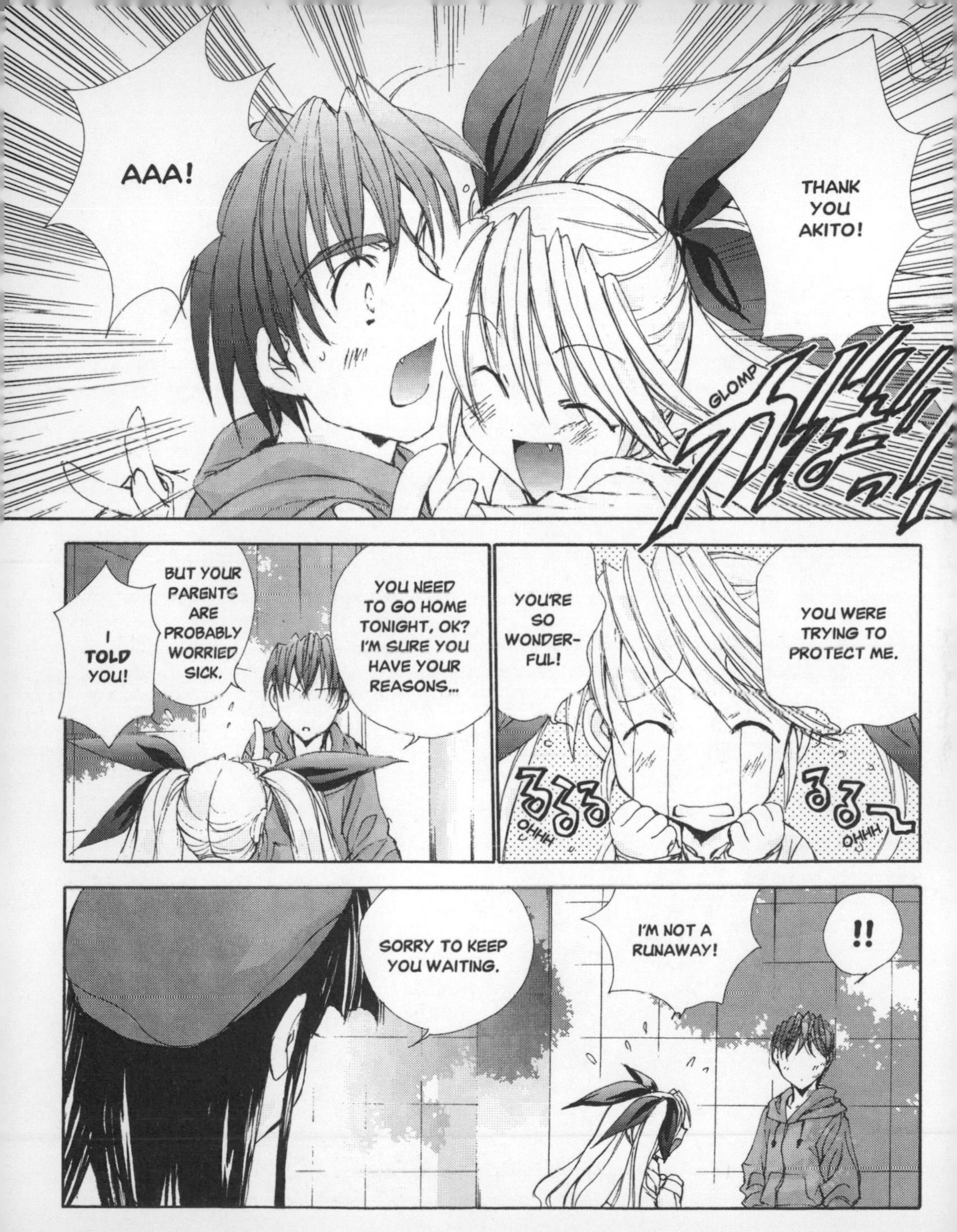
THANK YOU AKITO!
AAA!
GLOMP
YOU WERE TRYING TO PROTECT ME.
YOU'RE SO WONDER-FUL!
OHHH
OHHH
YOU NEED TO GO HOME TONIGHT, OK? I'M SURE YOU HAVE YOUR REASONS...
BUT YOUR PARENTS ARE PROBABLY WORRIED SICK.
I TOLD YOU!
!!
I'M NOT A RUNAWAY!
SORRY TO KEEP YOU WAITING.

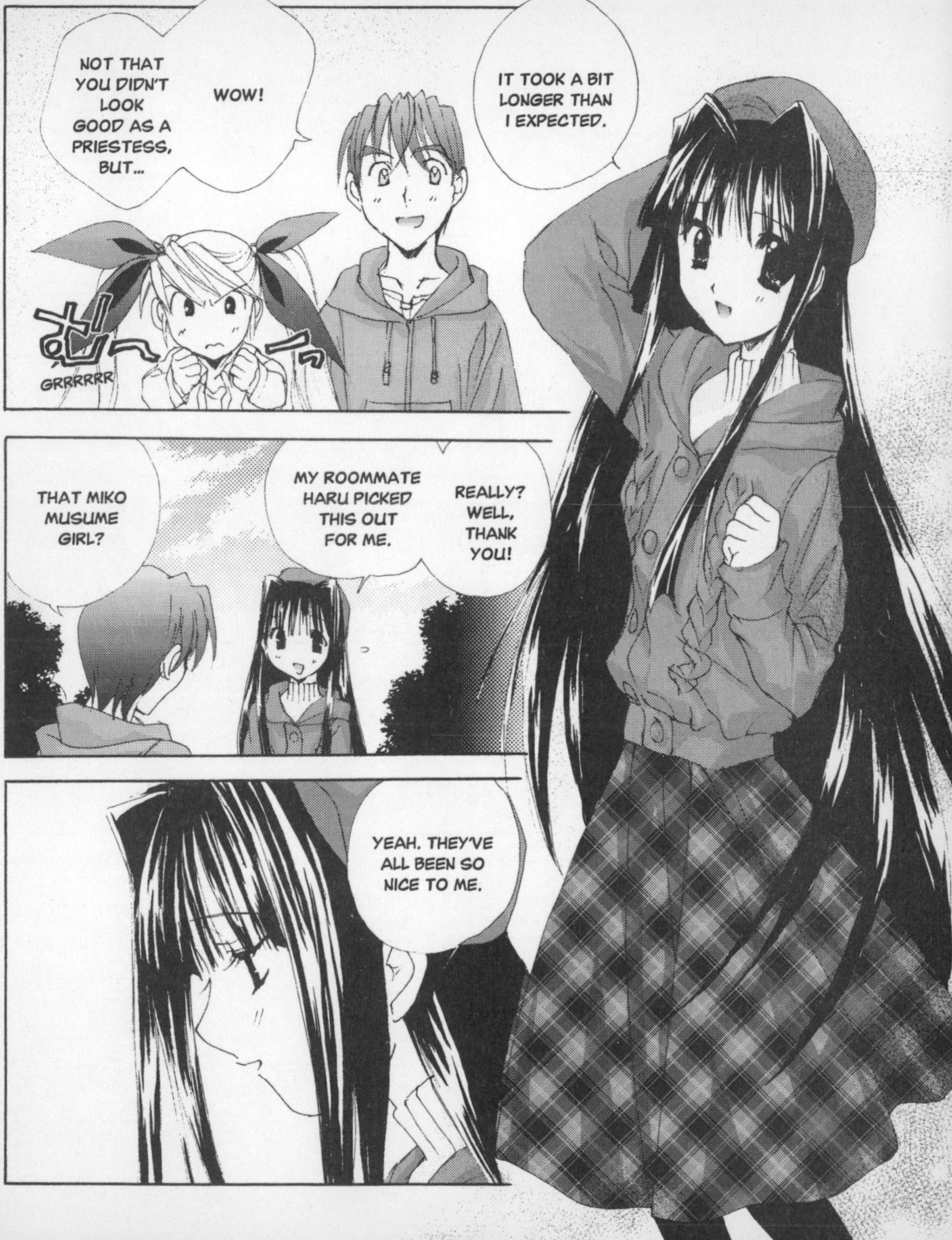
IT TOOK A BIT LONGER THAN I EXPECTED.
WOW!
NOT THAT YOU DIDN'T LOOK GOOD AS A PRIESTESS, BUT...
GRRRRRR
REALLY? WELL, THANK YOU!
MY ROOMMATE HARU PICKED THIS OUT FOR ME.
THAT MIKO MUSUME GIRL?
YEAH. THEY'VE ALL BEEN SO NICE TO ME.

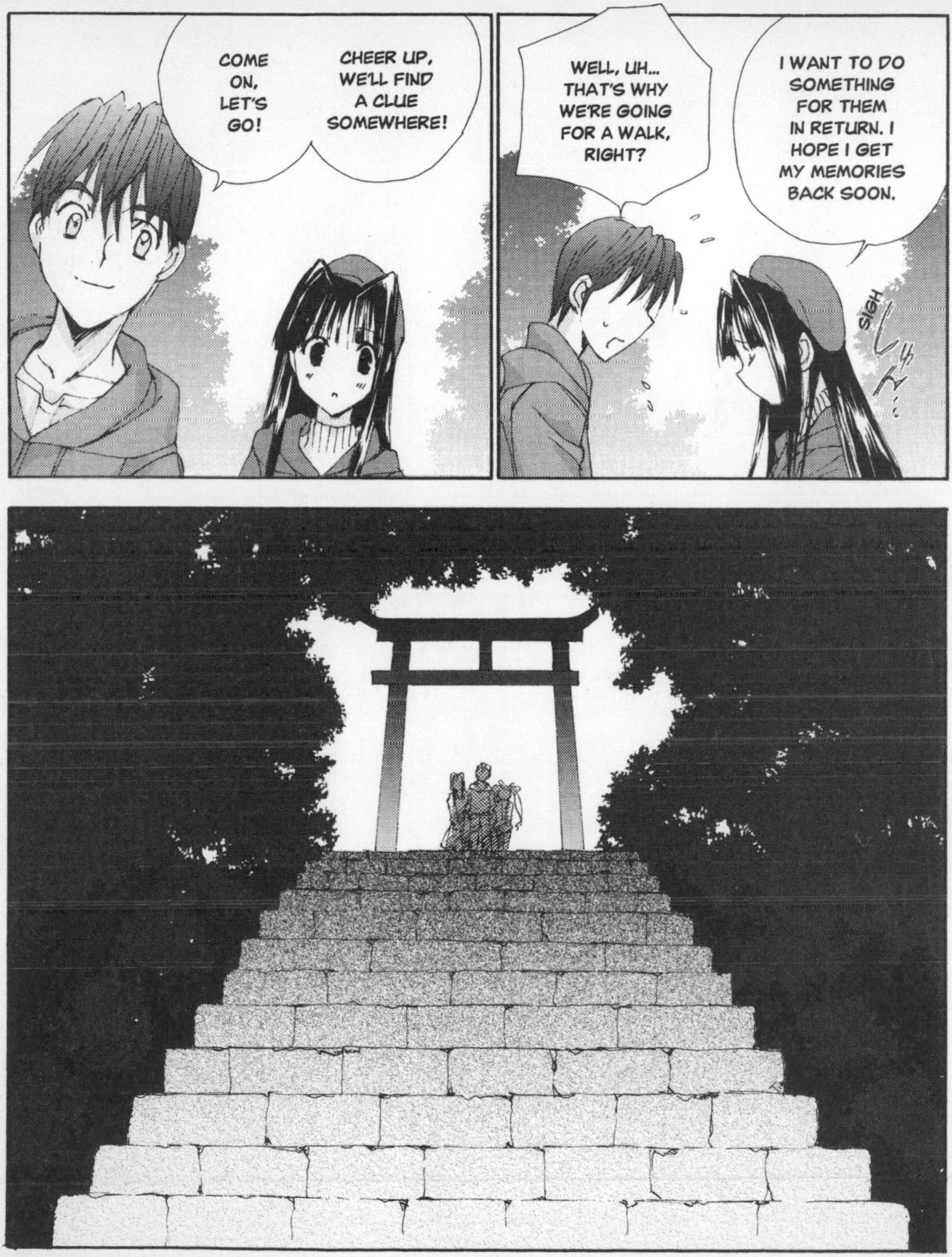
I WANT TO DO SOMETHING FOR THEM IN RETURN. I HOPE I GET MY MEMORIES BACK SOON.
WELL, UH... THAT'S WHY WE'RE GOING FOR A WALK, RIGHT?
SIGH
CHEER UP, WE'LL FIND A CLUE SOMEWHERE!
COME ON, LET'S GO!

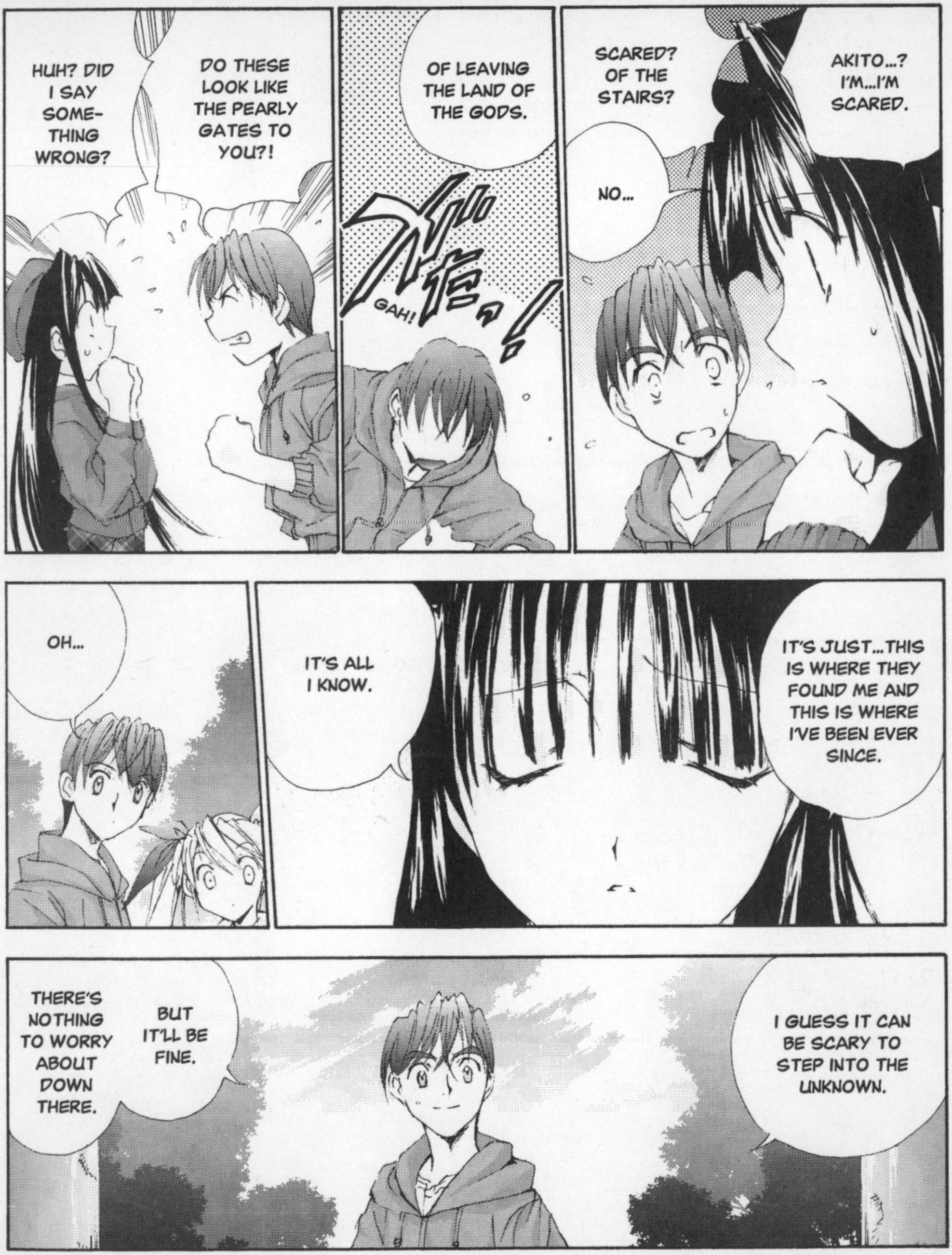
AKITO...? I'M...I'M SCARED.
SCARED? OF THE STAIRS?
NO...
OF LEAVING THE LAND OF THE GODS.
GAH!
DO THESE LOOK LIKE THE PEARLY GATES TO YOU?!
HUH? DID I SAY SOME-THING WRONG?
IT'S JUST...THIS IS WHERE THEY FOUND ME AND THIS IS WHERE I'VE BEEN EVER SINCE.
IT'S ALL I KNOW.
OH...
I GUESS IT CAN BE SCARY TO STEP INTO THE UNKNOWN.
BUT IT'LL BE FINE.
THERE'S NOTHING TO WORRY ABOUT DOWN THERE.

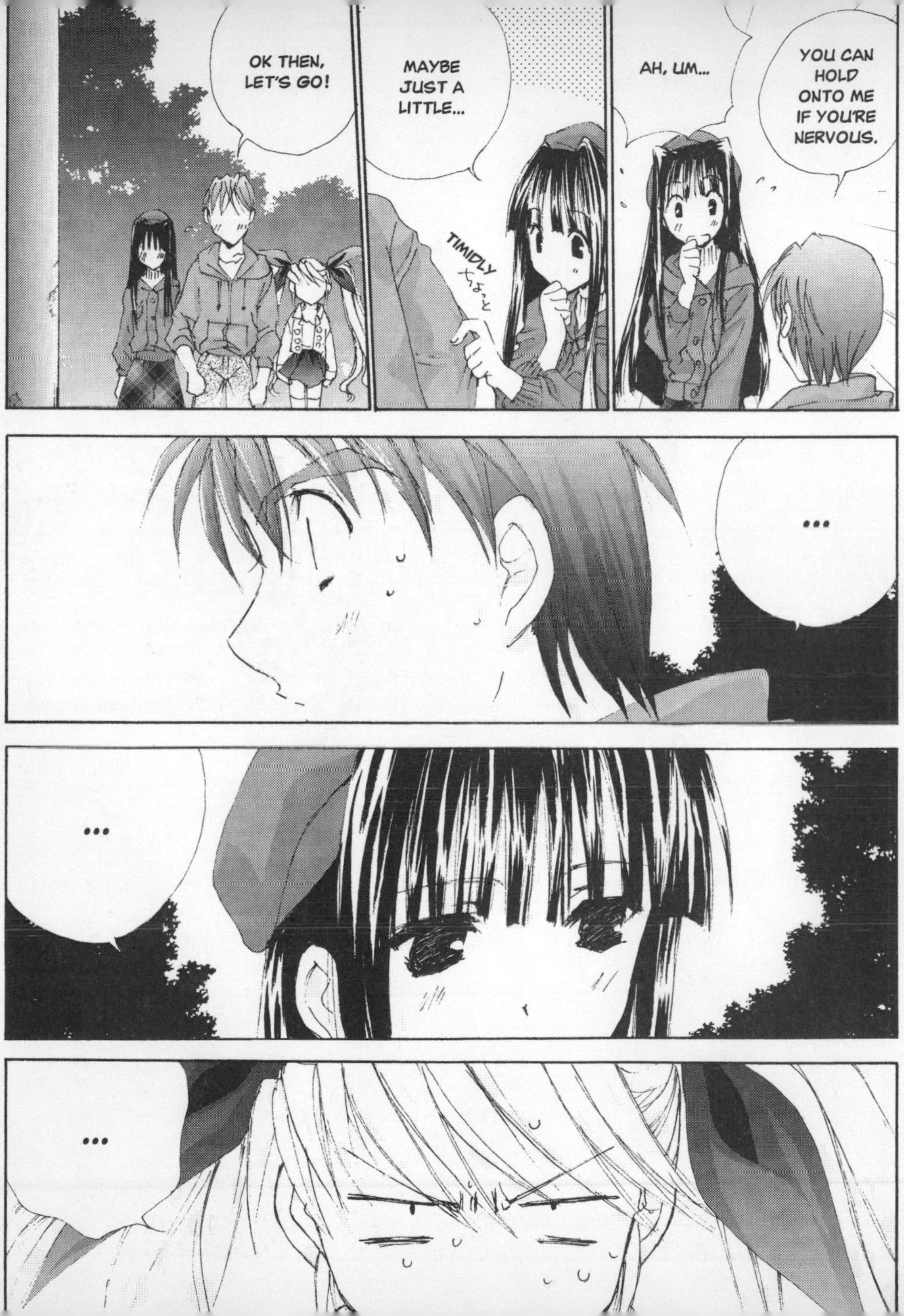
YOU CAN HOLD ONTO ME IF YOU'RE NERVOUS.
AH, UM...
MAYBE JUST A LITTLE...
TIMIDLY
OK THEN, LET'S GO!
...
...
...

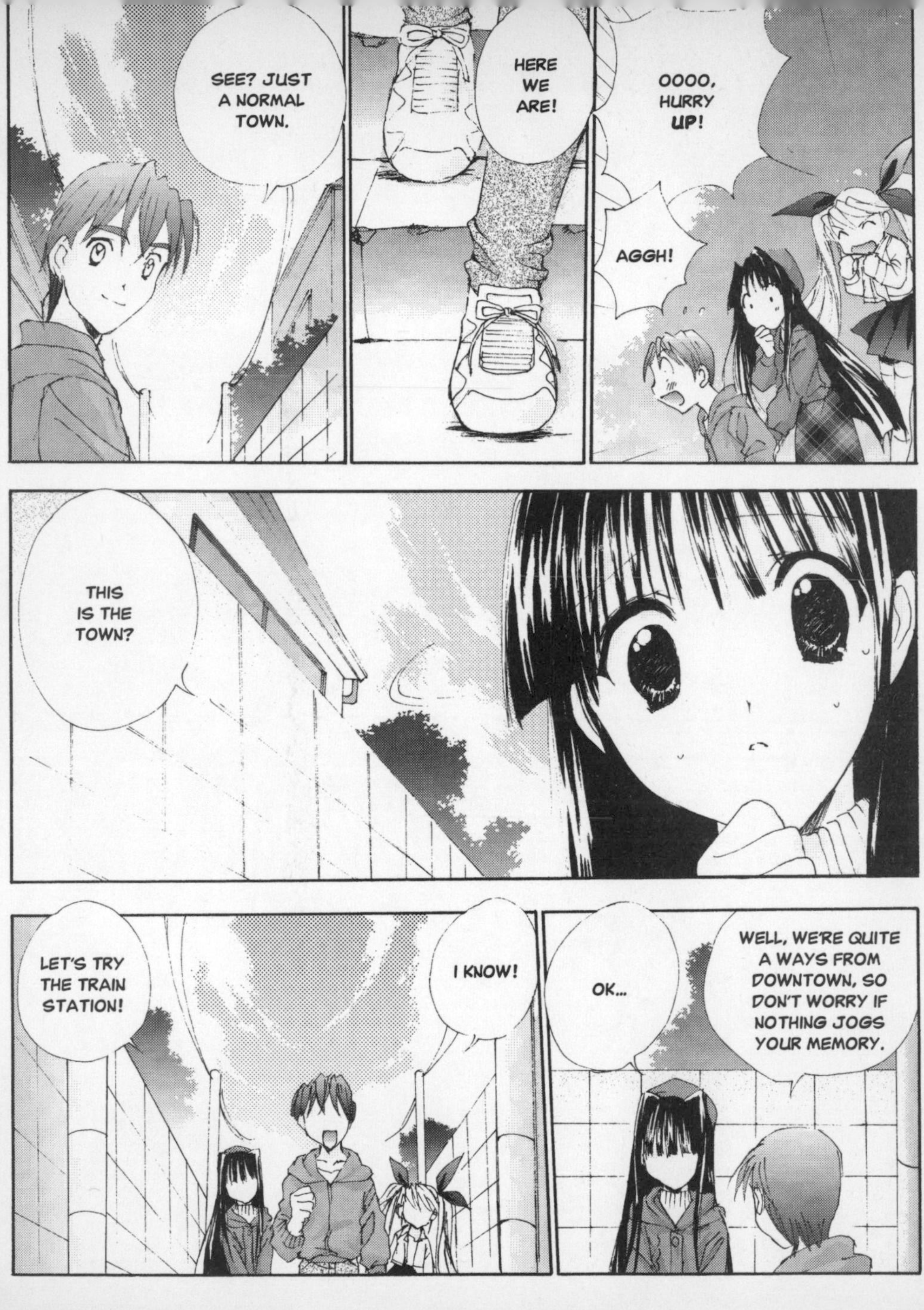
OOOO, HURRY UP!
AGGH!
HERE WE ARE!
SEE? JUST A NORMAL TOWN.
THIS IS THE TOWN?
WELL, WE'RE QUITE A WAYS FROM DOWNTOWN, SO DON'T WORRY IF NOTHING JOGS YOUR MEMORY.
OK...
I KNOW!
LET'S TRY THE TRAIN STATION!

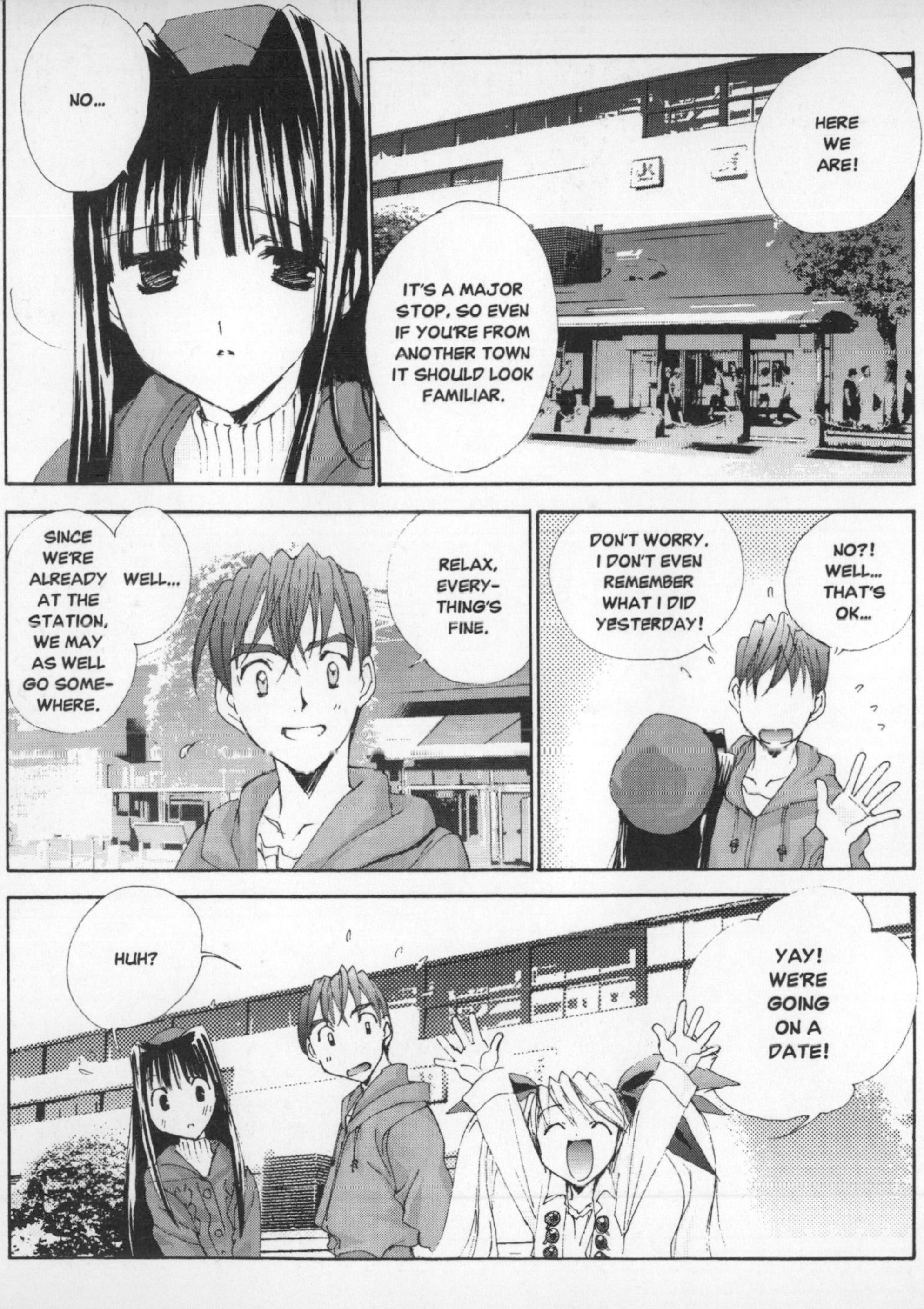
HERE WE ARE!
IT'S A MAJOR STOP, SO EVEN IF YOU'RE FROM ANOTHER TOWN IT SHOULD LOOK FAMILIAR.
NO...
NO?! WELL... THAT'S OK...
DON'T WORRY. I DON'T EVEN REMEMBER WHAT I DID YESTERDAY!
RELAX, EVERY-THING'S FINE.
WELL...
SINCE WE'RE ALREADY AT THE STATION, WE MAY AS WELL GO SOME-WHERE.
YAY! WE'RE GOING ON A DATE!
HUH?

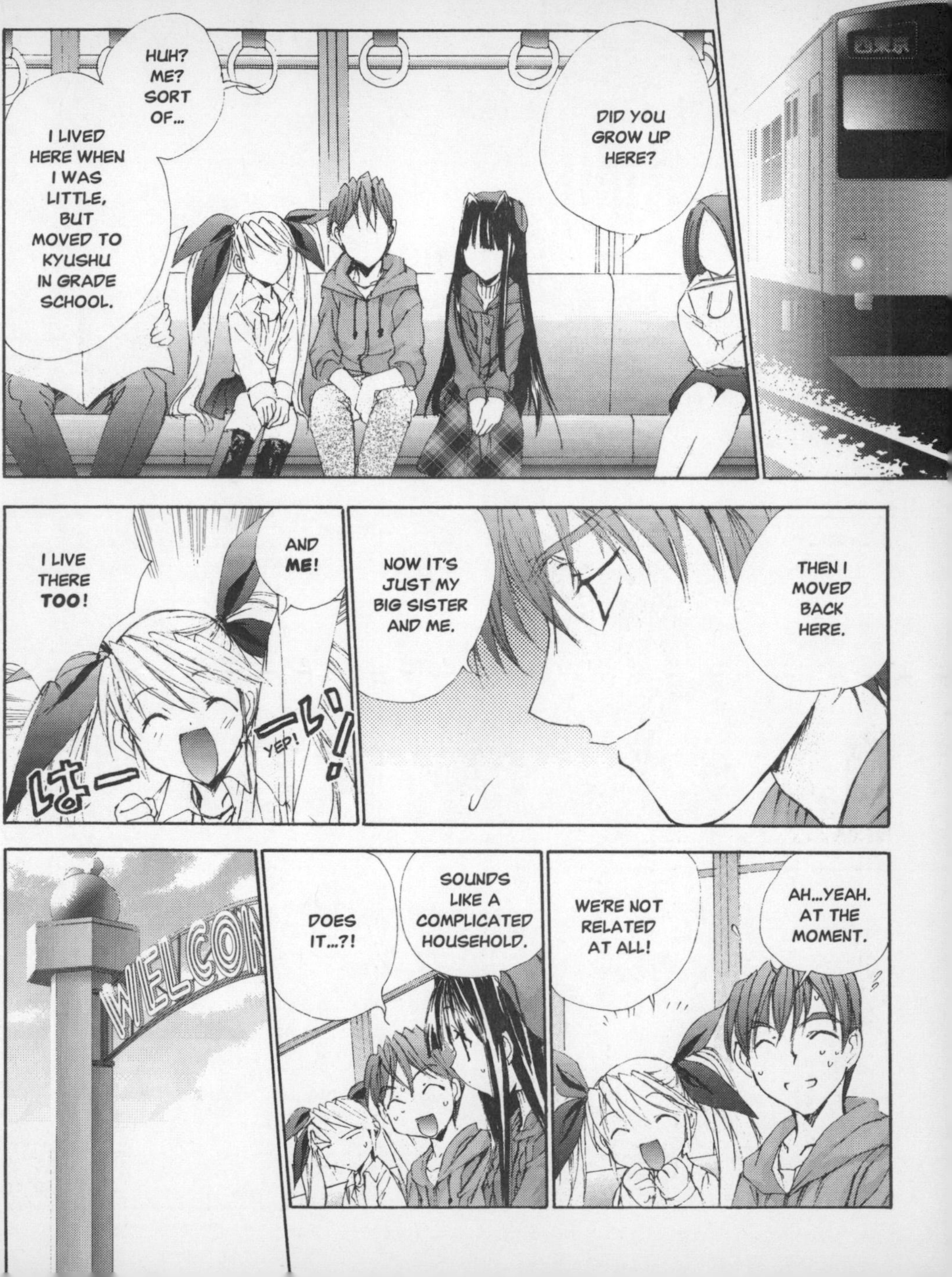
DID YOU GROW UP HERE?
HUH? ME? SORT OF...
I LIVED HERE WHEN I WAS LITTLE, BUT MOVED TO KYUSHU IN GRADE SCHOOL.
THEN I MOVED BACK HERE.
NOW IT'S JUST MY BIG SISTER AND ME.
AND ME!
I LIVE THERE TOO!
YEP!
AH...YEAH. AT THE MOMENT.
WE'RE NOT RELATED AT ALL!
SOUNDS LIKE A COMPLICATED HOUSEHOLD.
DOES IT...?!
WELCOM

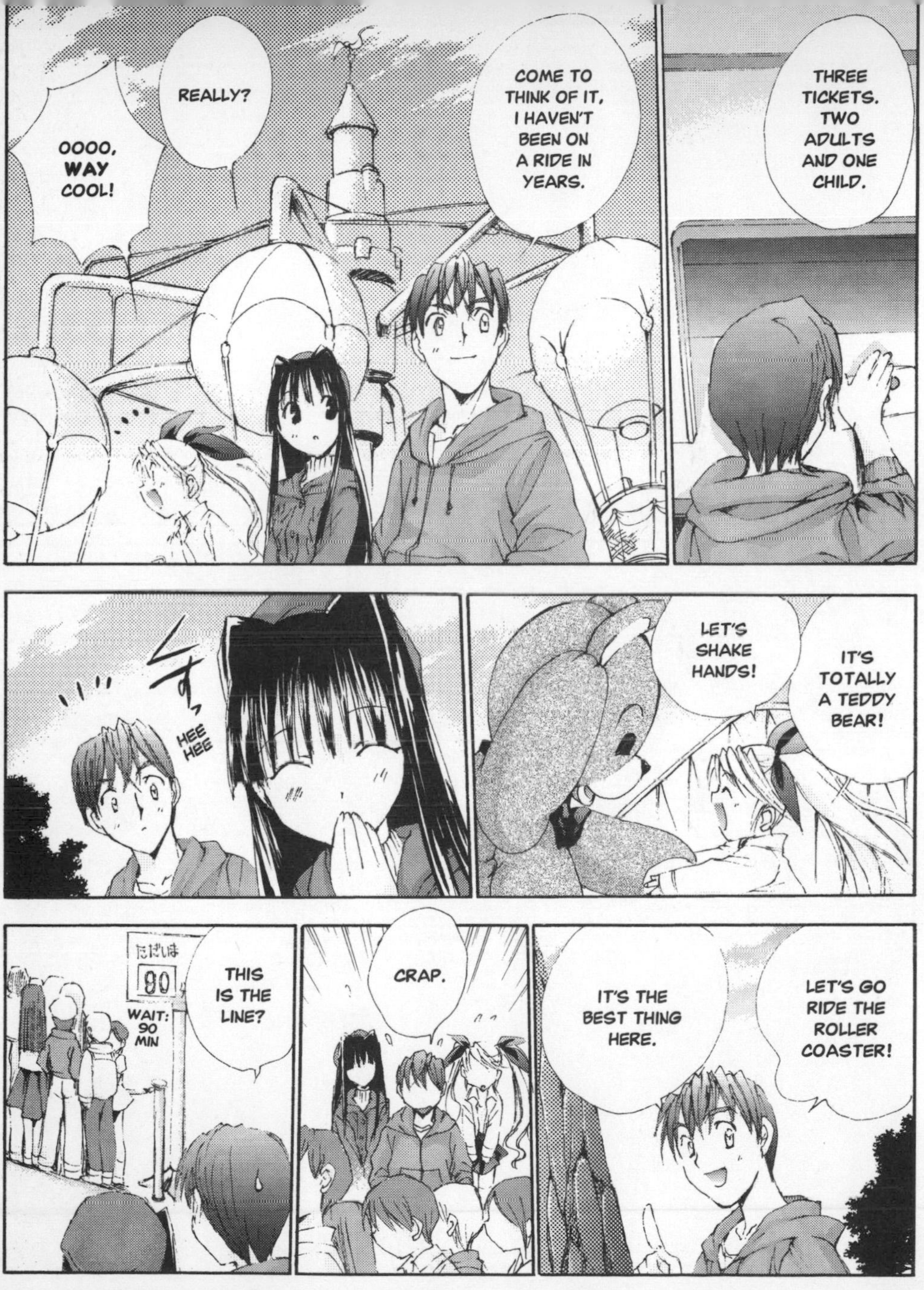
THREE TICKETS. TWO ADULTS AND ONE CHILD.
COME TO THINK OF IT, I HAVEN'T BEEN ON A RIDE IN YEARS.
REALLY?
OOOO, WAY COOL!
IT'S TOTALLY A TEDDY BEAR!
LET'S SHAKE HANDS!
HEE HEE
LET'S GO RIDE THE ROLLER COASTER!
IT'S THE BEST THING HERE.
CRAP.
THIS IS THE LINE?
90
WAIT: 90 MIN

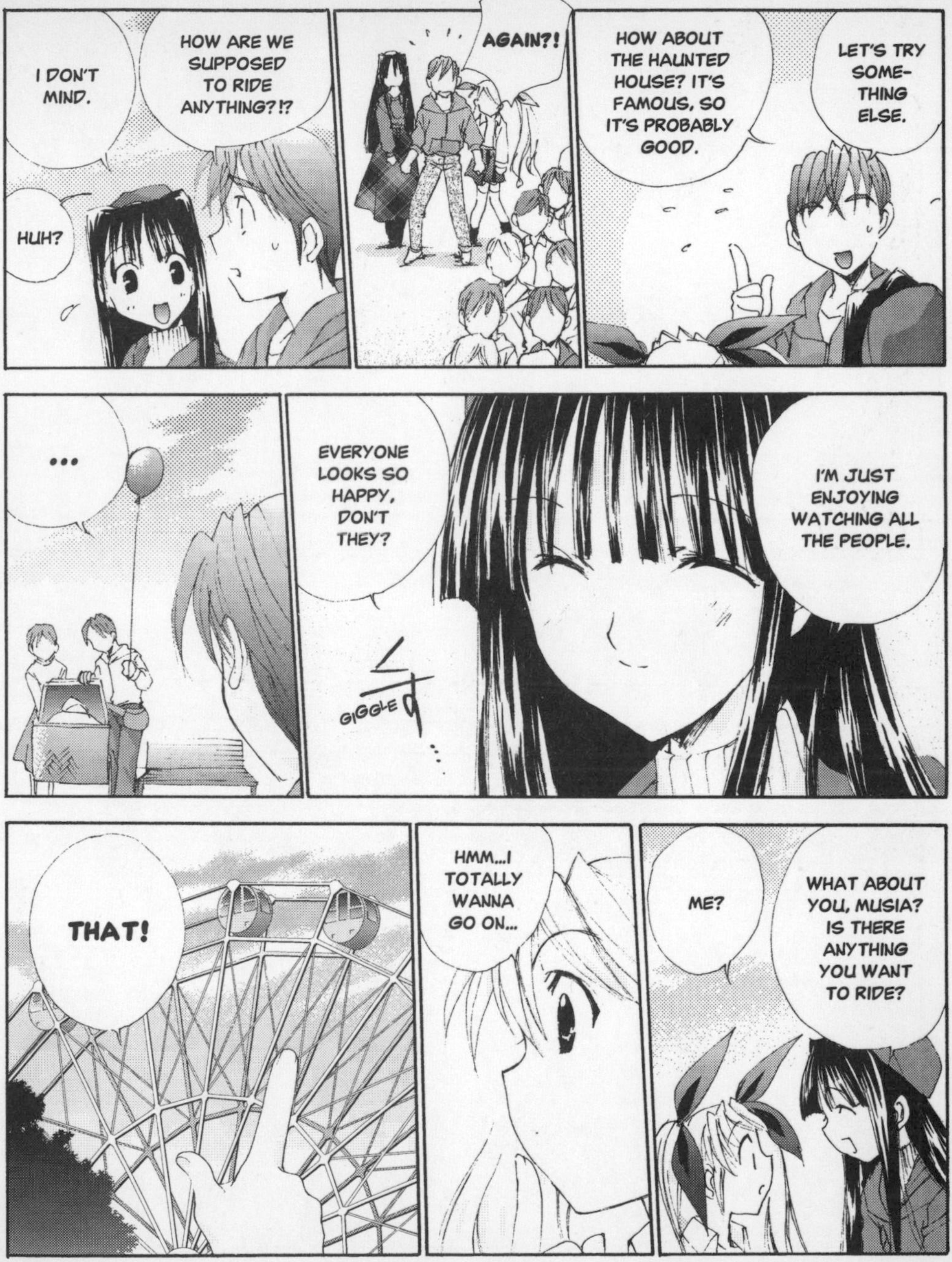
LET'S TRY SOME-THING ELSE.
HOW ABOUT THE HAUNTED HOUSE? IT'S FAMOUS, SO IT'S PROBABLY GOOD.
AGAIN?!
HOW ARE WE SUPPOSED TO RIDE ANYTHING?!?
I DON'T MIND.
HUH?
I'M JUST ENJOYING WATCHING ALL THE PEOPLE.
EVERYONE LOOKS SO HAPPY, DON'T THEY?
GIGGLE
...
WHAT ABOUT YOU, MUSIA? IS THERE ANYTHING YOU WANT TO RIDE?
ME?
HMM...I TOTALLY WANNA GO ON...
THAT!

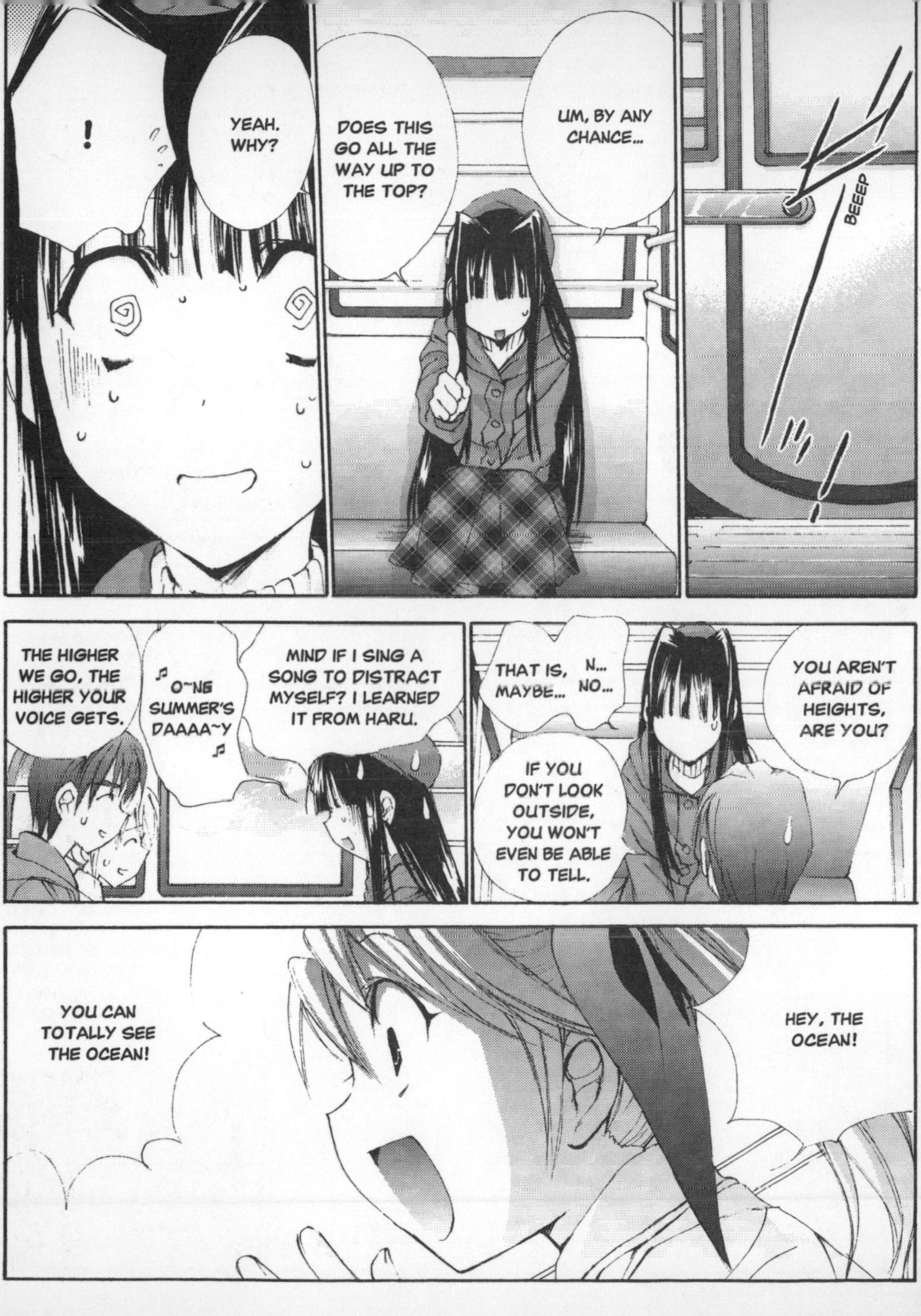

BEEEP
!
UM, BY ANY CHANCE...
DOES THIS GO ALL THE WAY UP TO THE TOP?
YEAH. WHY?
!
YOU AREN'T AFRAID OF HEIGHTS, ARE YOU?
N... NO...
THAT IS, MAYBE...
IF YOU DON'T LOOK OUTSIDE, YOU WON'T EVEN BE ABLE TO TELL.
MIND IF I SING A SONG TO DISTRACT MYSELF? I LEARNED IT FROM HARU.
♪ O~NE SUMMER'S DAAAA~Y ♪
THE HIGHER WE GO, THE HIGHER YOUR VOICE GETS.
HEY, THE OCEAN!
YOU CAN TOTALLY SEE THE OCEAN!

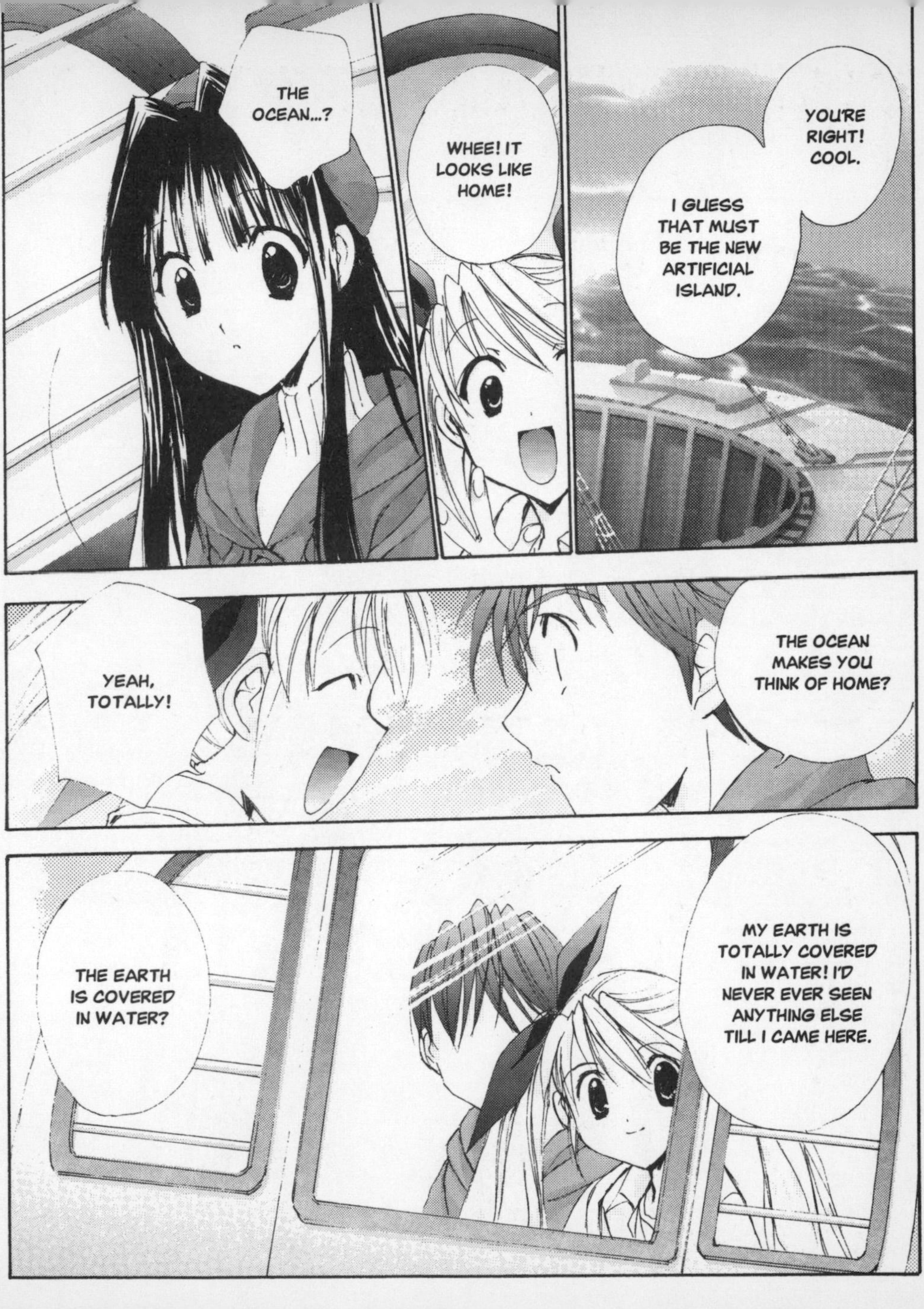
YOU'RE RIGHT! COOL.
I GUESS THAT MUST BE THE NEW ARTIFICIAL ISLAND.
WHEE! IT LOOKS LIKE HOME!
THE OCEAN...?
THE OCEAN MAKES YOU THINK OF HOME?
YEAH, TOTALLY!
MY EARTH IS TOTALLY COVERED IN WATER! I'D NEVER EVER SEEN ANYTHING ELSE TILL I CAME HERE.
THE EARTH IS COVERED IN WATER?

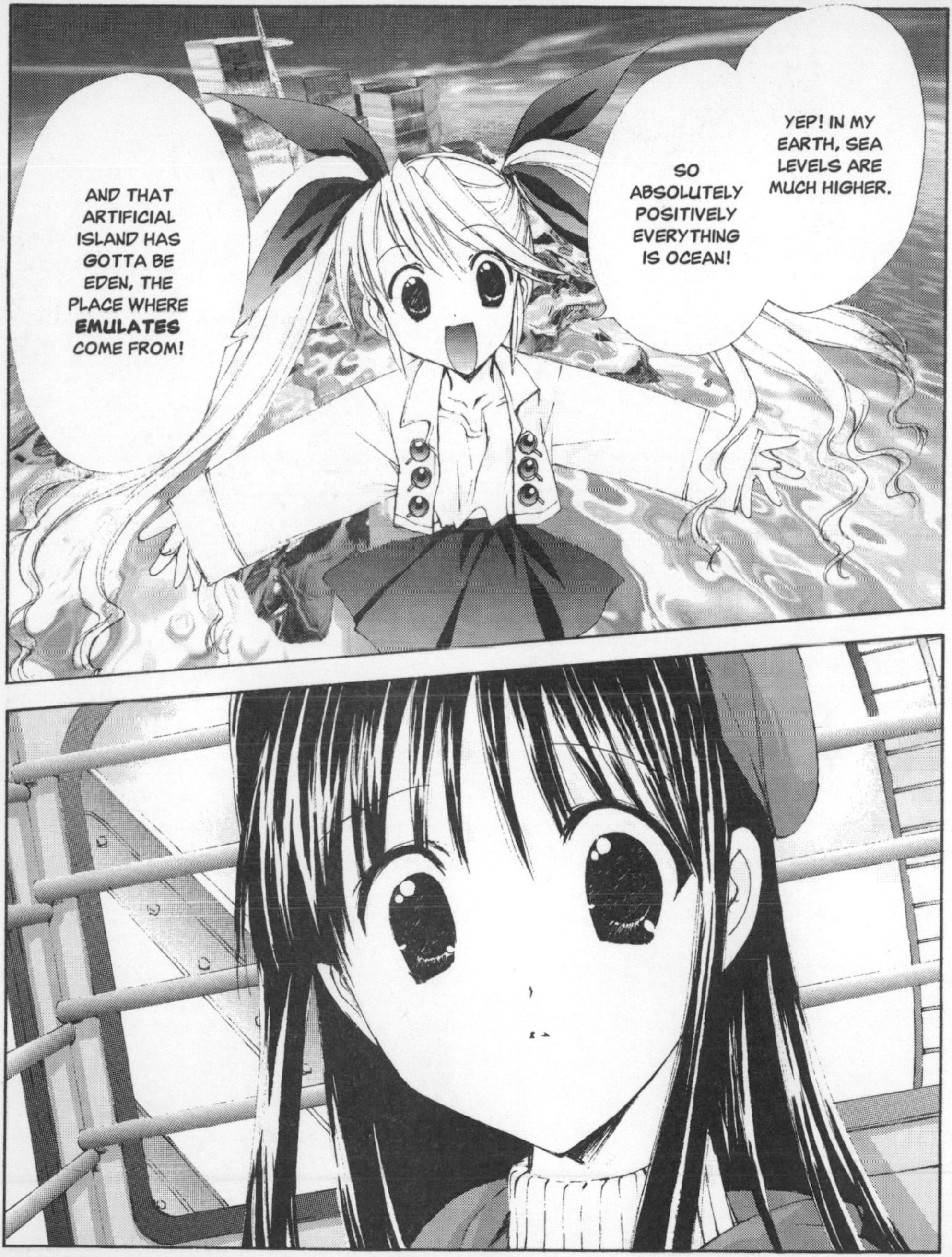
YEP! IN MY EARTH, SEA LEVELS ARE MUCH HIGHER.
SO ABSOLUTELY POSITIVELY EVERYTHING IS OCEAN!
AND THAT ARTIFICIAL ISLAND HAS GOTTA BE EDEN, THE PLACE WHERE **EMULATES** COME FROM!

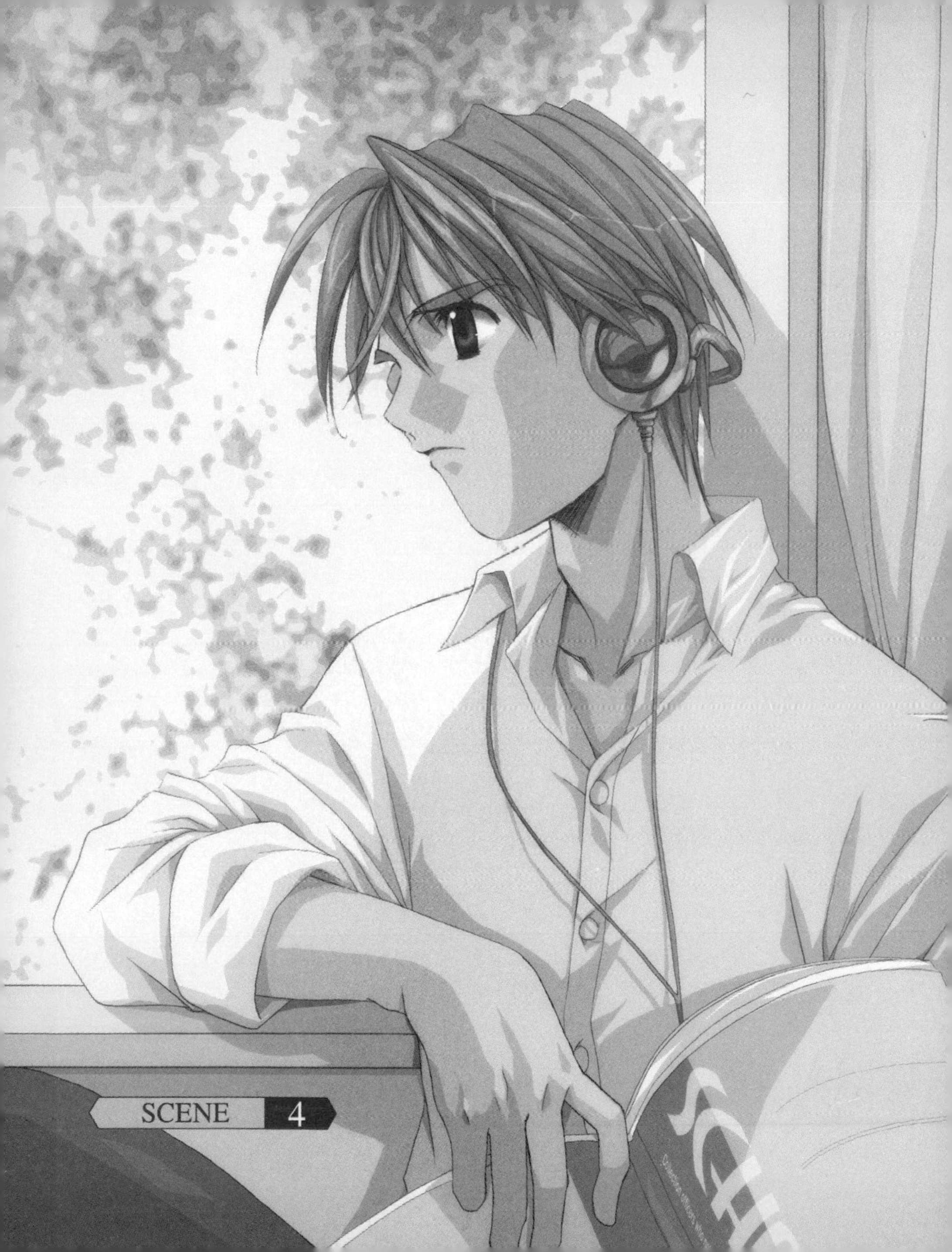
SCENE 4

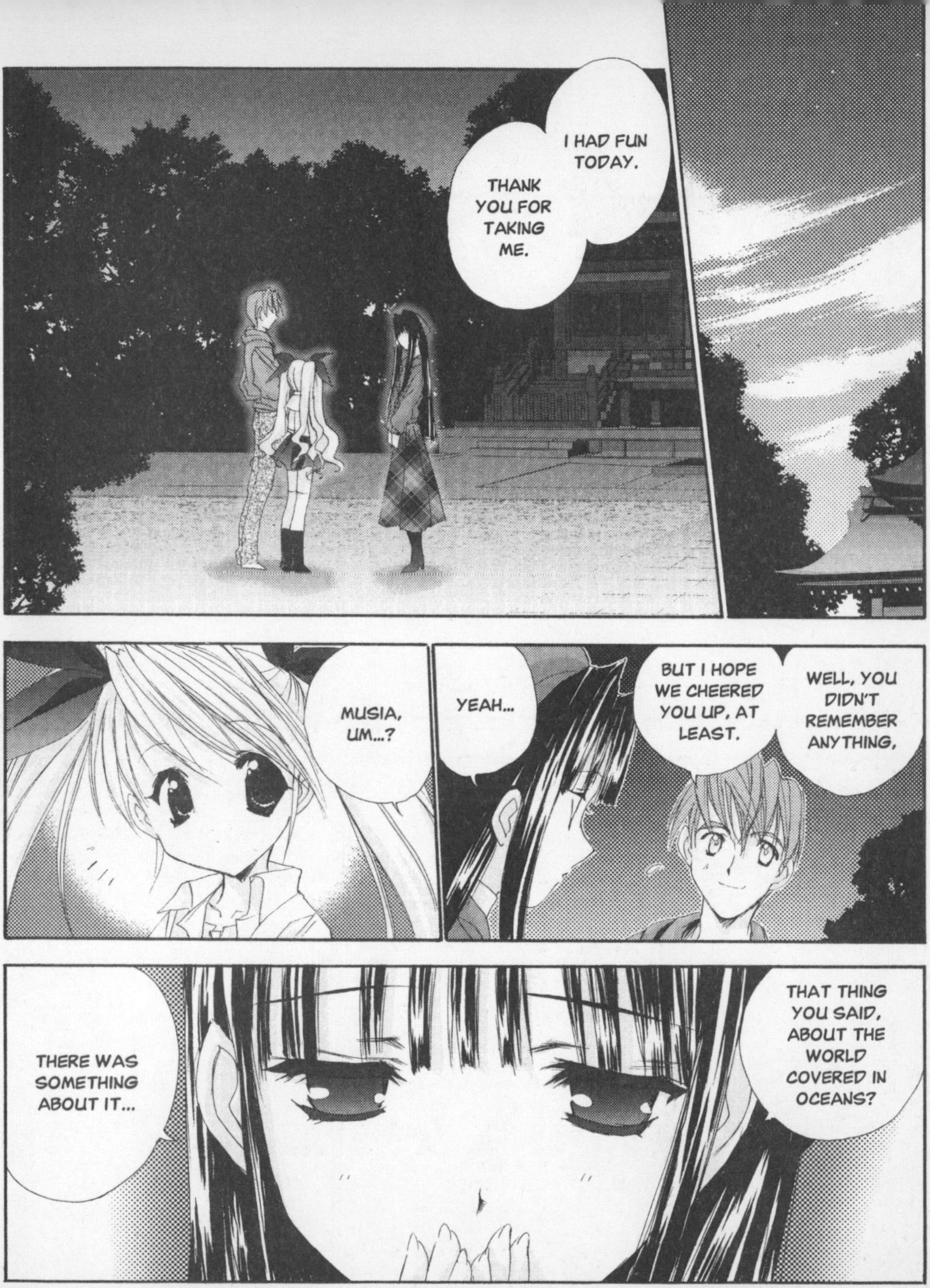
I HAD FUN TODAY.
THANK YOU FOR TAKING ME.
WELL, YOU DIDN'T REMEMBER ANYTHING,
BUT I HOPE WE CHEERED YOU UP, AT LEAST.
YEAH...
MUSIA, UM...?
THAT THING YOU SAID, ABOUT THE WORLD COVERED IN OCEANS?
THERE WAS SOMETHING ABOUT IT...

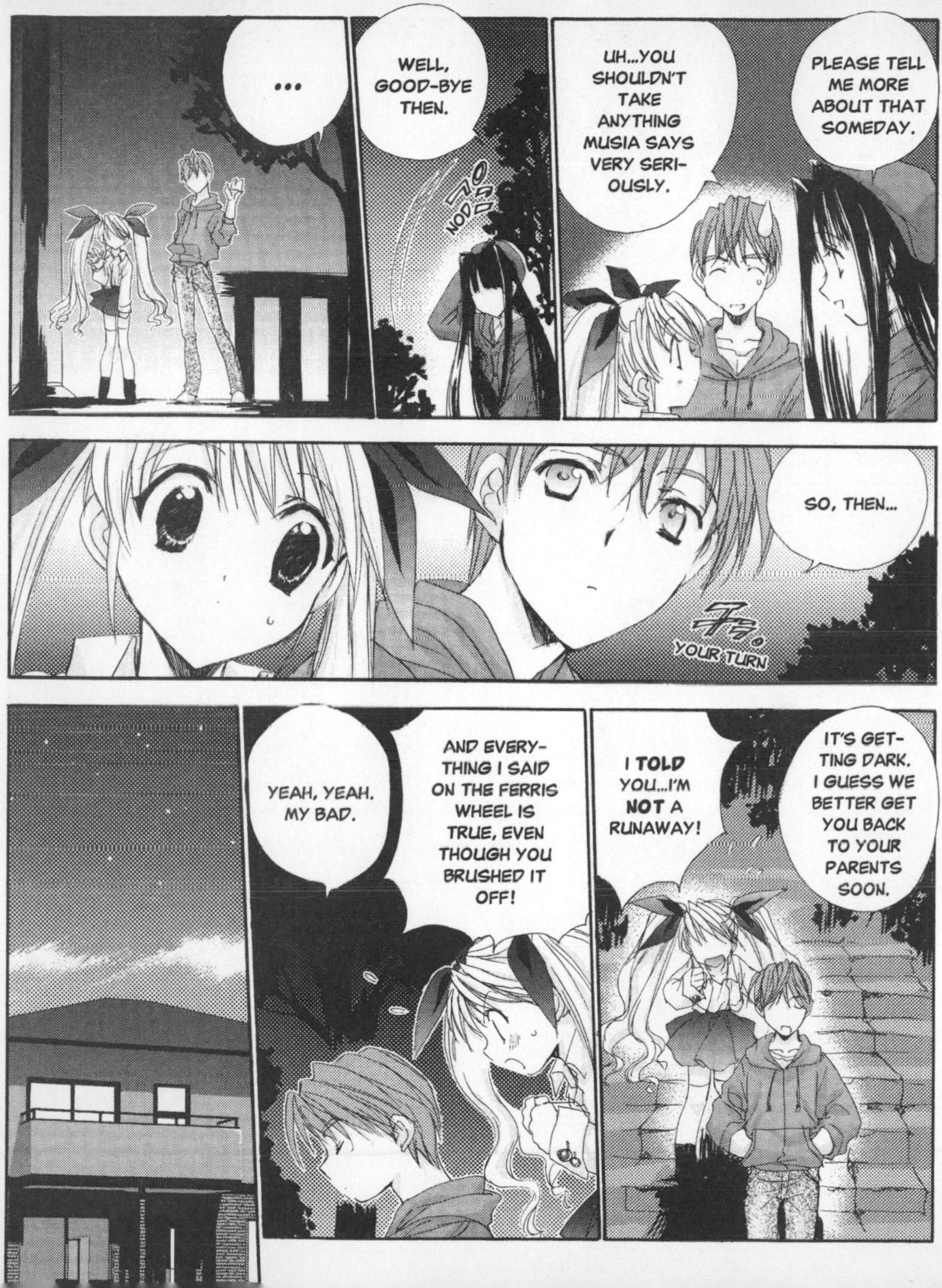
PLEASE TELL ME MORE ABOUT THAT SOMEDAY.
UH...YOU SHOULDN'T TAKE ANYTHING MUSIA SAYS VERY SERI-OUSLY.
WELL, GOOD-BYE THEN.
NOD
...
SO, THEN...
YOUR TURN
IT'S GET-TING DARK. I GUESS WE BETTER GET YOU BACK TO YOUR PARENTS SOON.
I **TOLD** YOU...I'M **NOT** A RUNAWAY!
AND EVERY-THING I SAID ON THE FERRIS WHEEL IS TRUE, EVEN THOUGH YOU BRUSHED IT OFF!
YEAH, YEAH. MY BAD.

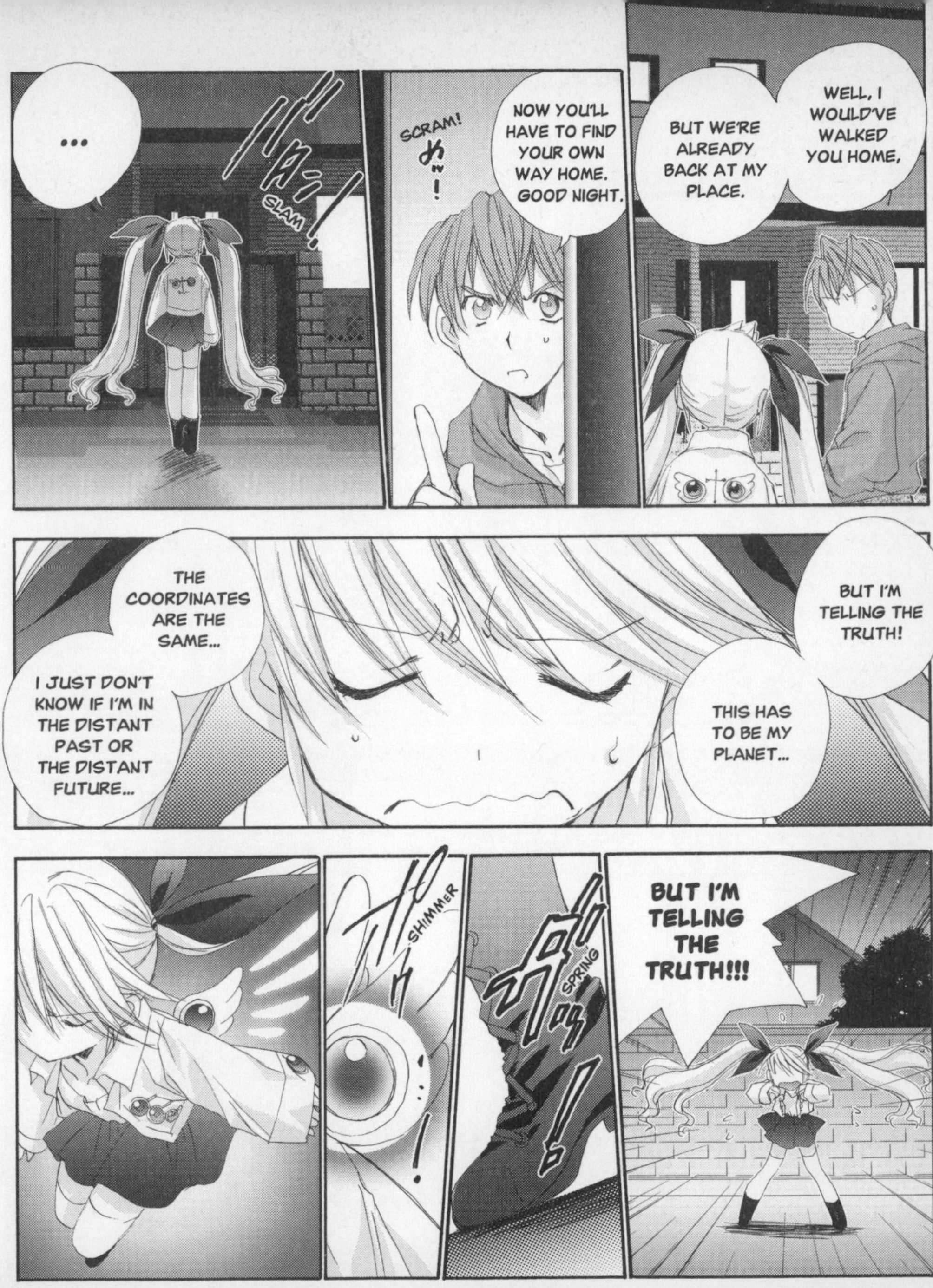
WELL, I WOULD'VE WALKED YOU HOME,
BUT WE'RE ALREADY BACK AT MY PLACE.
NOW YOU'LL HAVE TO FIND YOUR OWN WAY HOME. GOOD NIGHT.
SCRAM!
SLAM
...
BUT I'M TELLING THE TRUTH!
THIS HAS TO BE MY PLANET...
THE COORDINATES ARE THE SAME...
I JUST DON'T KNOW IF I'M IN THE DISTANT PAST OR THE DISTANT FUTURE...
BUT I'M TELLING THE TRUTH!!!
SPRING
SHIMMER

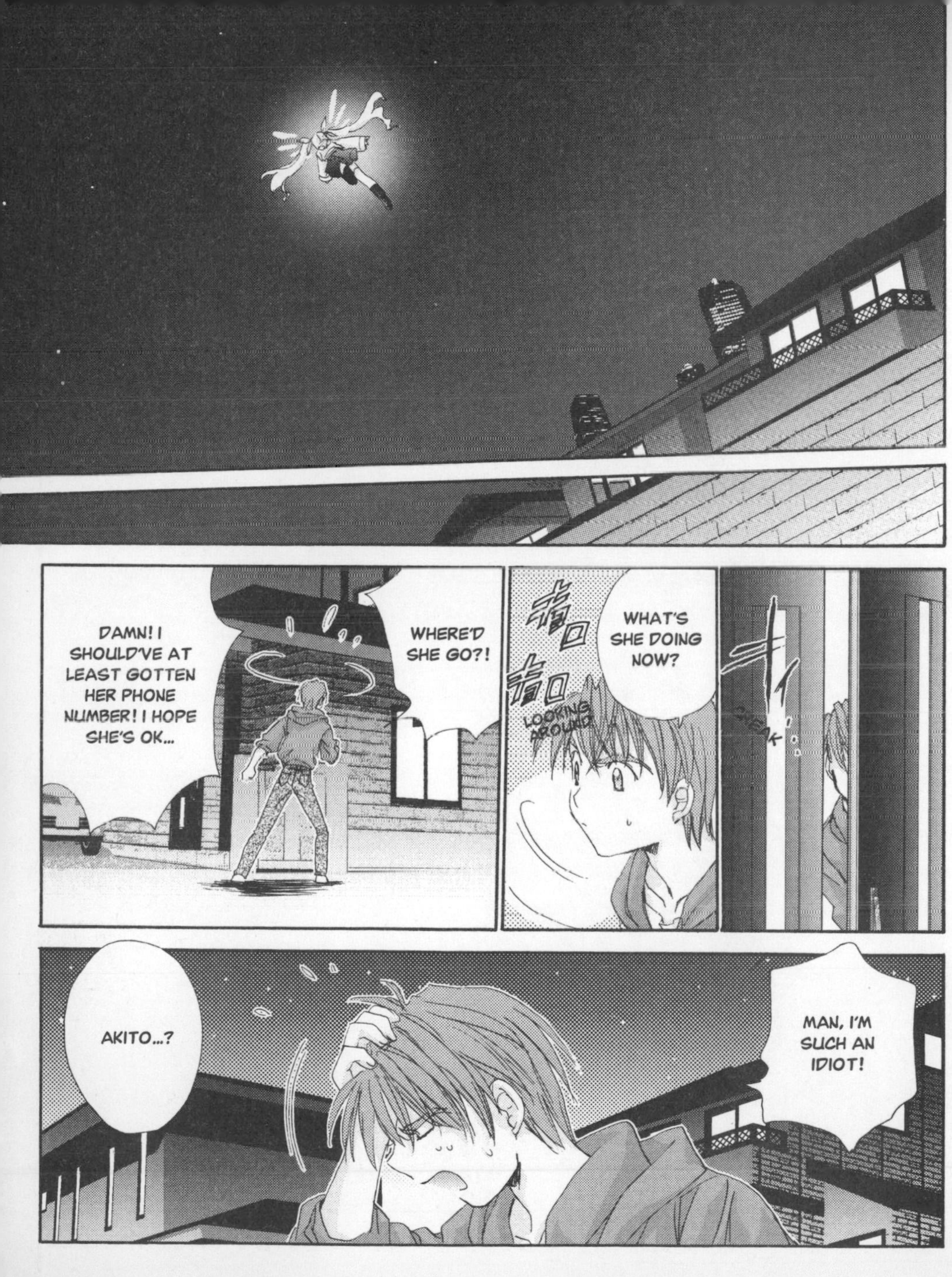
WHAT'S SHE DOING NOW?
LOOKING AROUND
WHERE'D SHE GO?!
DAMN! I SHOULD'VE AT LEAST GOTTEN HER PHONE NUMBER! I HOPE SHE'S OK...
MAN, I'M SUCH AN IDIOT!
AKITO...?

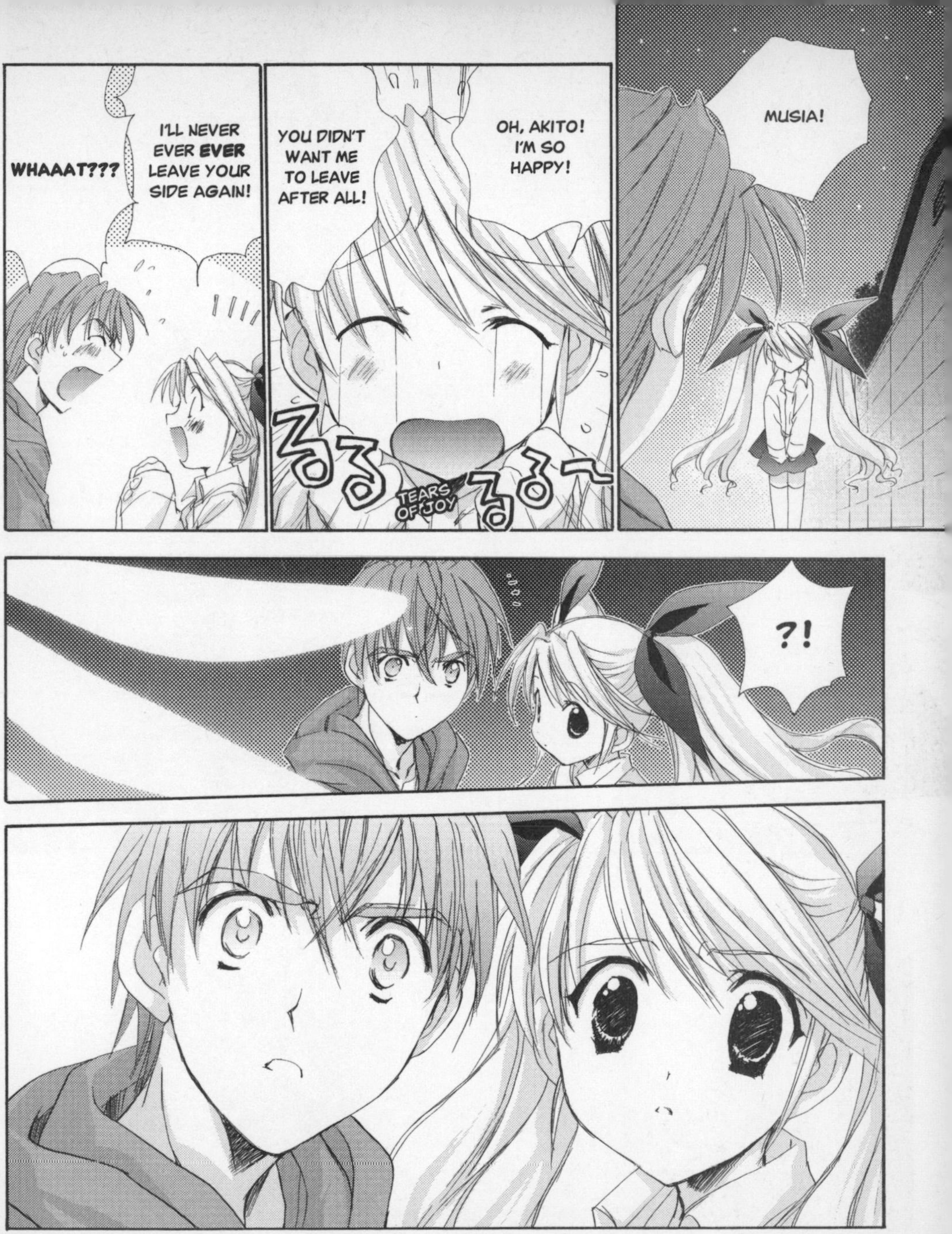
MUSIA!
OH, AKITO! I'M SO HAPPY!
YOU DIDN'T WANT ME TO LEAVE AFTER ALL!
るる
TEARS OF JOY
るる〜
I'LL NEVER EVER **EVER** LEAVE YOUR SIDE AGAIN!
WHAAAT???
?!

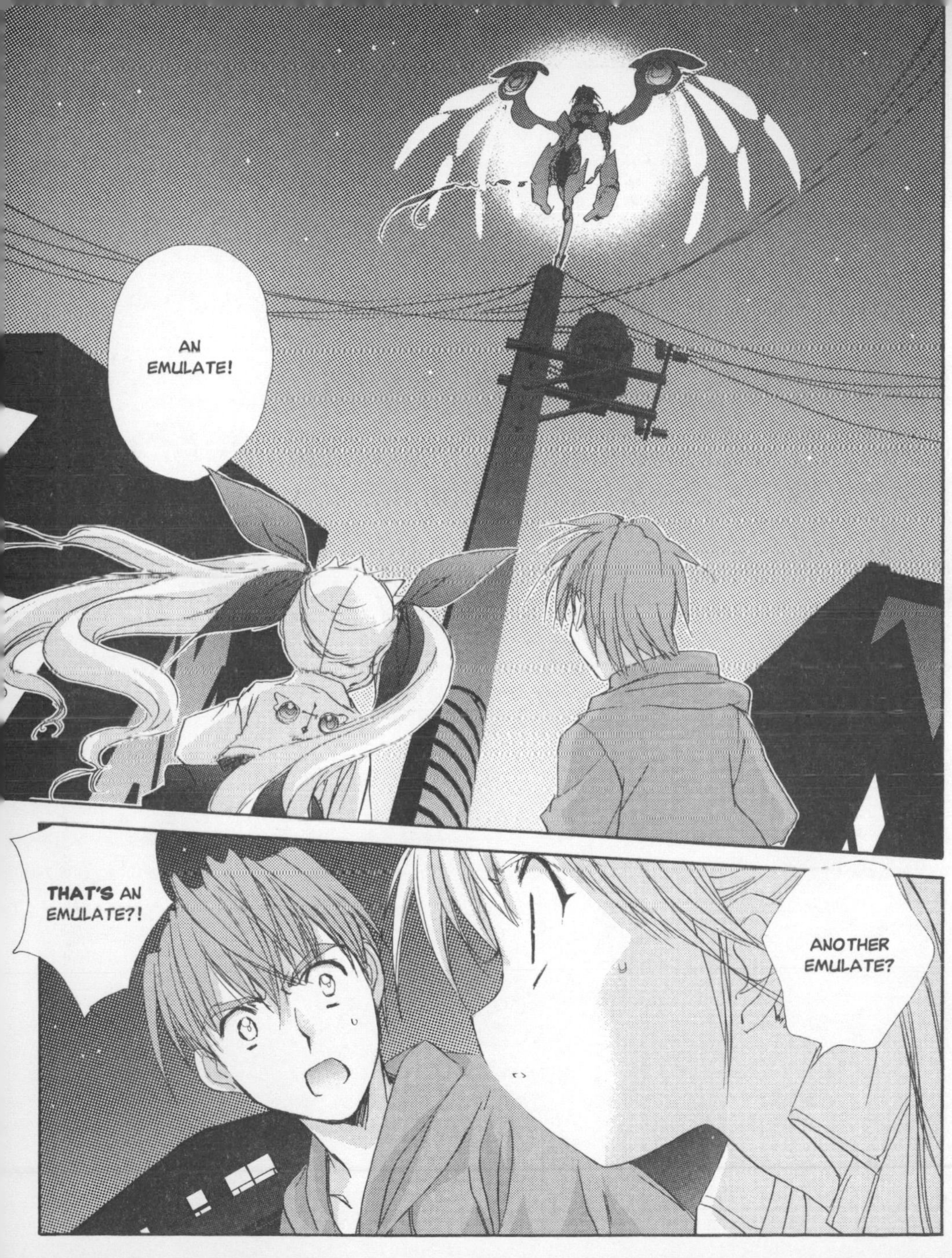
AN EMULATE!
THAT'S AN EMULATE?!
ANOTHER EMULATE?

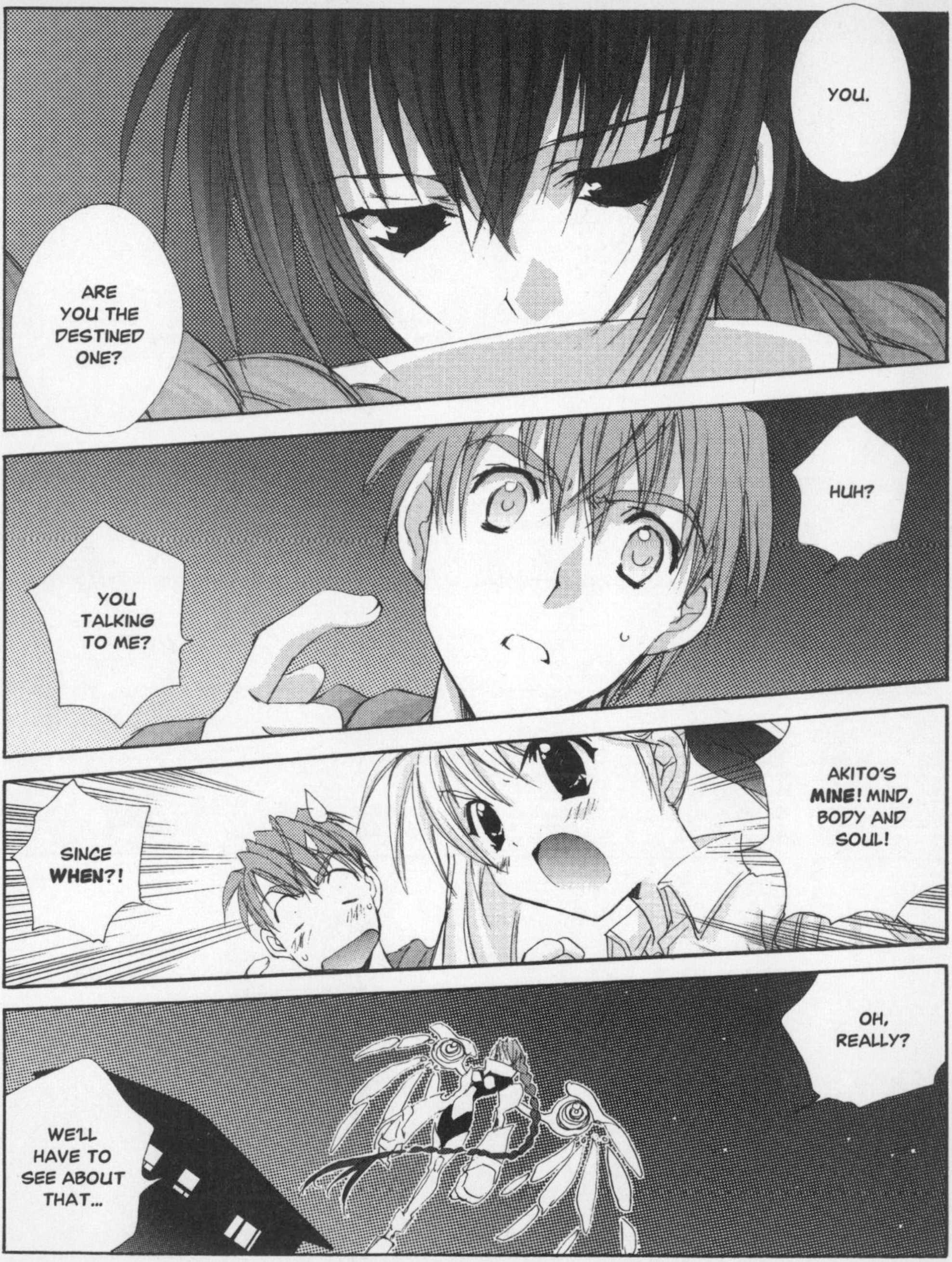
YOU.
ARE YOU THE DESTINED ONE?
HUH?
YOU TALKING TO ME?
AKITO'S **MINE!** MIND, BODY AND SOUL!
SINCE **WHEN?!**
OH, REALLY?
WE'LL HAVE TO SEE ABOUT THAT...

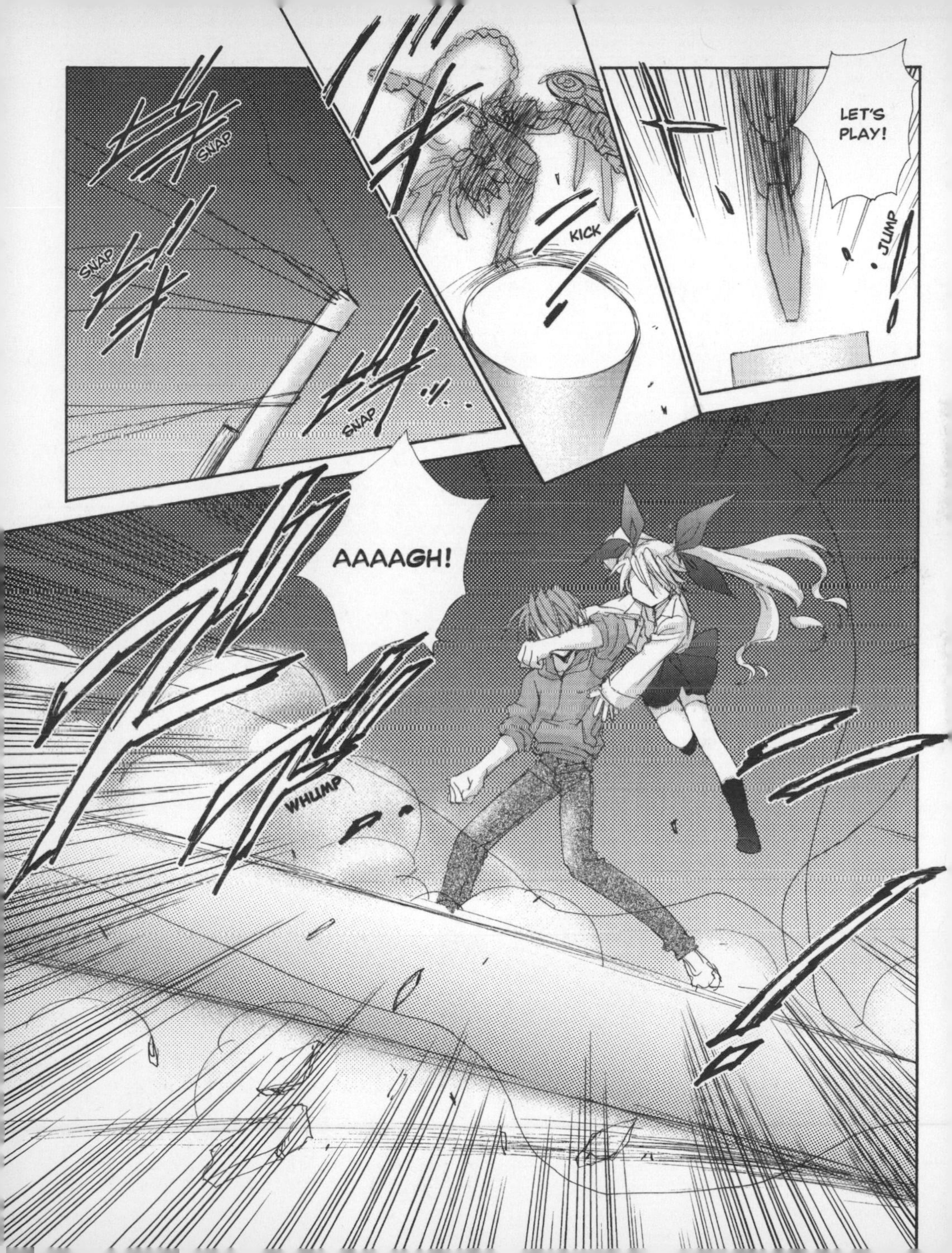
LET'S PLAY!
JUMP
KICK
SNAP
SNAP
SNAP
AAAAGH!
WHUMP

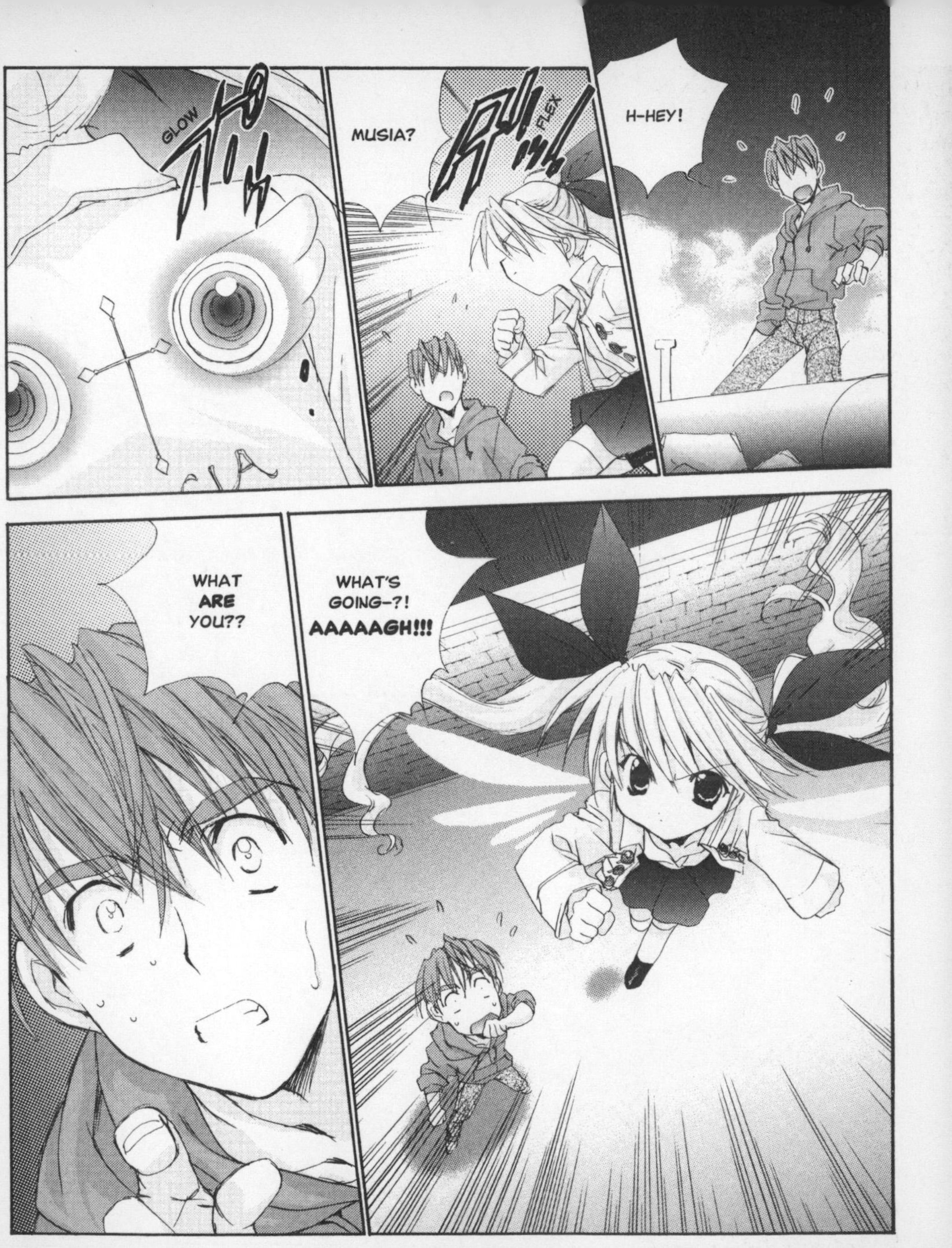
H-HEY!
MUSIA?
FLEX
GLOW
WHAT'S GOING-?! **AAAAAGH!!!**
WHAT **ARE** YOU??

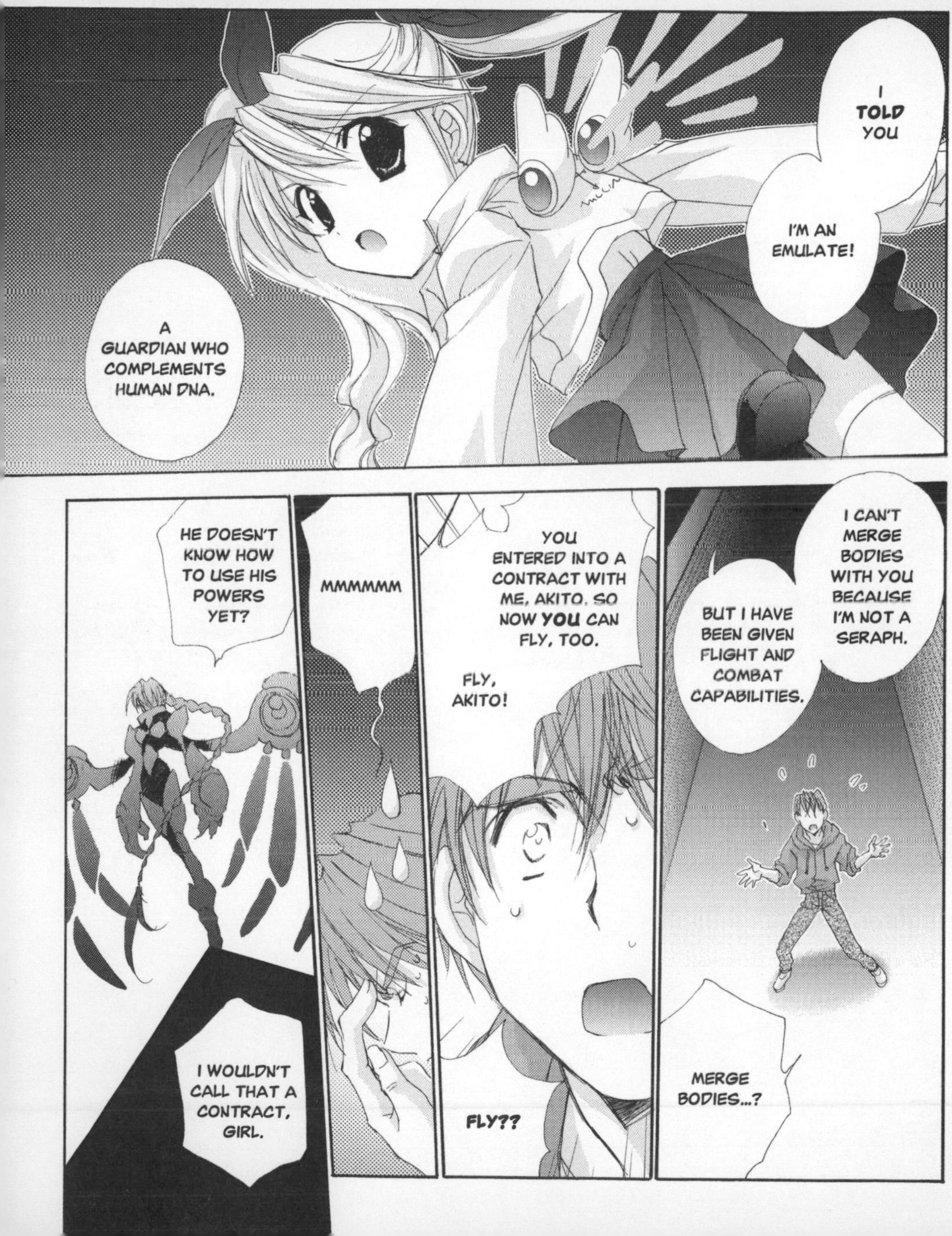
I TOLD YOU
I'M AN EMULATE!
A GUARDIAN WHO COMPLEMENTS HUMAN DNA.
I CAN'T MERGE BODIES WITH YOU BECAUSE I'M NOT A SERAPH.
BUT I HAVE BEEN GIVEN FLIGHT AND COMBAT CAPABILITIES.
MERGE BODIES...?
YOU ENTERED INTO A CONTRACT WITH ME, AKITO, SO NOW YOU CAN FLY, TOO.
FLY, AKITO!
FLY??
MMMMMM
HE DOESN'T KNOW HOW TO USE HIS POWERS YET?
I WOULDN'T CALL THAT A CONTRACT, GIRL.

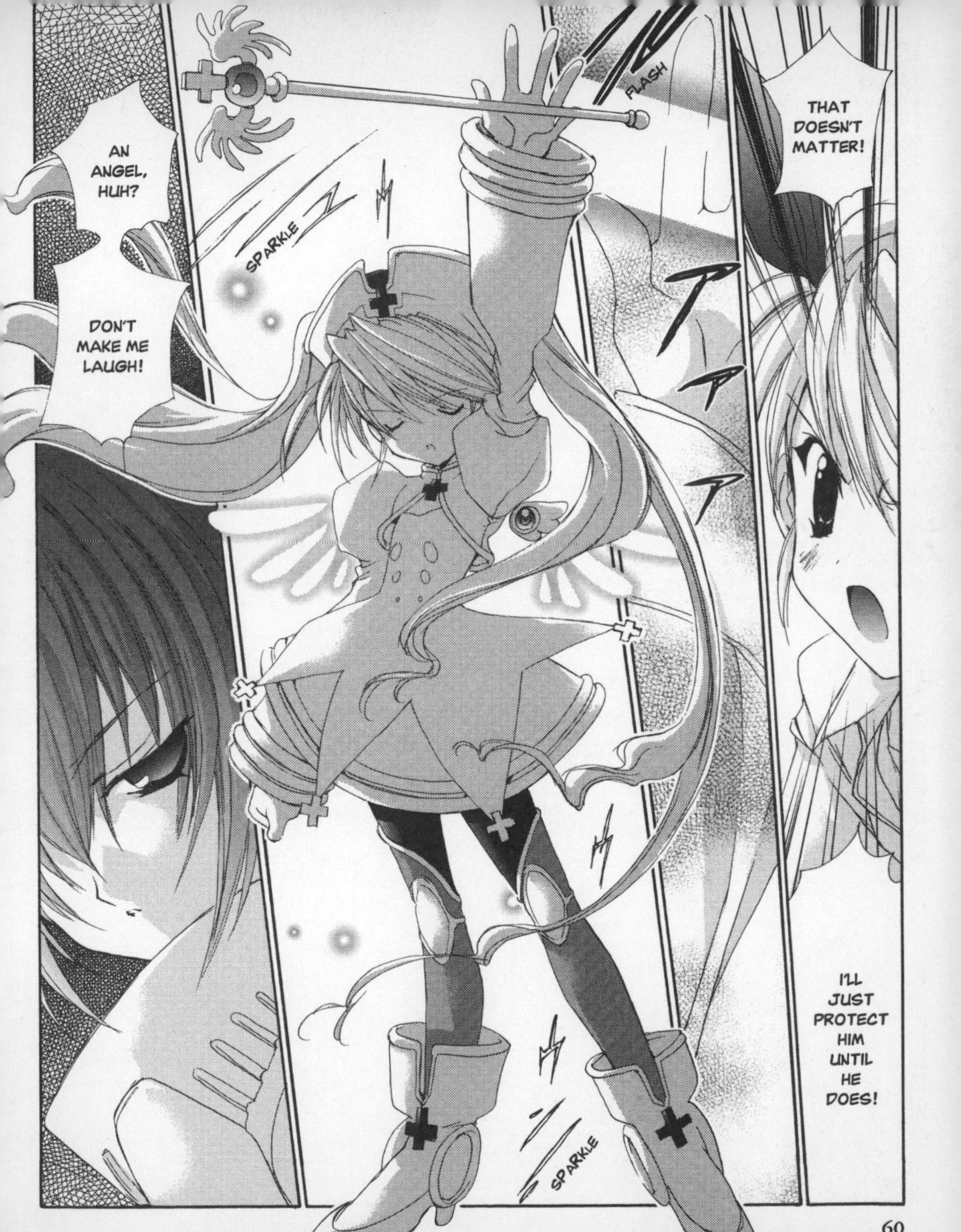
THAT DOESN'T MATTER!
FLASH
AN ANGEL, HUH?
DON'T MAKE ME LAUGH!
SPARKLE
I'LL JUST PROTECT HIM UNTIL HE DOES!
SPARKLE

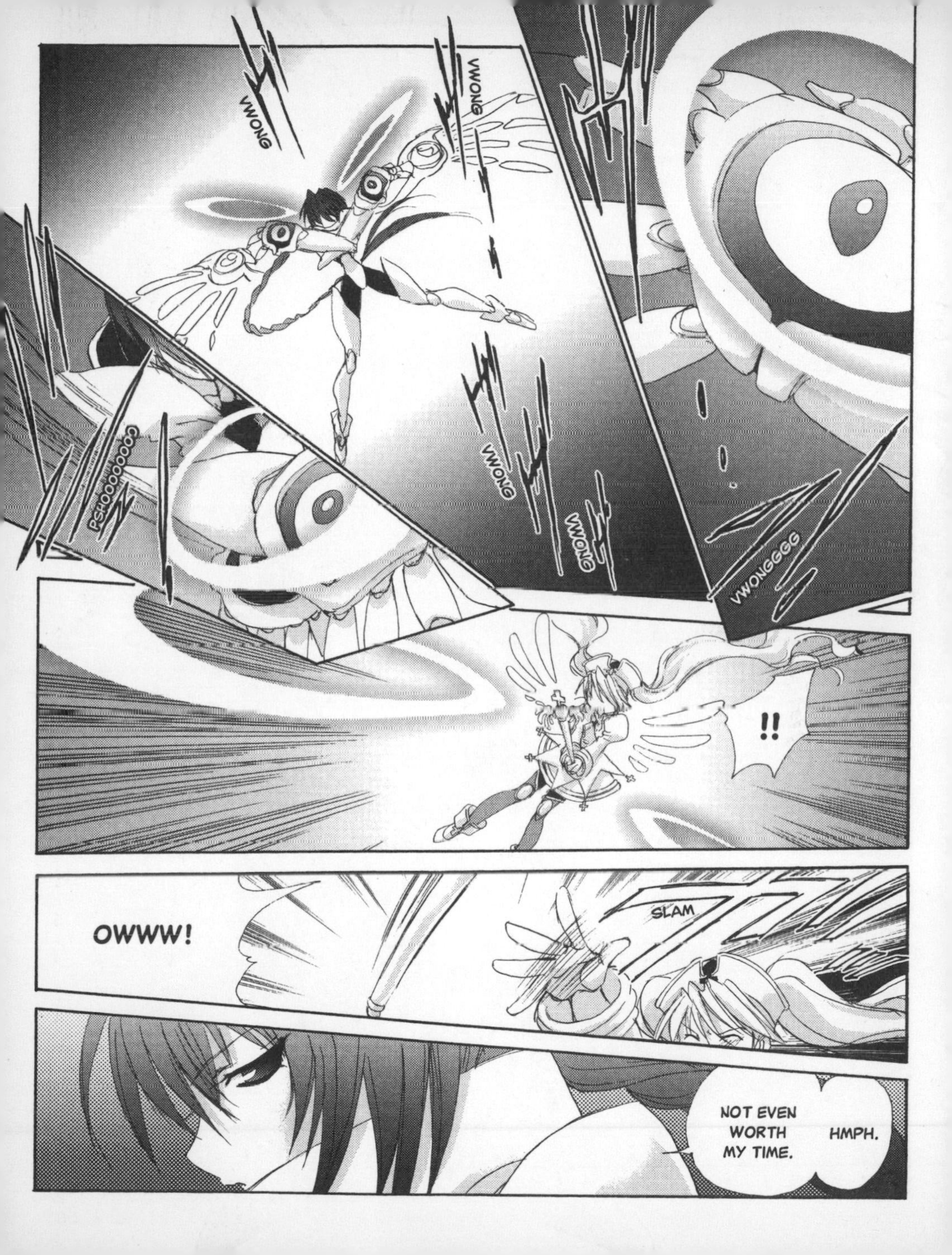
VWONG
VWONG
PSHOOOOOOOOO
VWONG
VWONG
VWONGGGG
!!
OWWW!
SLAM
NOT EVEN WORTH MY TIME.
HMPH.

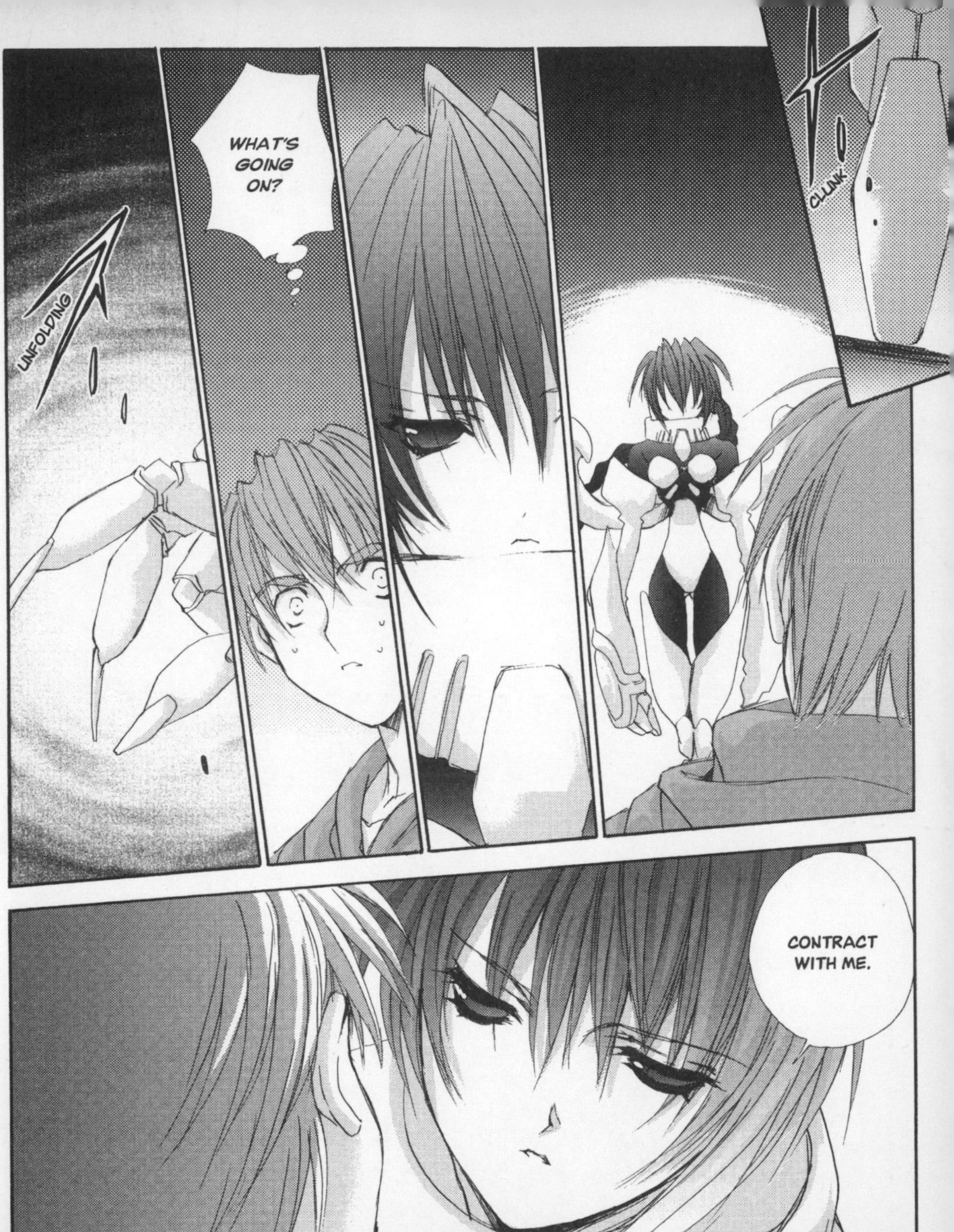
CLUNK
WHAT'S GOING ON?
UNFOLDING
CONTRACT WITH ME.

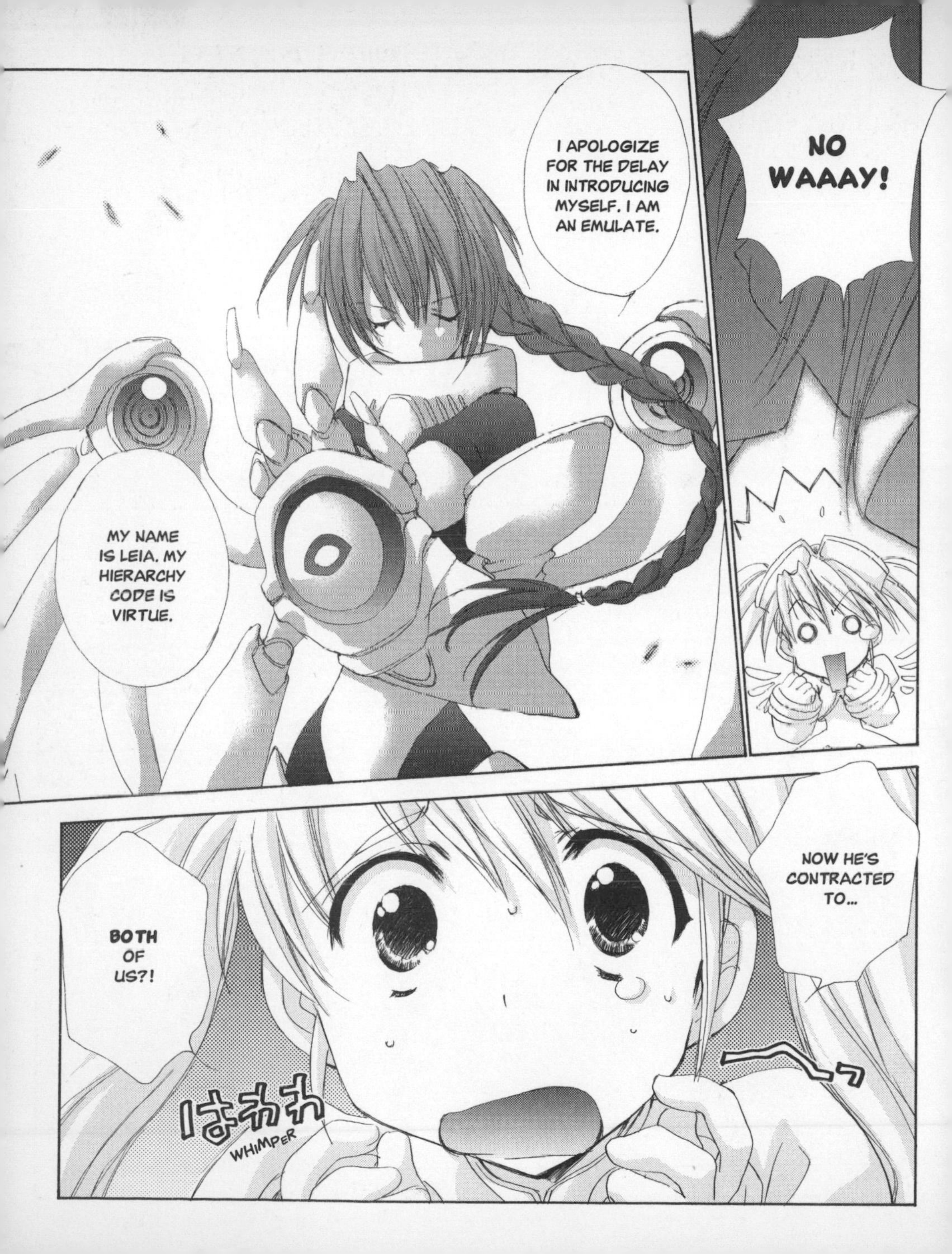
NO WAAAY!
I APOLOGIZE FOR THE DELAY IN INTRODUCING MYSELF. I AM AN EMULATE.
MY NAME IS LEIA. MY HIERARCHY CODE IS VIRTUE.
NOW HE'S CONTRACTED TO...
BOTH OF US?!
はわわ
WHIMPER

SCENE 5

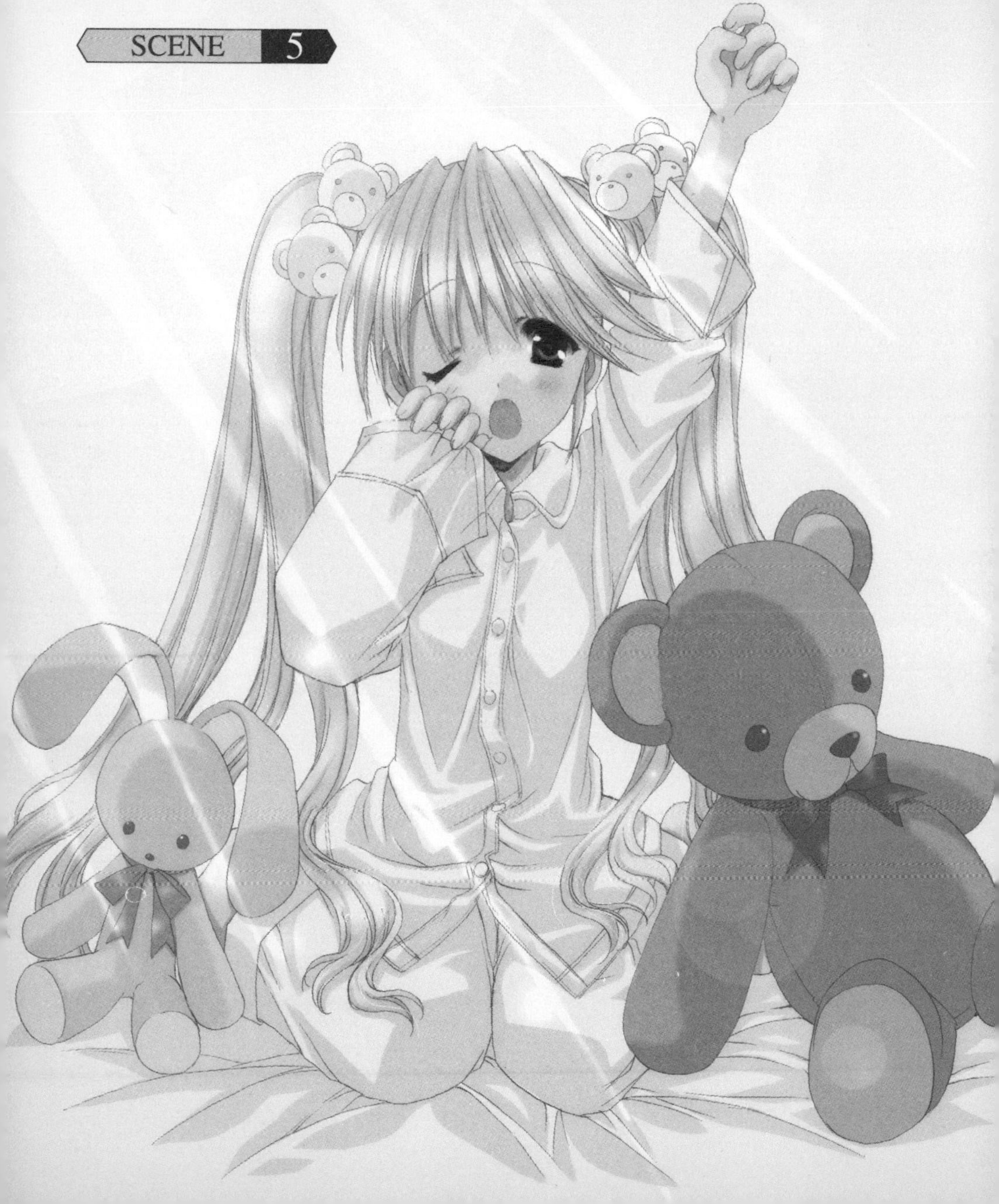

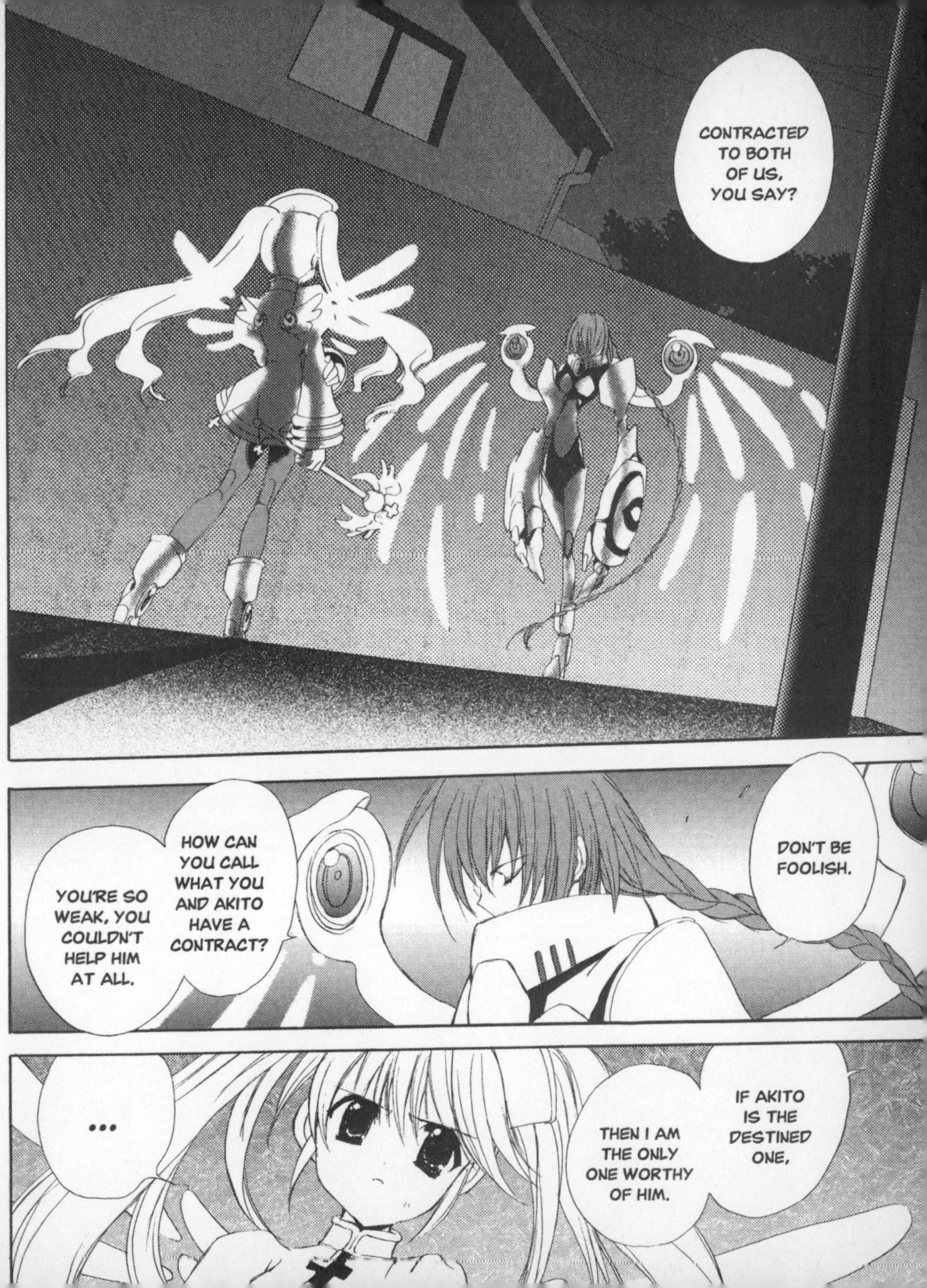
CONTRACTED TO BOTH OF US, YOU SAY?
DON'T BE FOOLISH.
HOW CAN YOU CALL WHAT YOU AND AKITO HAVE A CONTRACT?
YOU'RE SO WEAK, YOU COULDN'T HELP HIM AT ALL.
IF AKITO IS THE DESTINED ONE,
THEN I AM THE ONLY ONE WORTHY OF HIM.
...

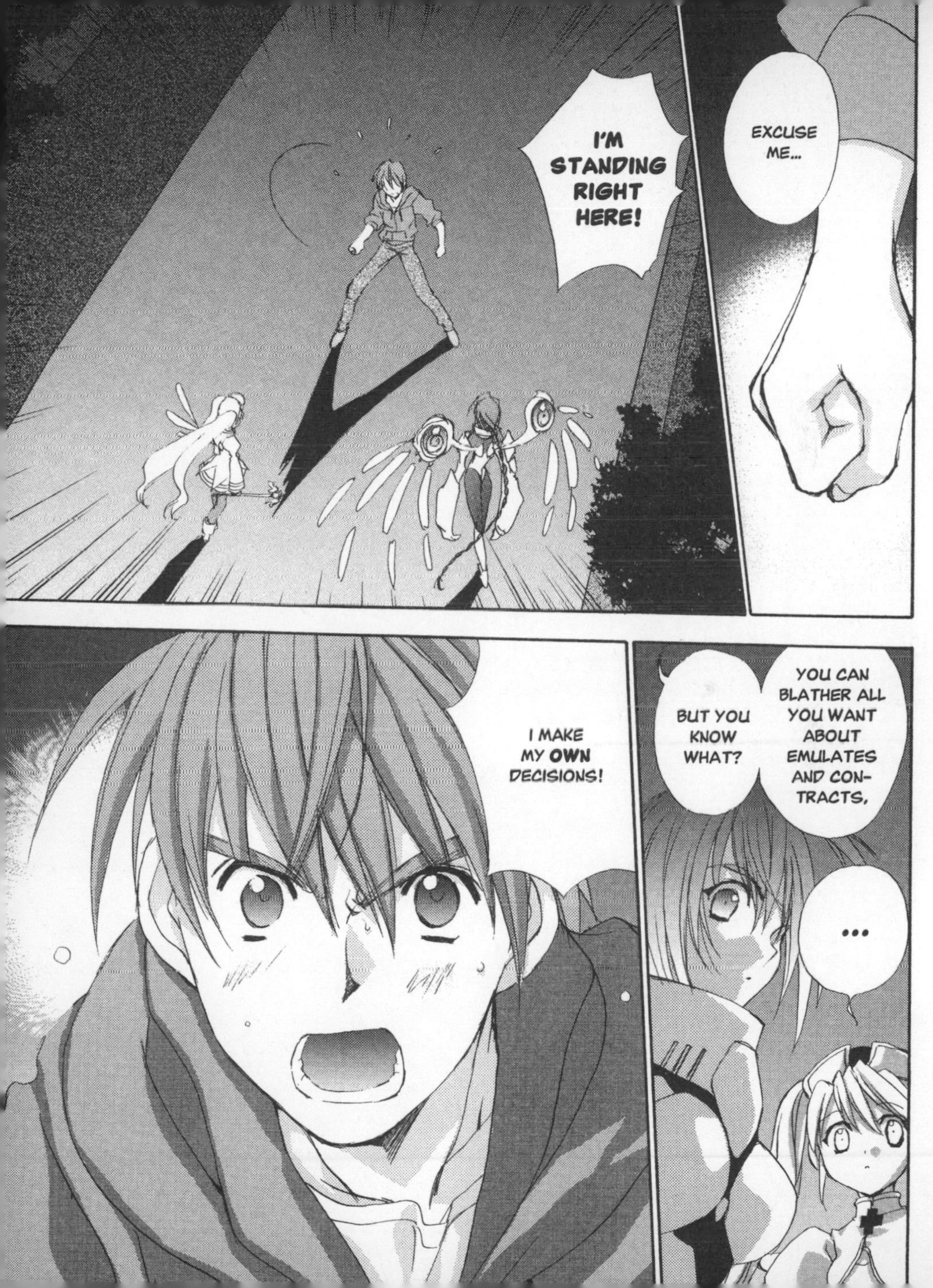
EXCUSE ME...
I'M STANDING RIGHT HERE!
YOU CAN BLATHER ALL YOU WANT ABOUT EMULATES AND CON-TRACTS,
BUT YOU KNOW WHAT?
...
I MAKE MY OWN DECISIONS!

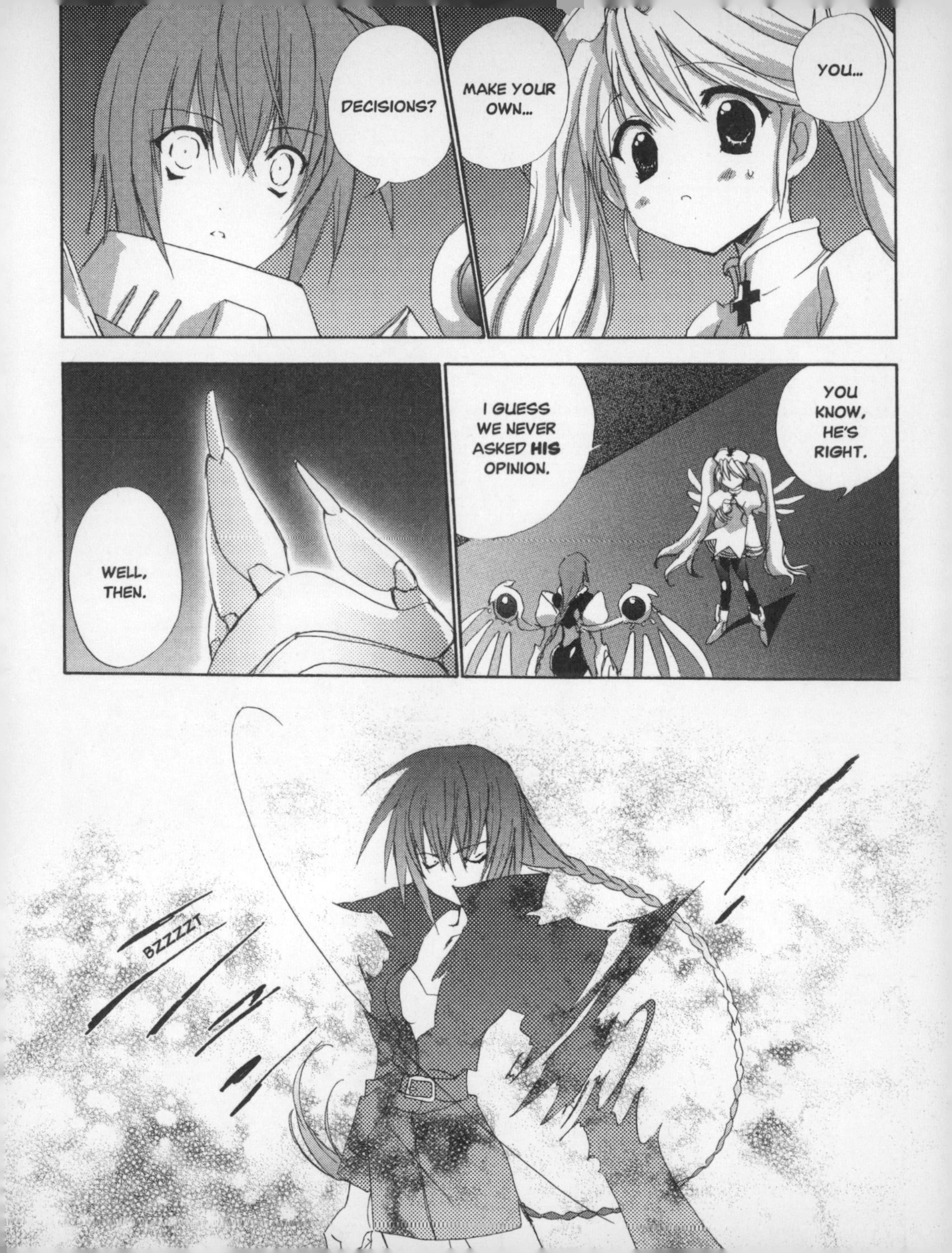

YOU...
MAKE YOUR OWN...
DECISIONS?
YOU KNOW, HE'S RIGHT.
I GUESS WE NEVER ASKED **HIS** OPINION.
WELL, THEN.
BZZZZT

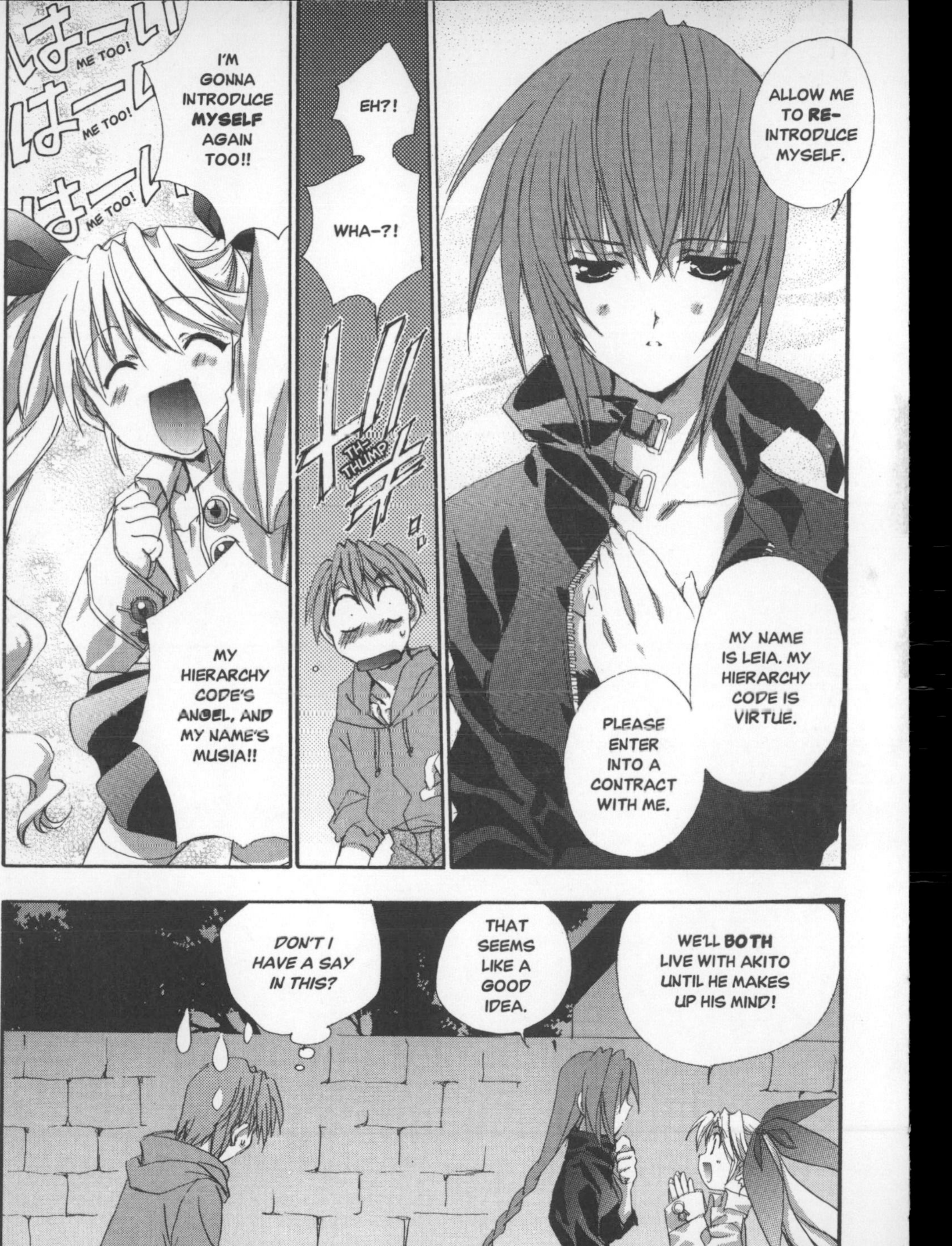
ALLOW ME TO RE-INTRODUCE MYSELF.
MY NAME IS LEIA. MY HIERARCHY CODE IS VIRTUE.
PLEASE ENTER INTO A CONTRACT WITH ME.
EH?!
WHA-?!
TH-THUMP
はーい
ME TOO!
はーい
ME TOO!
はーい
ME TOO!
I'M GONNA INTRODUCE MYSELF AGAIN TOO!!
MY HIERARCHY CODE'S ANGEL, AND MY NAME'S MUSIA!!
WE'LL BOTH LIVE WITH AKITO UNTIL HE MAKES UP HIS MIND!
THAT SEEMS LIKE A GOOD IDEA.
DON'T I HAVE A SAY IN THIS?

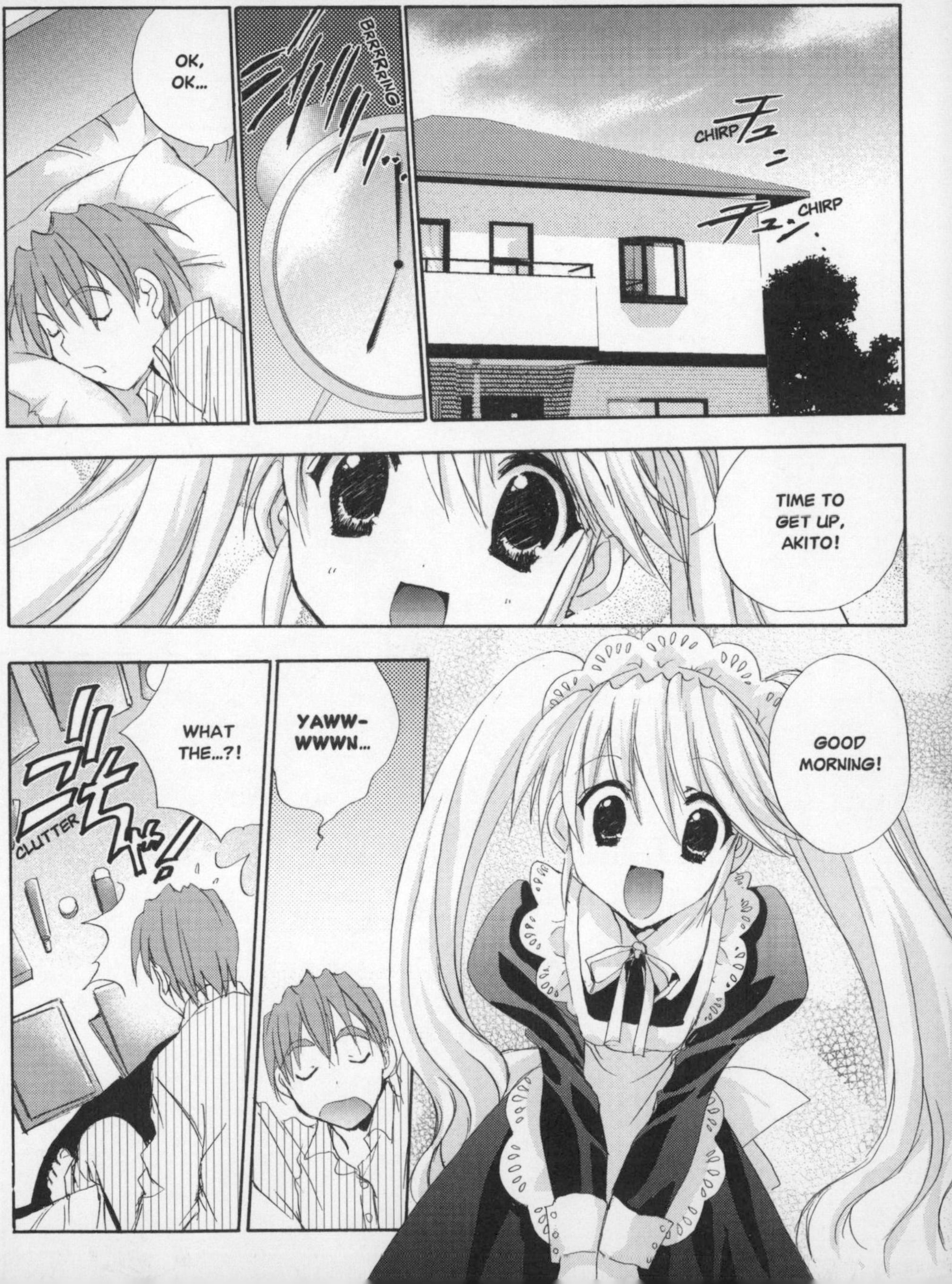
CHIRP
CHIRP
BRRRRRING
OK, OK...
TIME TO GET UP, AKITO!
GOOD MORNING!
YAWW-WWWN...
WHAT THE...?!
CLUTTER

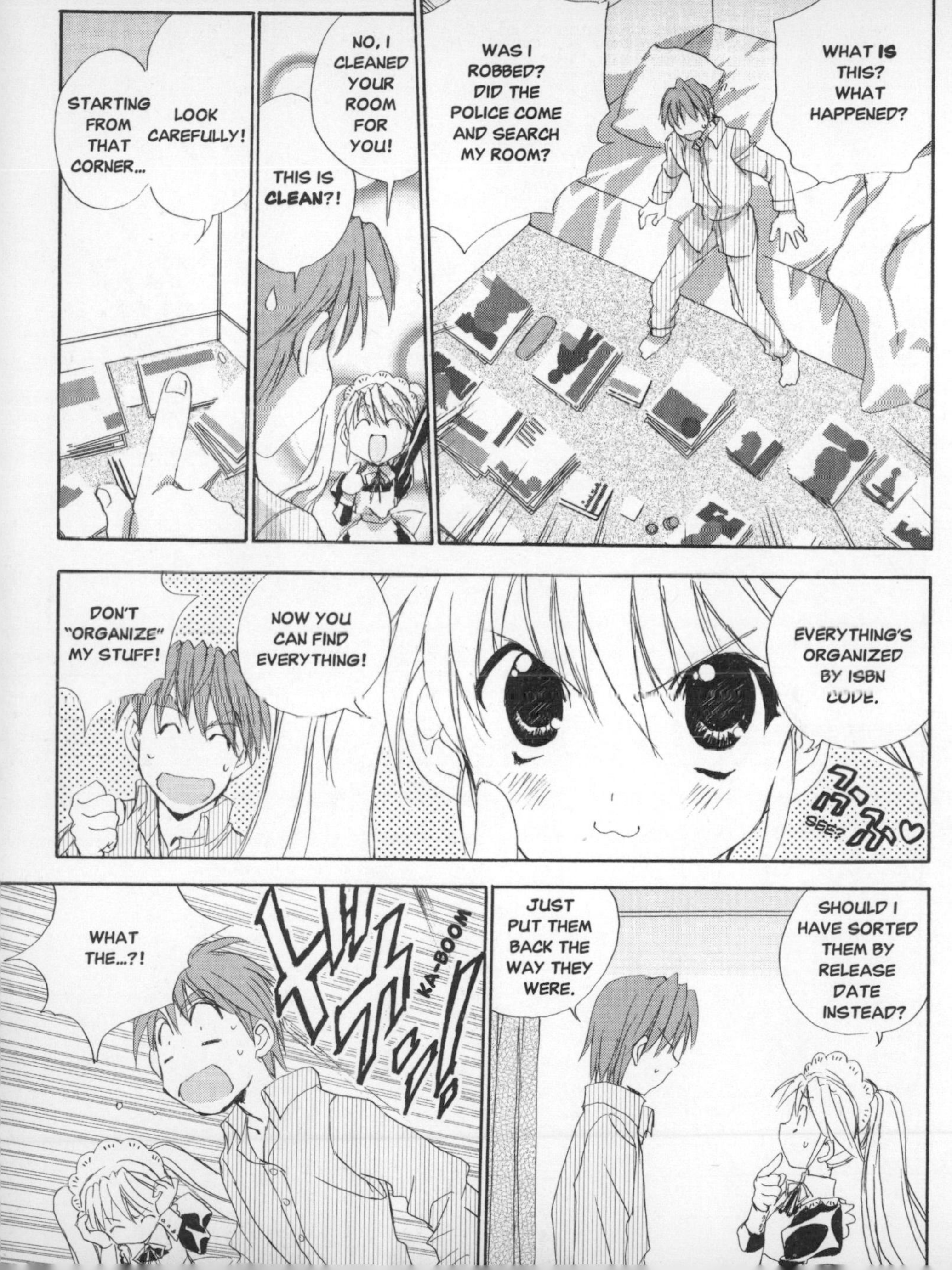
WHAT IS THIS? WHAT HAPPENED?
WAS I ROBBED? DID THE POLICE COME AND SEARCH MY ROOM?
NO, I CLEANED YOUR ROOM FOR YOU!
THIS IS CLEAN?!
LOOK CAREFULLY!
STARTING FROM THAT CORNER...
EVERYTHING'S ORGANIZED BY ISBN CODE.
SEE?
NOW YOU CAN FIND EVERYTHING!
DON'T "ORGANIZE" MY STUFF!
SHOULD I HAVE SORTED THEM BY RELEASE DATE INSTEAD?
JUST PUT THEM BACK THE WAY THEY WERE.
KA-BOOM
WHAT THE...?!

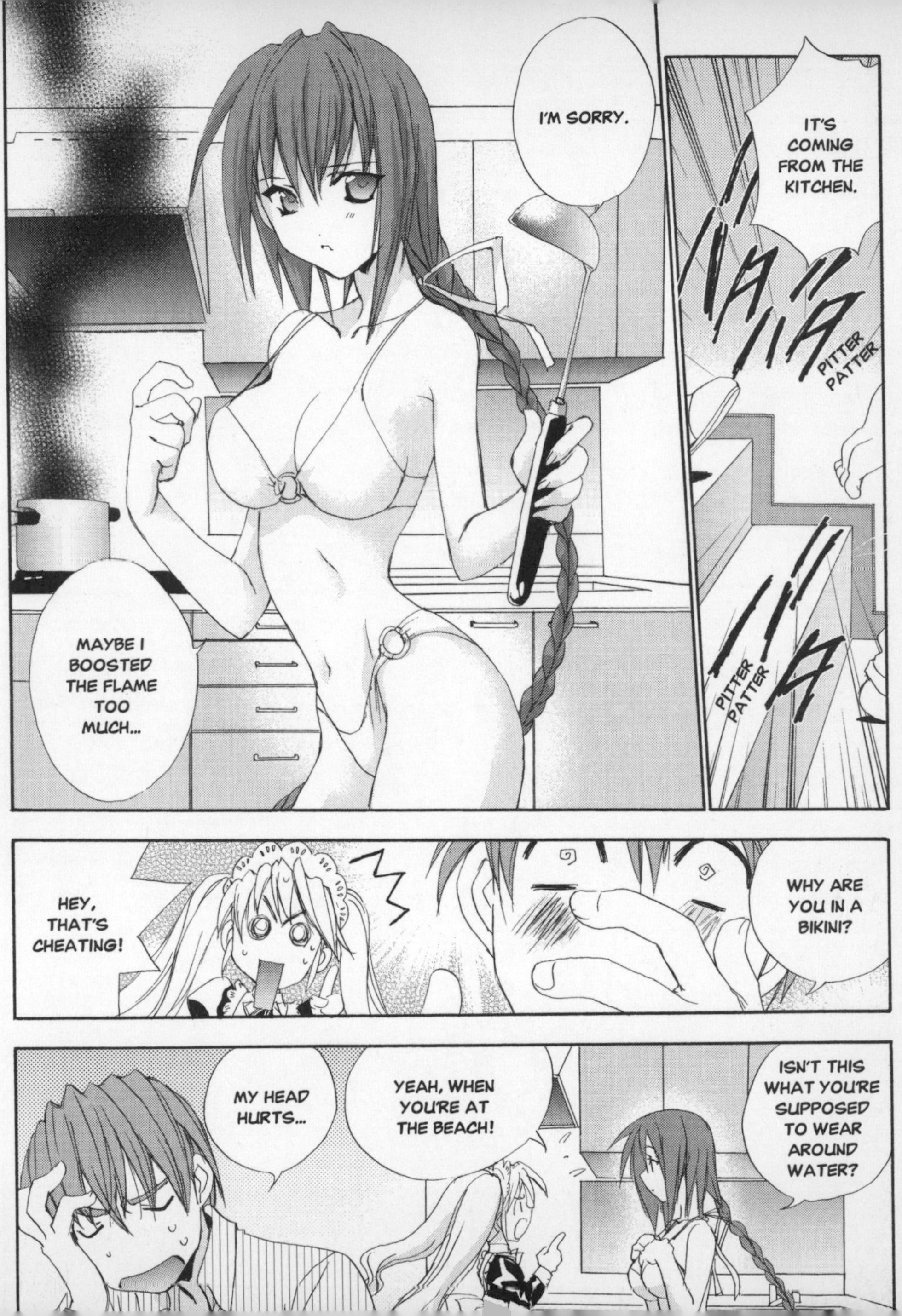
IT'S COMING FROM THE KITCHEN.
PITTER PATTER
PITTER PATTER
I'M SORRY.
MAYBE I BOOSTED THE FLAME TOO MUCH...
WHY ARE YOU IN A BIKINI?
HEY, THAT'S CHEATING!
ISN'T THIS WHAT YOU'RE SUPPOSED TO WEAR AROUND WATER?
YEAH, WHEN YOU'RE AT THE BEACH!
MY HEAD HURTS...

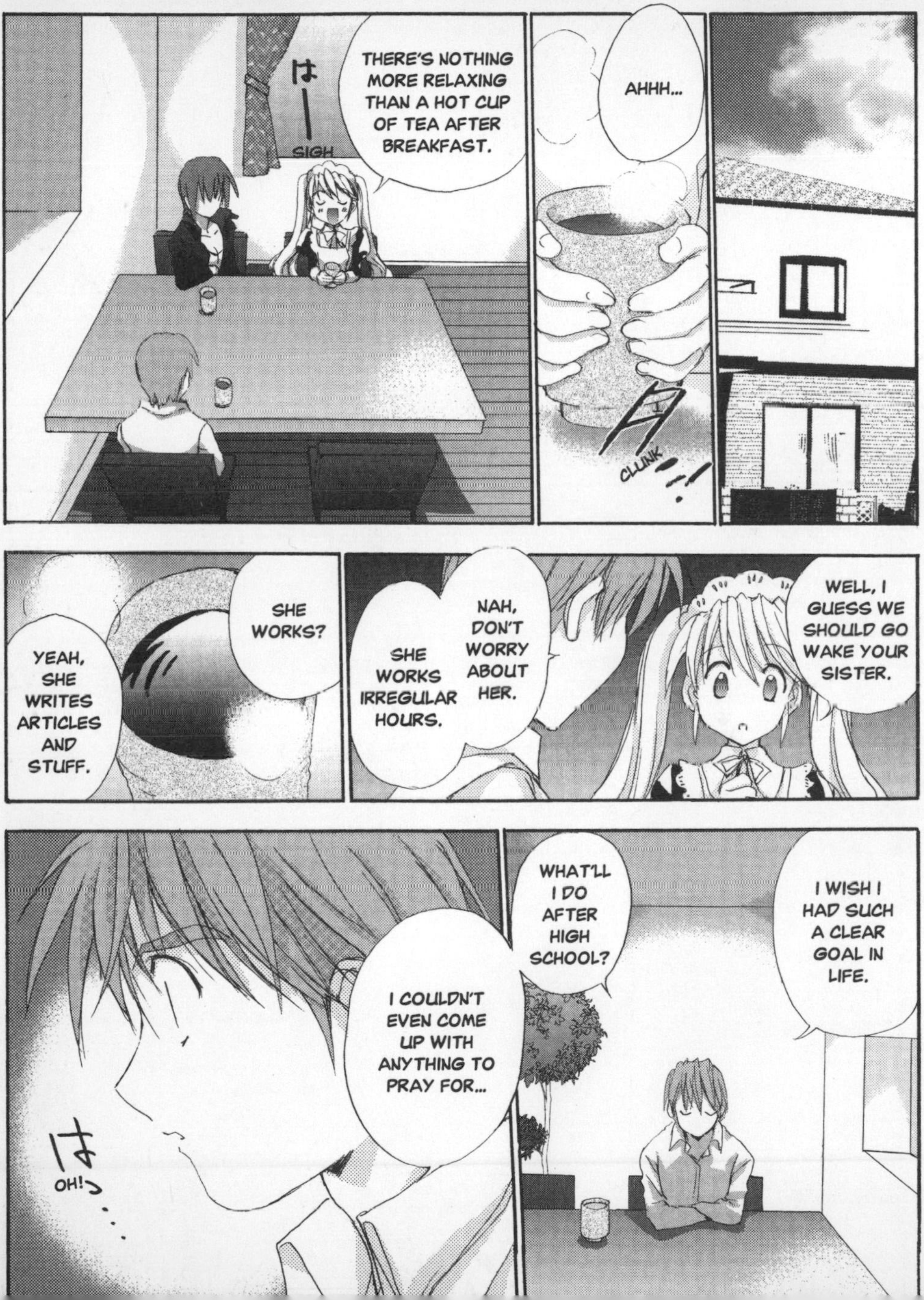
AHHH...
CLUNK
THERE'S NOTHING MORE RELAXING THAN A HOT CUP OF TEA AFTER BREAKFAST.
はー
SIGH
WELL, I GUESS WE SHOULD GO WAKE YOUR SISTER.
NAH, DON'T WORRY ABOUT HER.
SHE WORKS IRREGULAR HOURS.
SHE WORKS?
YEAH, SHE WRITES ARTICLES AND STUFF.
I WISH I HAD SUCH A CLEAR GOAL IN LIFE.
WHAT'LL I DO AFTER HIGH SCHOOL?
I COULDN'T EVEN COME UP WITH ANYTHING TO PRAY FOR...
は
OH!

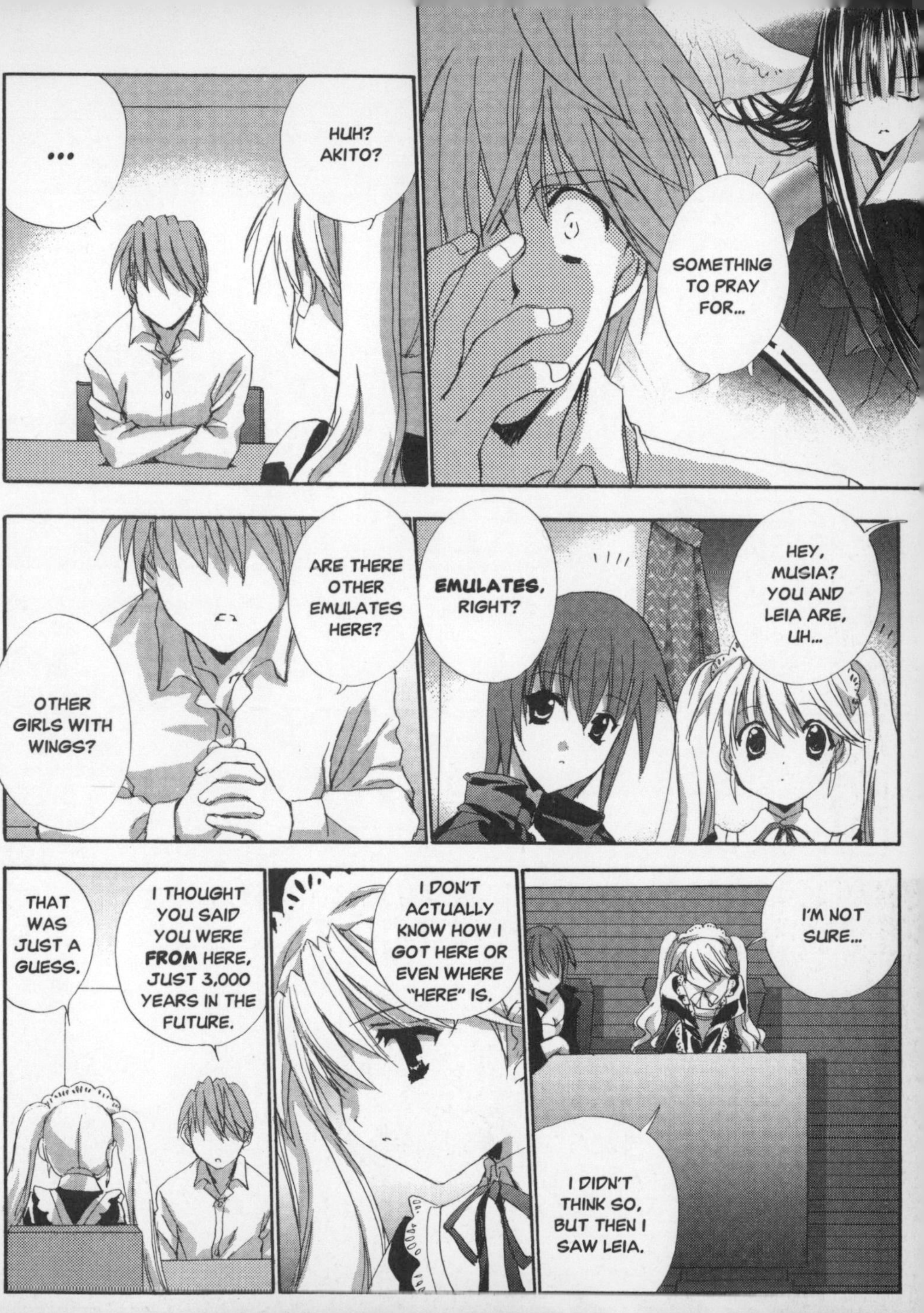

SOMETHING TO PRAY FOR...
HUH? AKITO?
...
HEY, MUSIA? YOU AND LEIA ARE, UH...
EMULATES, RIGHT?
ARE THERE OTHER EMULATES HERE?
OTHER GIRLS WITH WINGS?
I'M NOT SURE...
I DIDN'T THINK SO, BUT THEN I SAW LEIA.
I DON'T ACTUALLY KNOW HOW I GOT HERE OR EVEN WHERE "HERE" IS.
I THOUGHT YOU SAID YOU WERE FROM HERE, JUST 3,000 YEARS IN THE FUTURE.
THAT WAS JUST A GUESS.

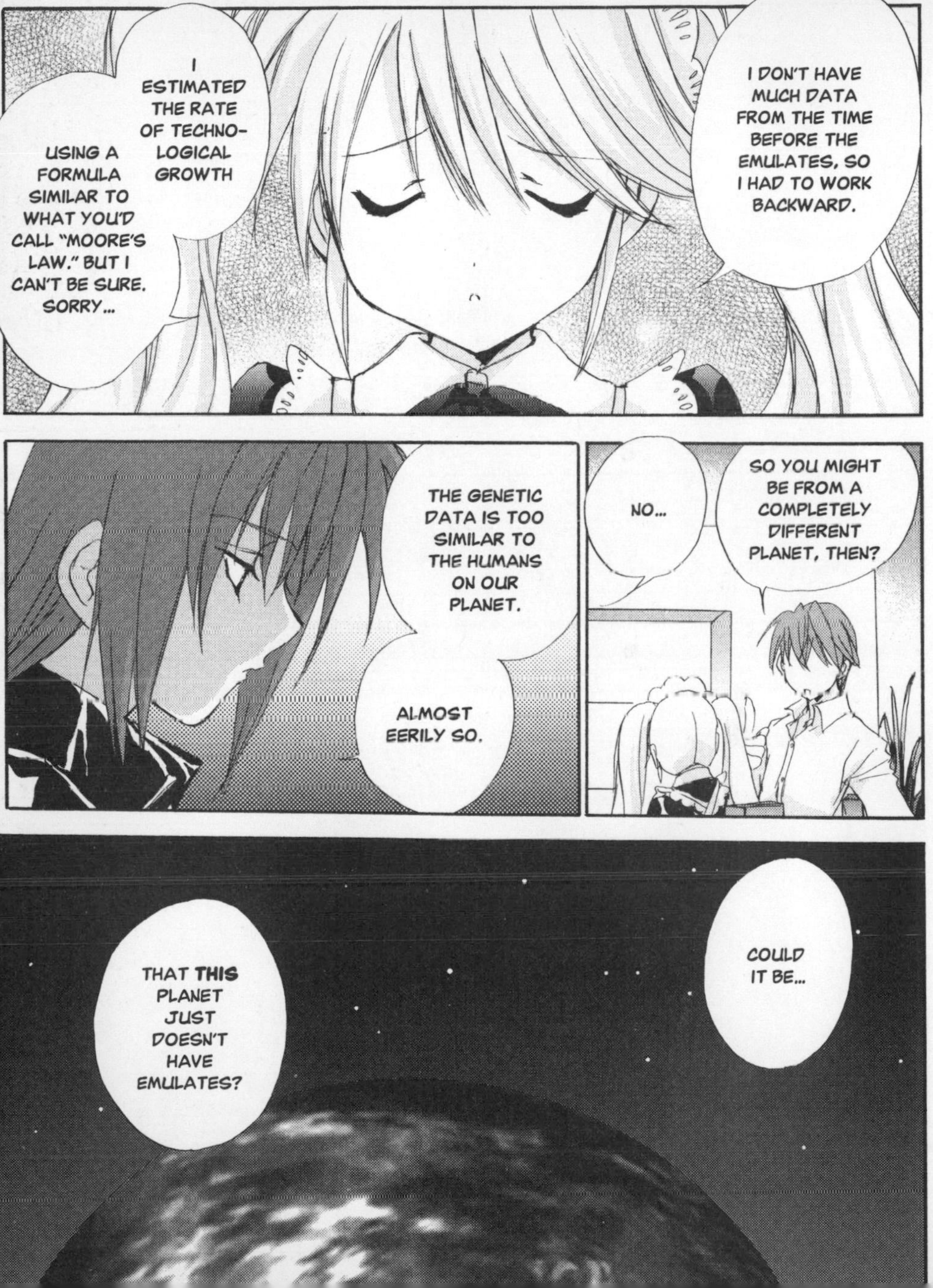
I DON'T HAVE MUCH DATA FROM THE TIME BEFORE THE EMULATES, SO I HAD TO WORK BACKWARD.
I ESTIMATED THE RATE OF TECHNO-LOGICAL GROWTH
USING A FORMULA SIMILAR TO WHAT YOU'D CALL "MOORE'S LAW." BUT I CAN'T BE SURE. SORRY...
SO YOU MIGHT BE FROM A COMPLETELY DIFFERENT PLANET, THEN?
NO...
THE GENETIC DATA IS TOO SIMILAR TO THE HUMANS ON OUR PLANET.
ALMOST EERILY SO.
COULD IT BE...
THAT **THIS** PLANET JUST DOESN'T HAVE EMULATES?

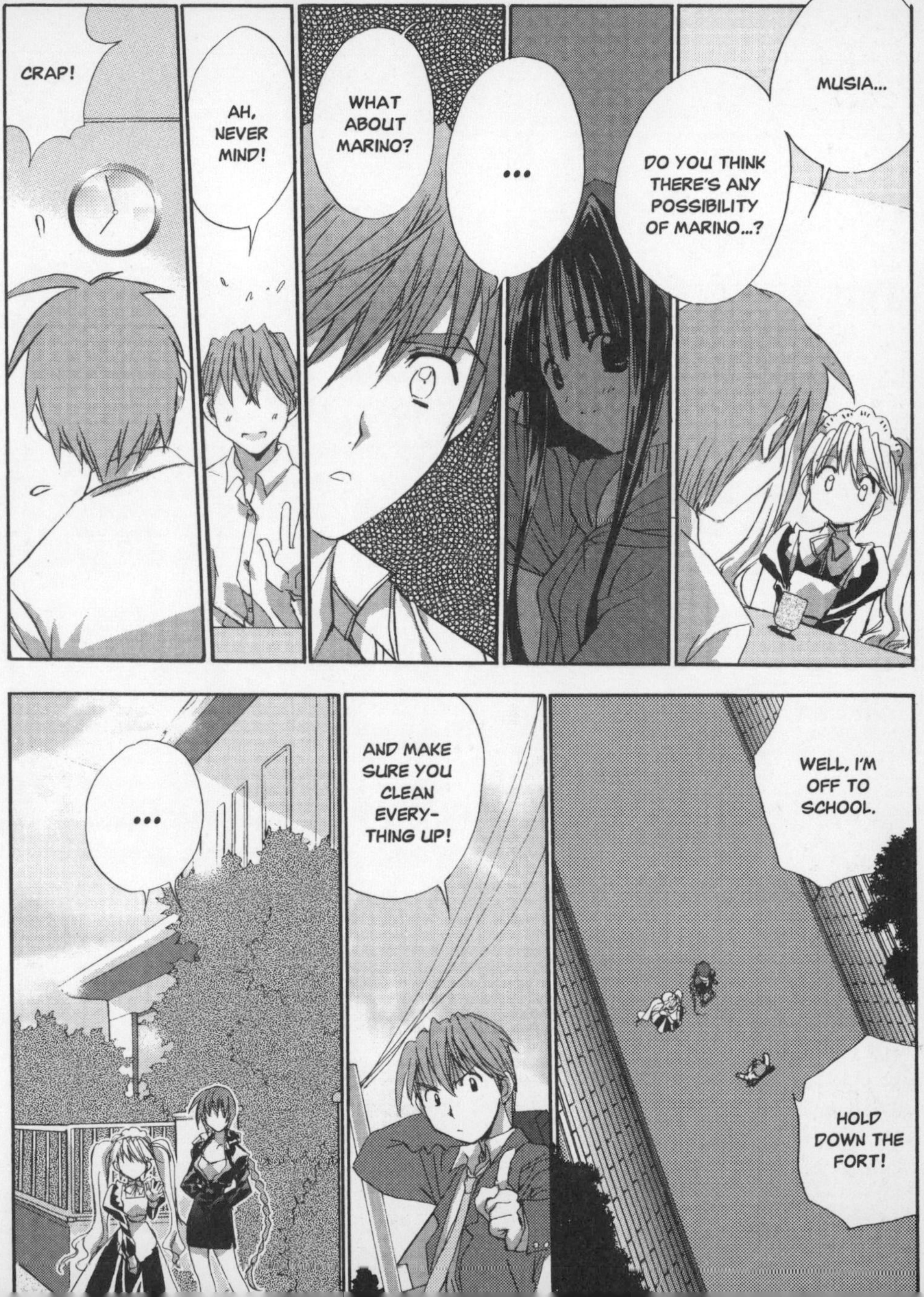
MUSIA...
DO YOU THINK THERE'S ANY POSSIBILITY OF MARINO...?
...
WHAT ABOUT MARINO?
AH, NEVER MIND!
CRAP!
WELL, I'M OFF TO SCHOOL.
HOLD DOWN THE FORT!
AND MAKE SURE YOU CLEAN EVERY-THING UP!
...

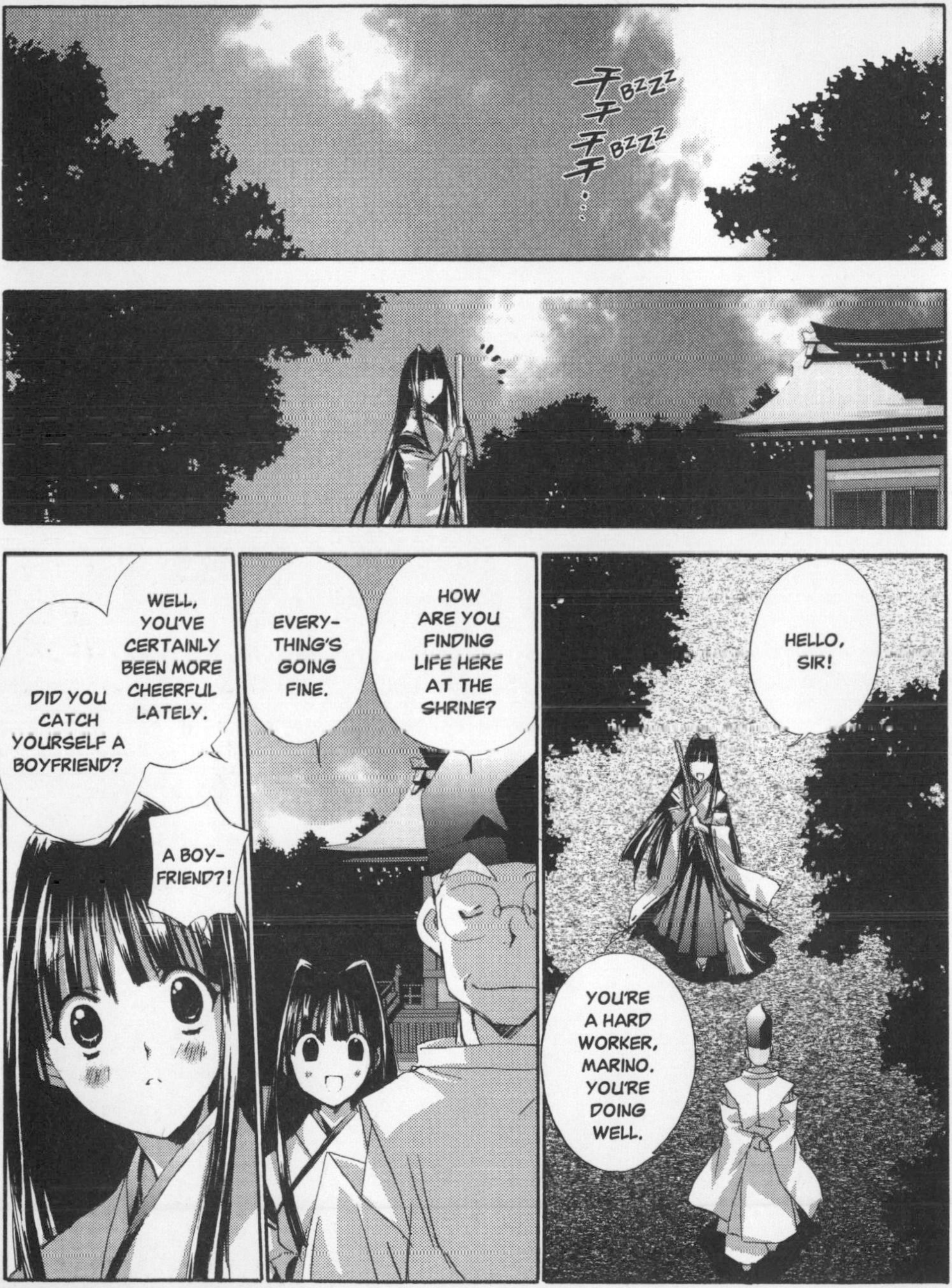

チチチチ...
BZZZ
BZZZ
HELLO, SIR!
YOU'RE A HARD WORKER, MARINO. YOU'RE DOING WELL.
HOW ARE YOU FINDING LIFE HERE AT THE SHRINE?
EVERY-THING'S GOING FINE.
WELL, YOU'VE CERTAINLY BEEN MORE CHEERFUL LATELY.
DID YOU CATCH YOURSELF A BOYFRIEND?
A BOY-FRIEND?!

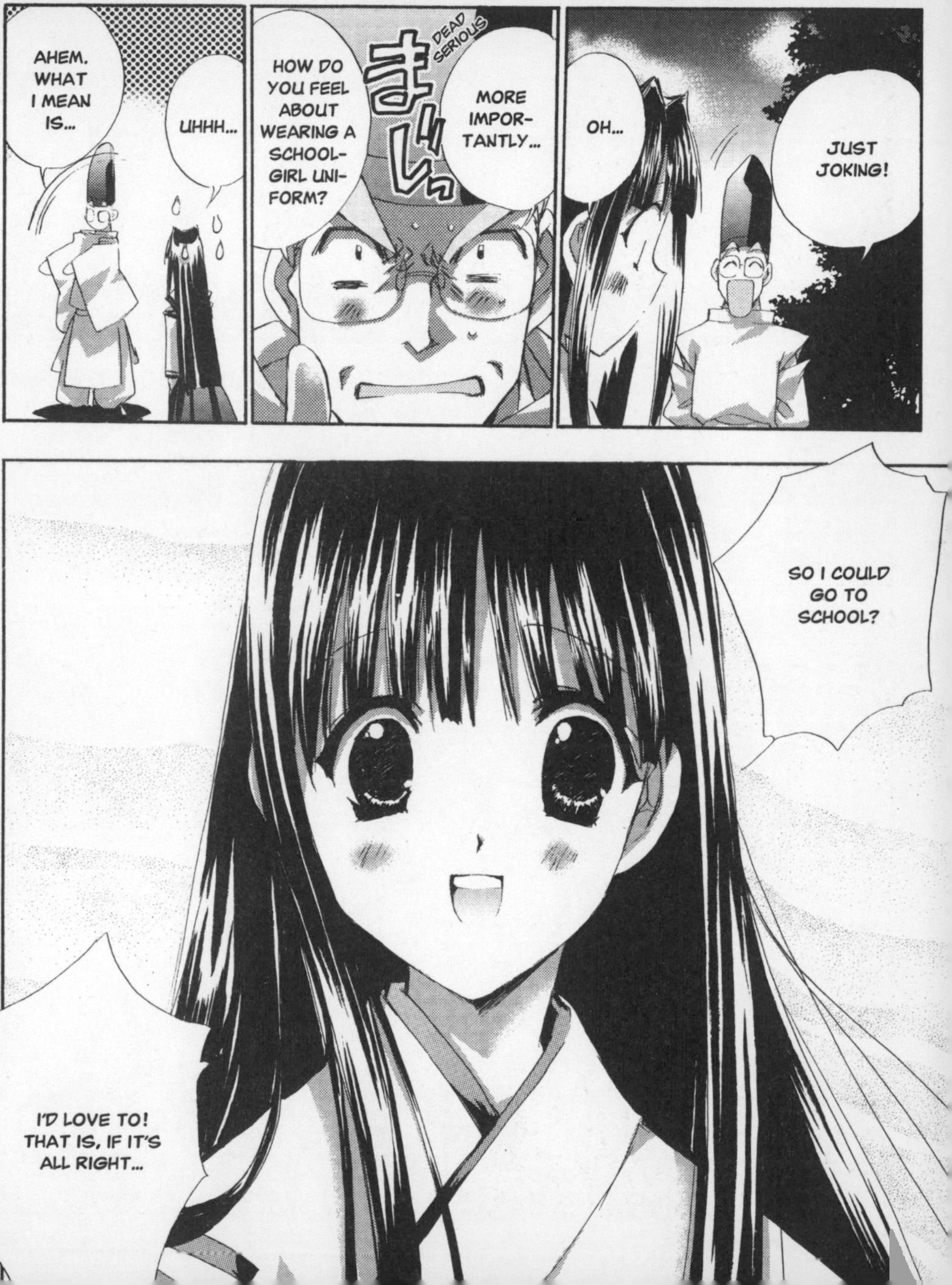
JUST JOKING!
OH...
MORE IMPORTANTLY...
DEAD SERIOUS
HOW DO YOU FEEL ABOUT WEARING A SCHOOLGIRL UNIFORM?
UHHH...
AHEM. WHAT I MEAN IS...
SO I COULD GO TO SCHOOL?
I'D LOVE TO! THAT IS, IF IT'S ALL RIGHT...

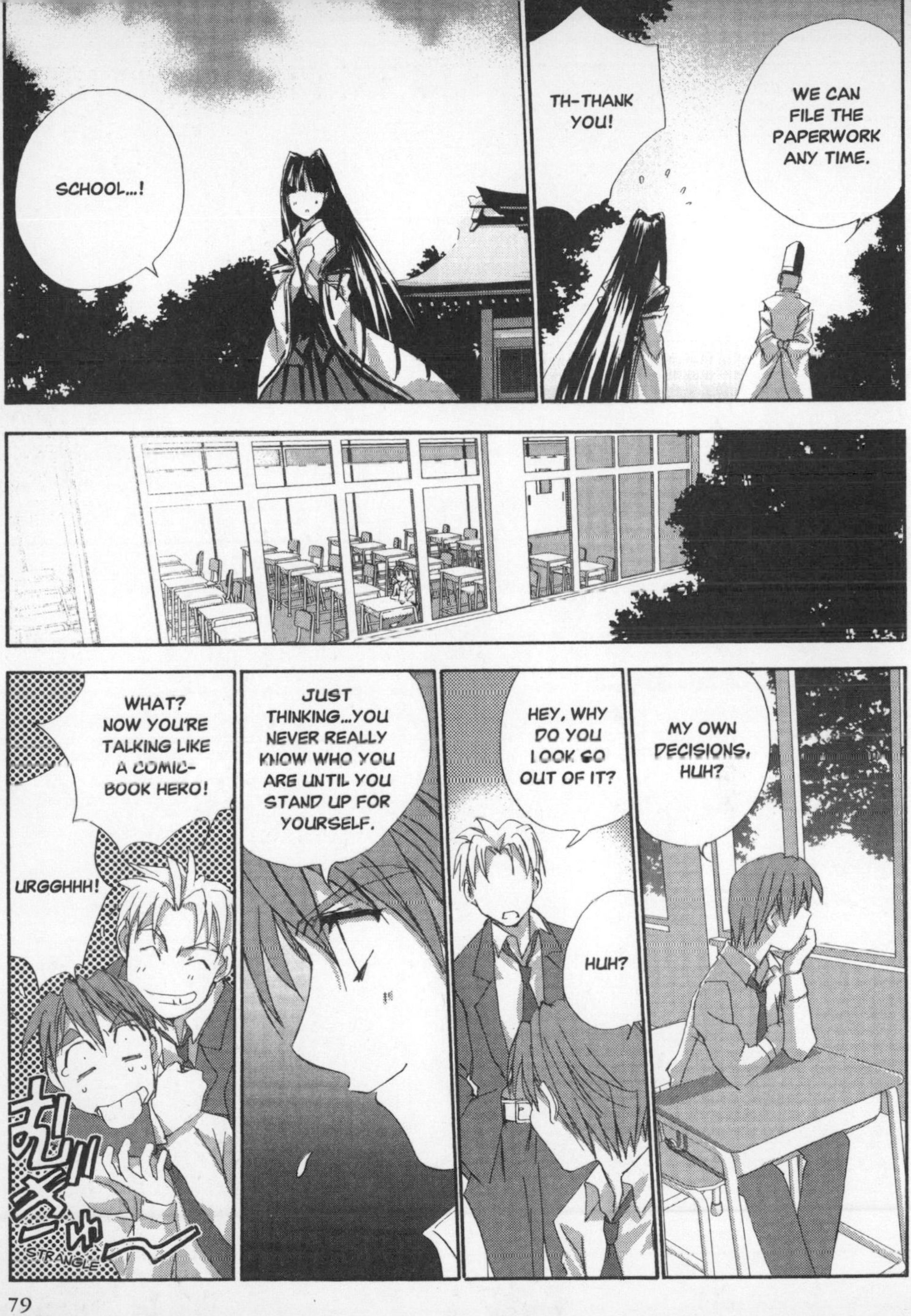
WE CAN FILE THE PAPERWORK ANY TIME.
TH-THANK YOU!
SCHOOL...!
MY OWN DECISIONS, HUH?
HEY, WHY DO YOU LOOK SO OUT OF IT?
HUH?
JUST THINKING...YOU NEVER REALLY KNOW WHO YOU ARE UNTIL YOU STAND UP FOR YOURSELF.
WHAT? NOW YOU'RE TALKING LIKE A COMIC-BOOK HERO!
URGGHHH!
STRANGLE

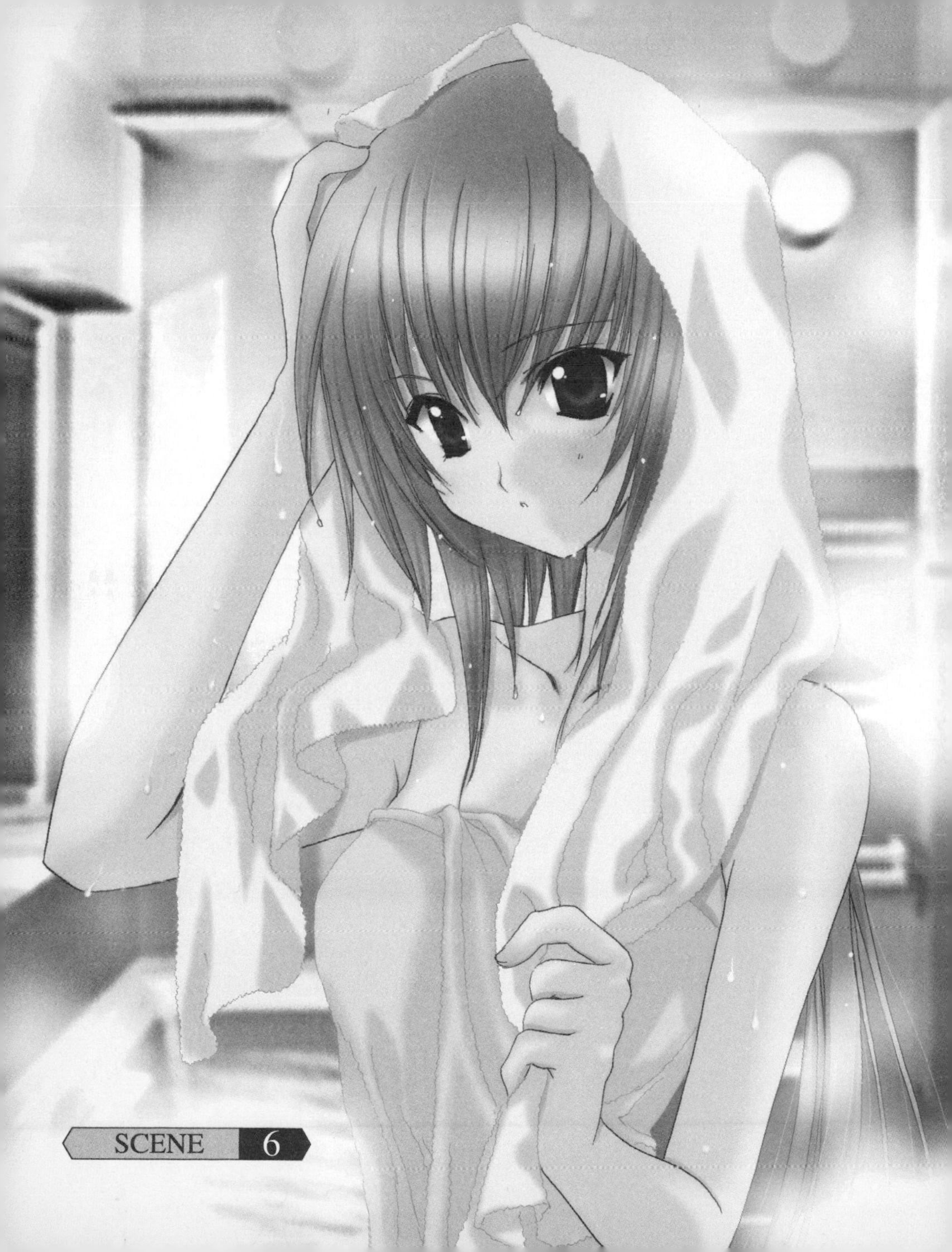
SCENE 6

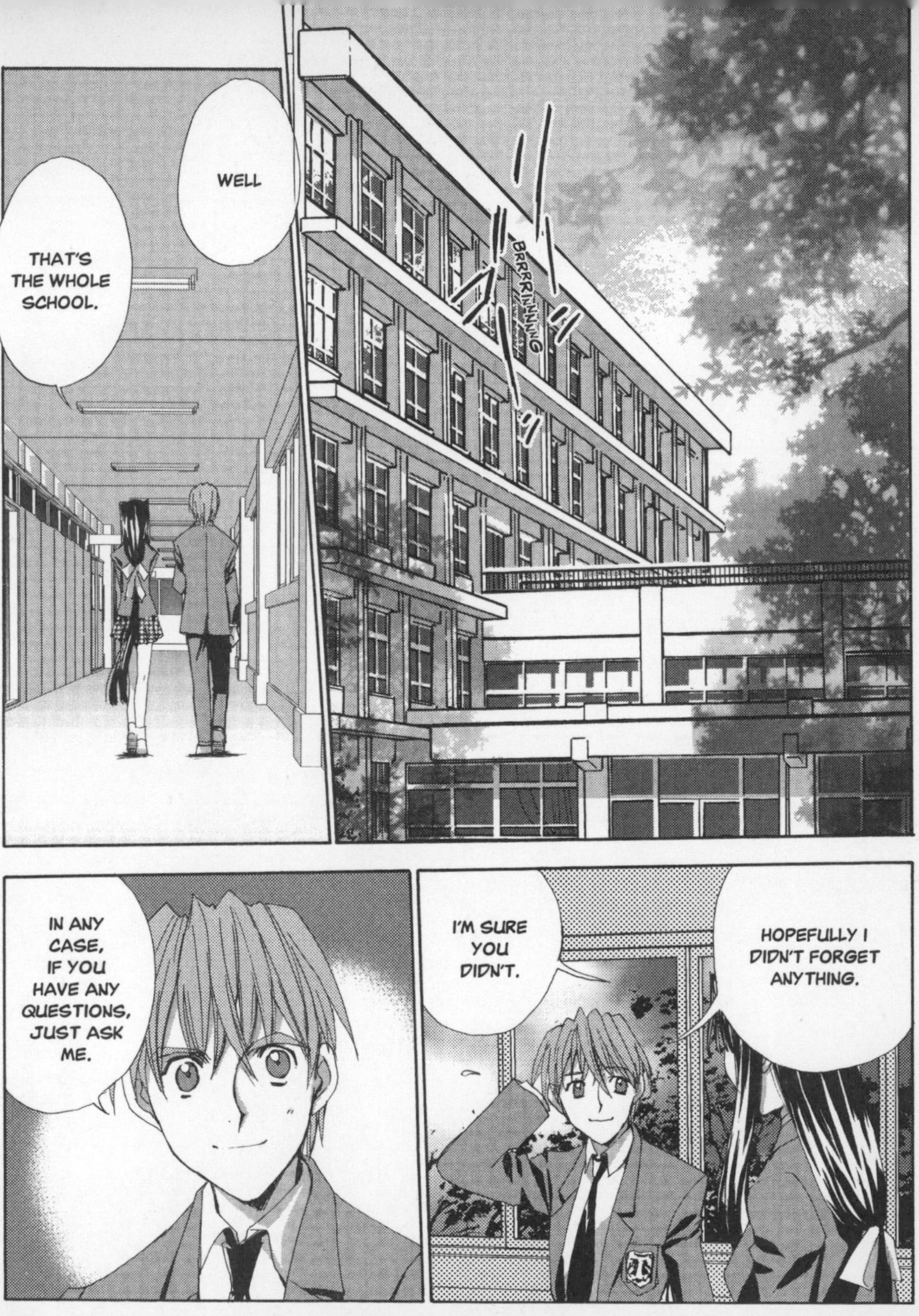
WELL
THAT'S THE WHOLE SCHOOL.
BRRRINNNG
HOPEFULLY I DIDN'T FORGET ANYTHING.
I'M SURE YOU DIDN'T.
IN ANY CASE, IF YOU HAVE ANY QUESTIONS, JUST ASK ME.

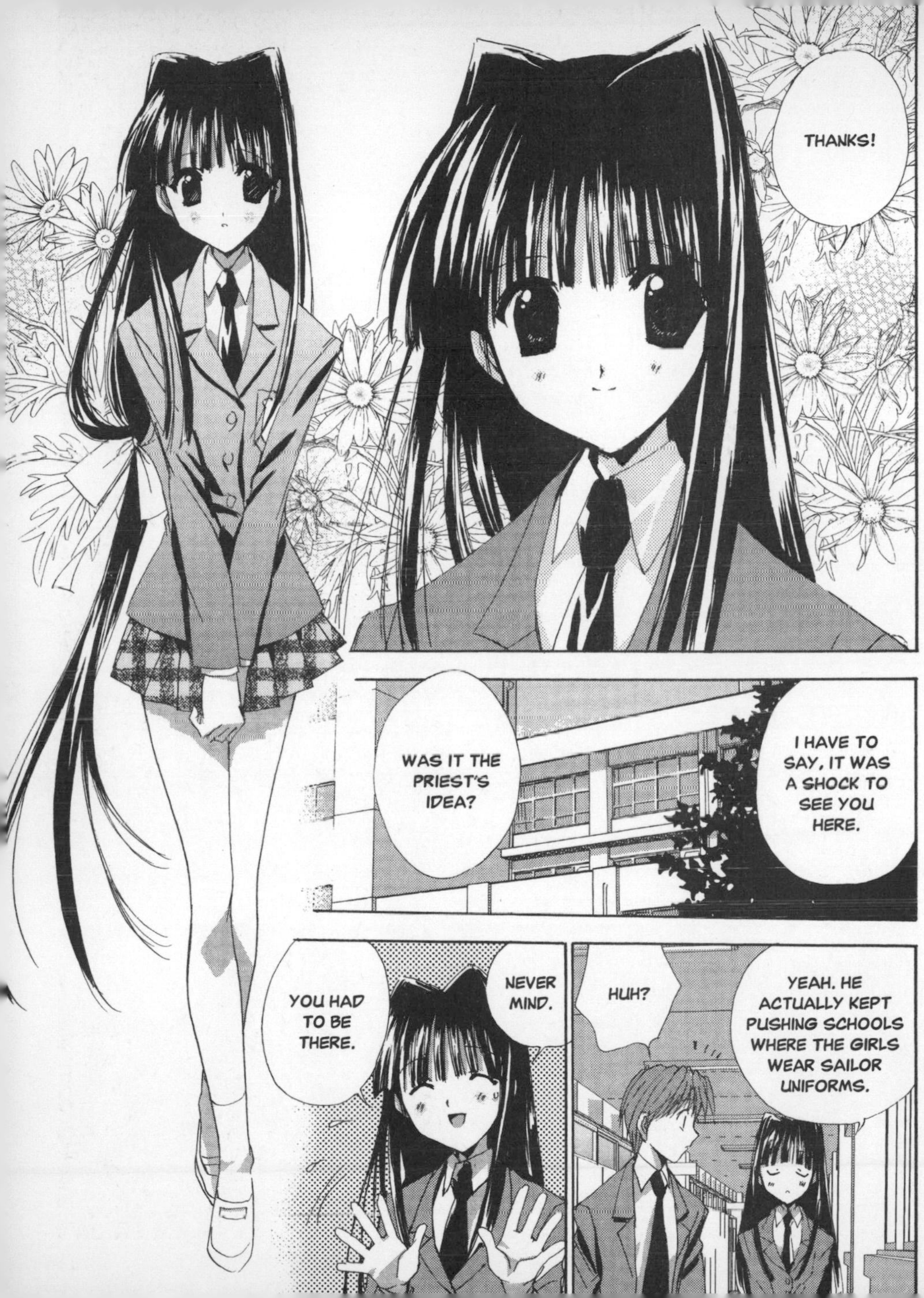
THANKS!
I HAVE TO SAY, IT WAS A SHOCK TO SEE YOU HERE.
WAS IT THE PRIEST'S IDEA?
YEAH. HE ACTUALLY KEPT PUSHING SCHOOLS WHERE THE GIRLS WEAR SAILOR UNIFORMS.
HUH?
NEVER MIND.
YOU HAD TO BE THERE.

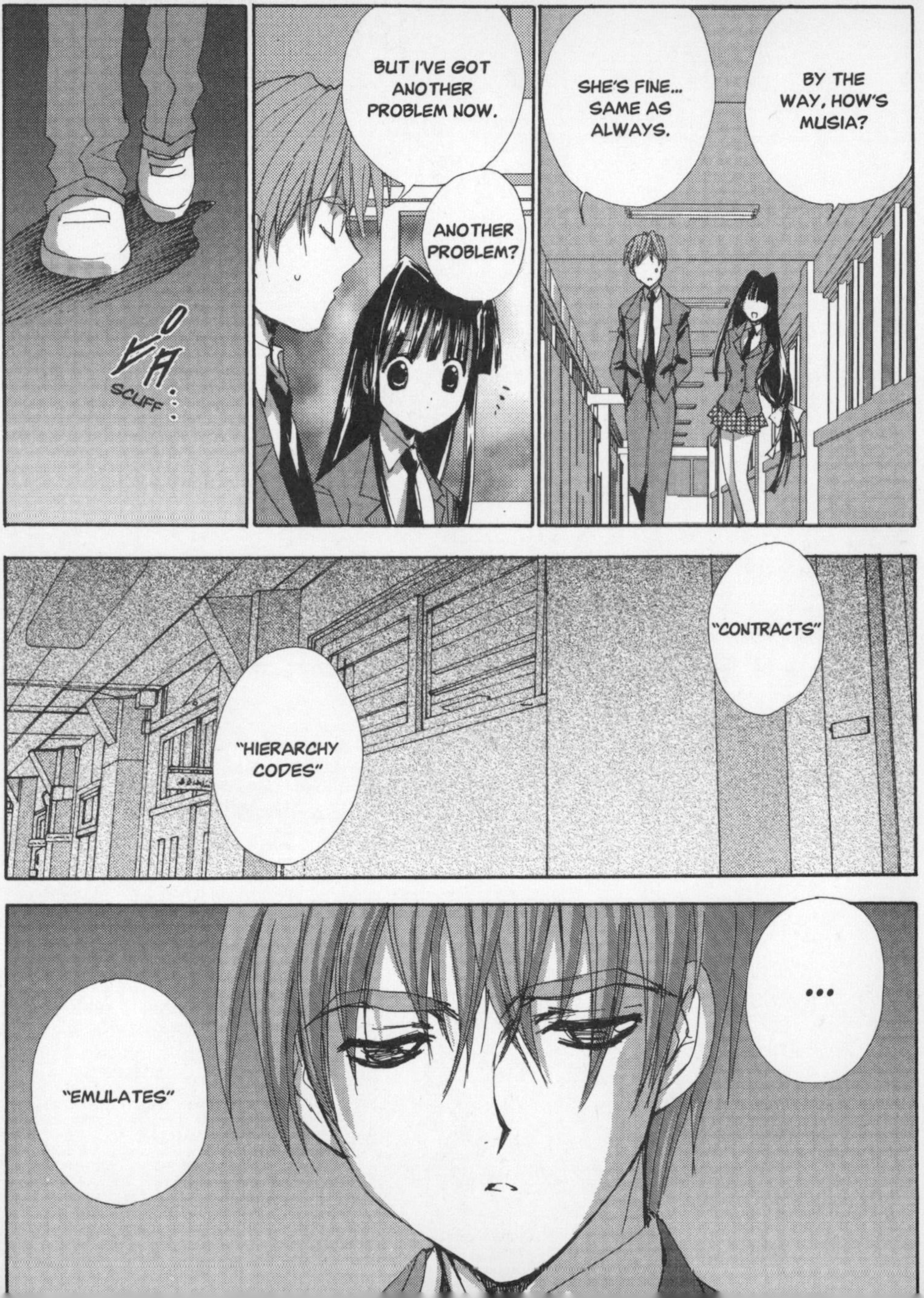
BY THE WAY, HOW'S MUSIA?
SHE'S FINE... SAME AS ALWAYS.
BUT I'VE GOT ANOTHER PROBLEM NOW.
ANOTHER PROBLEM?
SCUFF
"CONTRACTS"
"HIERARCHY CODES"
...
"EMULATES"

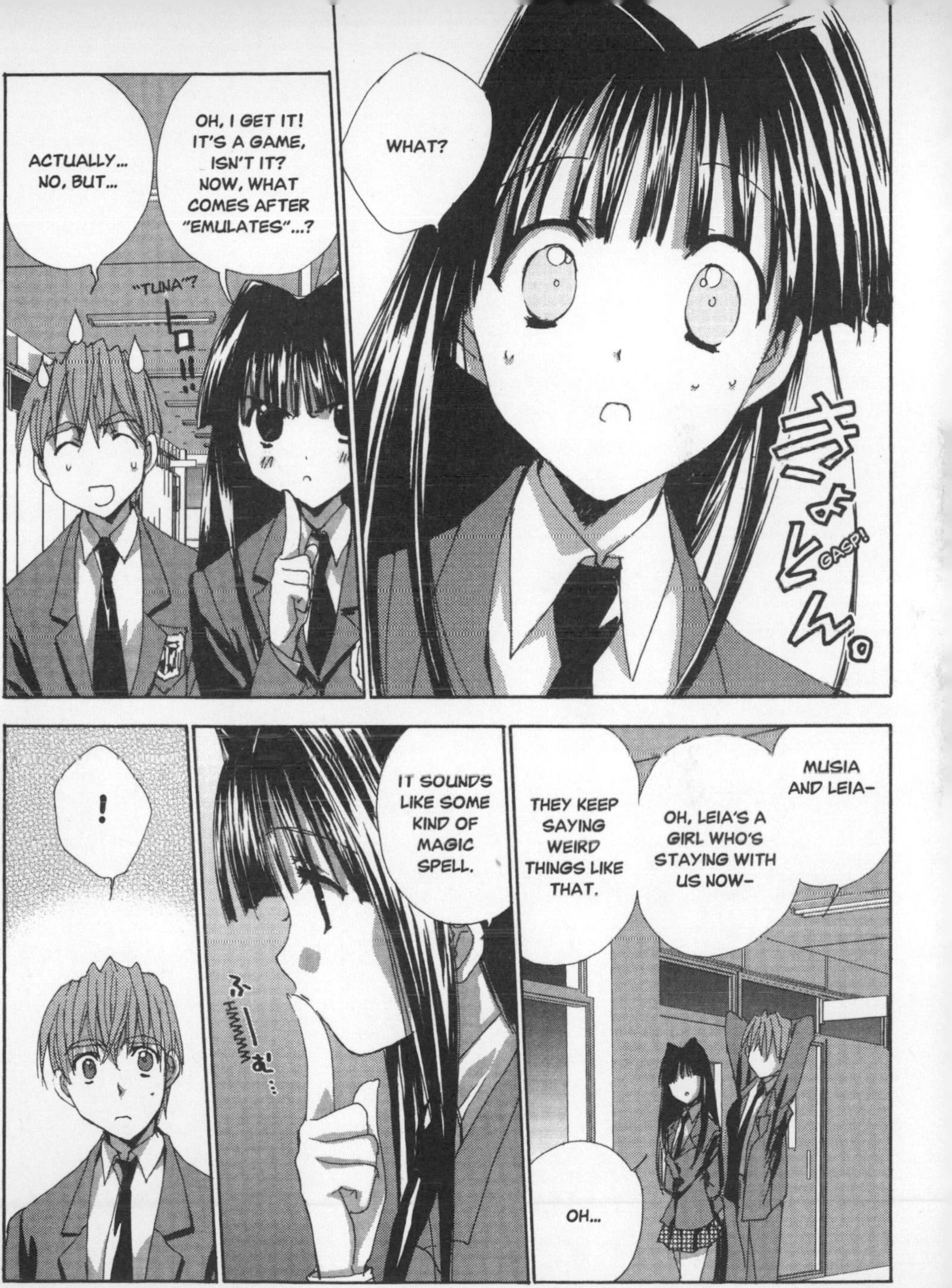
WHAT?
GASP!
OH, I GET IT! IT'S A GAME, ISN'T IT? NOW, WHAT COMES AFTER "EMULATES"...?
ACTUALLY... NO, BUT...
"TUNA"?
MUSIA AND LEIA-
OH, LEIA'S A GIRL WHO'S STAYING WITH US NOW-
THEY KEEP SAYING WEIRD THINGS LIKE THAT.
OH...
IT SOUNDS LIKE SOME KIND OF MAGIC SPELL.
HMMMM
!

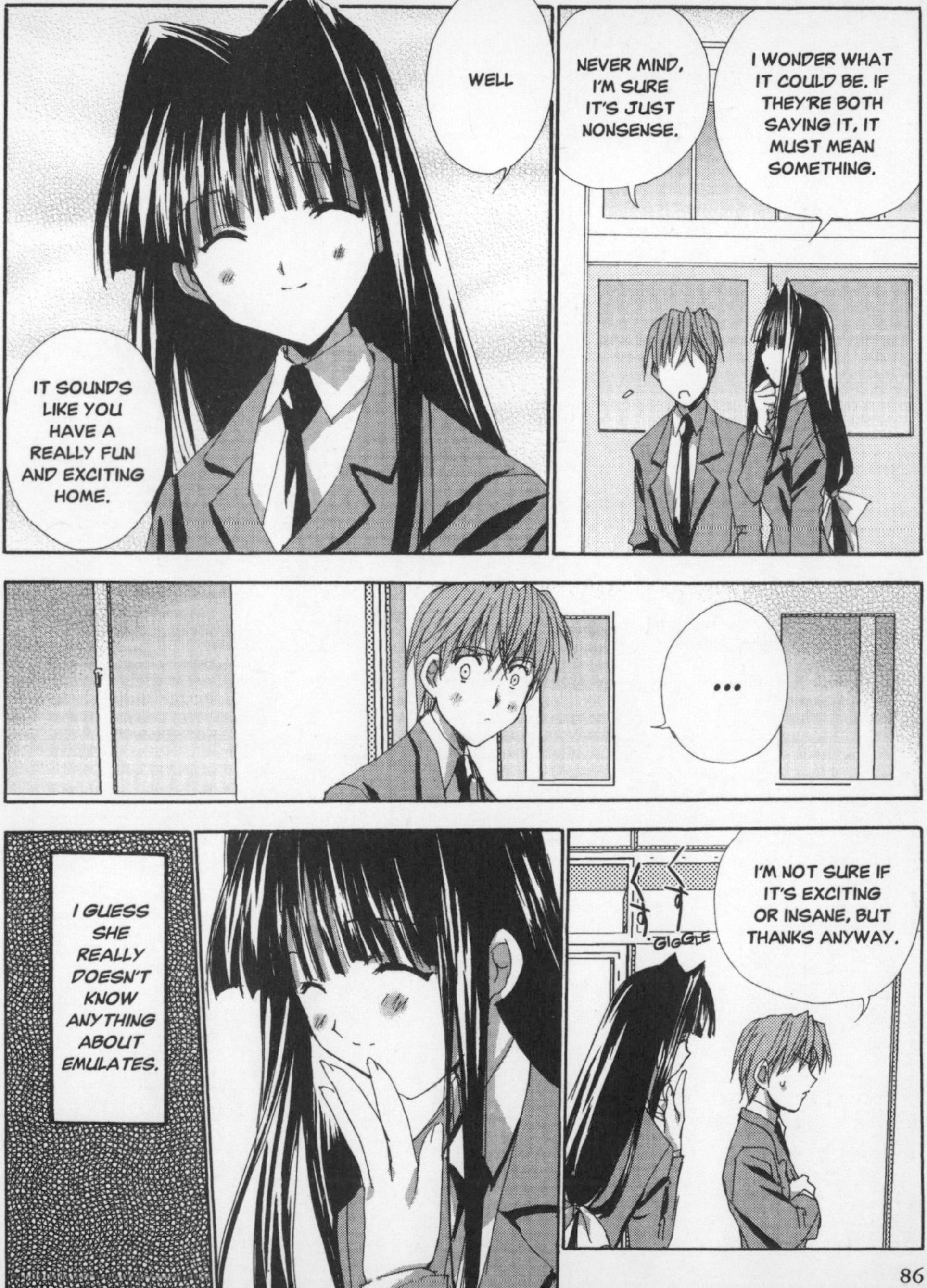
I WONDER WHAT IT COULD BE. IF THEY'RE BOTH SAYING IT, IT MUST MEAN SOMETHING.
NEVER MIND, I'M SURE IT'S JUST NONSENSE.
WELL
IT SOUNDS LIKE YOU HAVE A REALLY FUN AND EXCITING HOME.
...
I'M NOT SURE IF IT'S EXCITING OR INSANE, BUT THANKS ANYWAY.
くすくす
GIGGLE
I GUESS SHE REALLY DOESN'T KNOW ANYTHING ABOUT EMULATES.

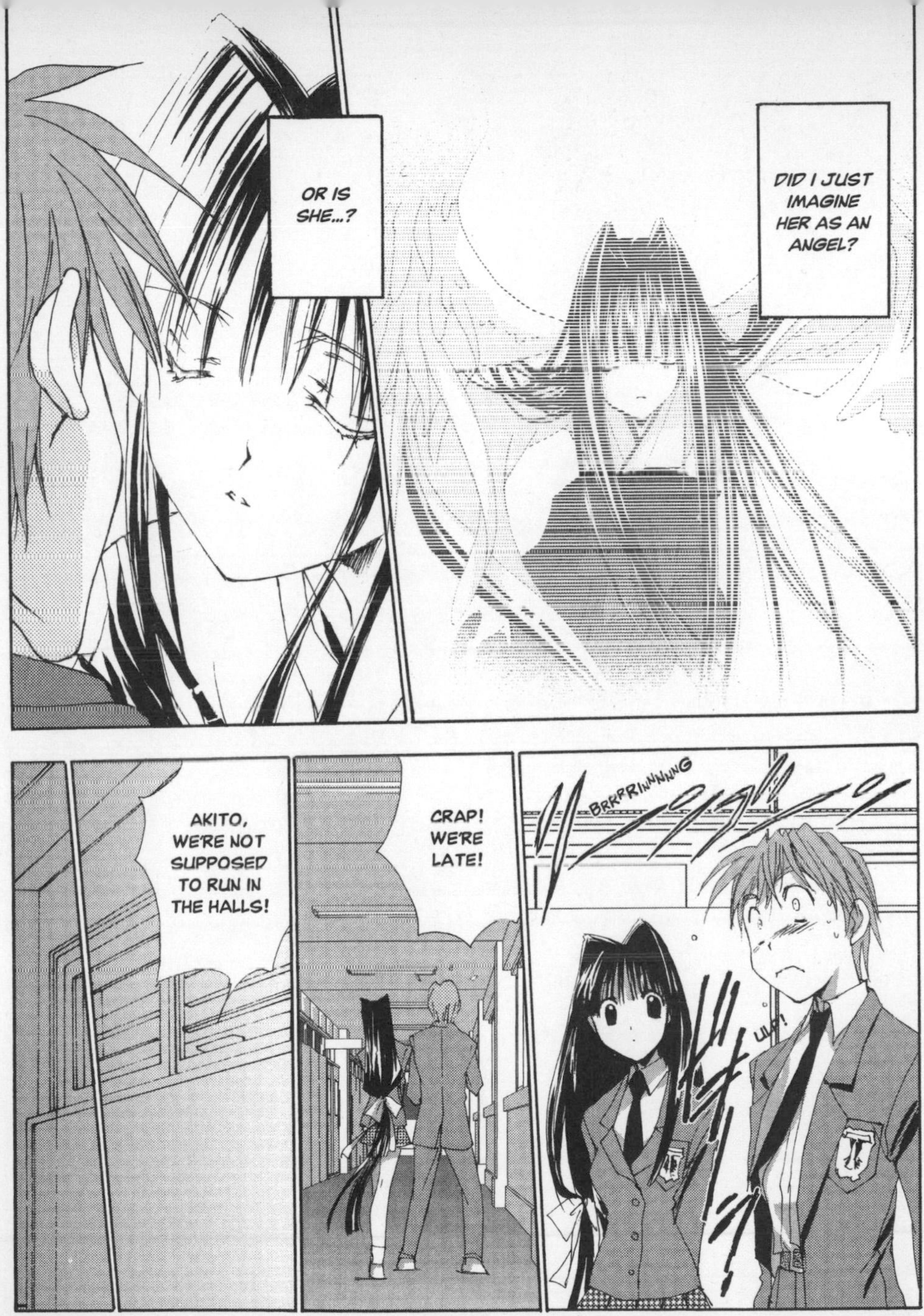
DID I JUST IMAGINE HER AS AN ANGEL?
OR IS SHE...?
BRRRRINNNNNG
ULP!
CRAP! WE'RE LATE!
AKITO, WE'RE NOT SUPPOSED TO RUN IN THE HALLS!

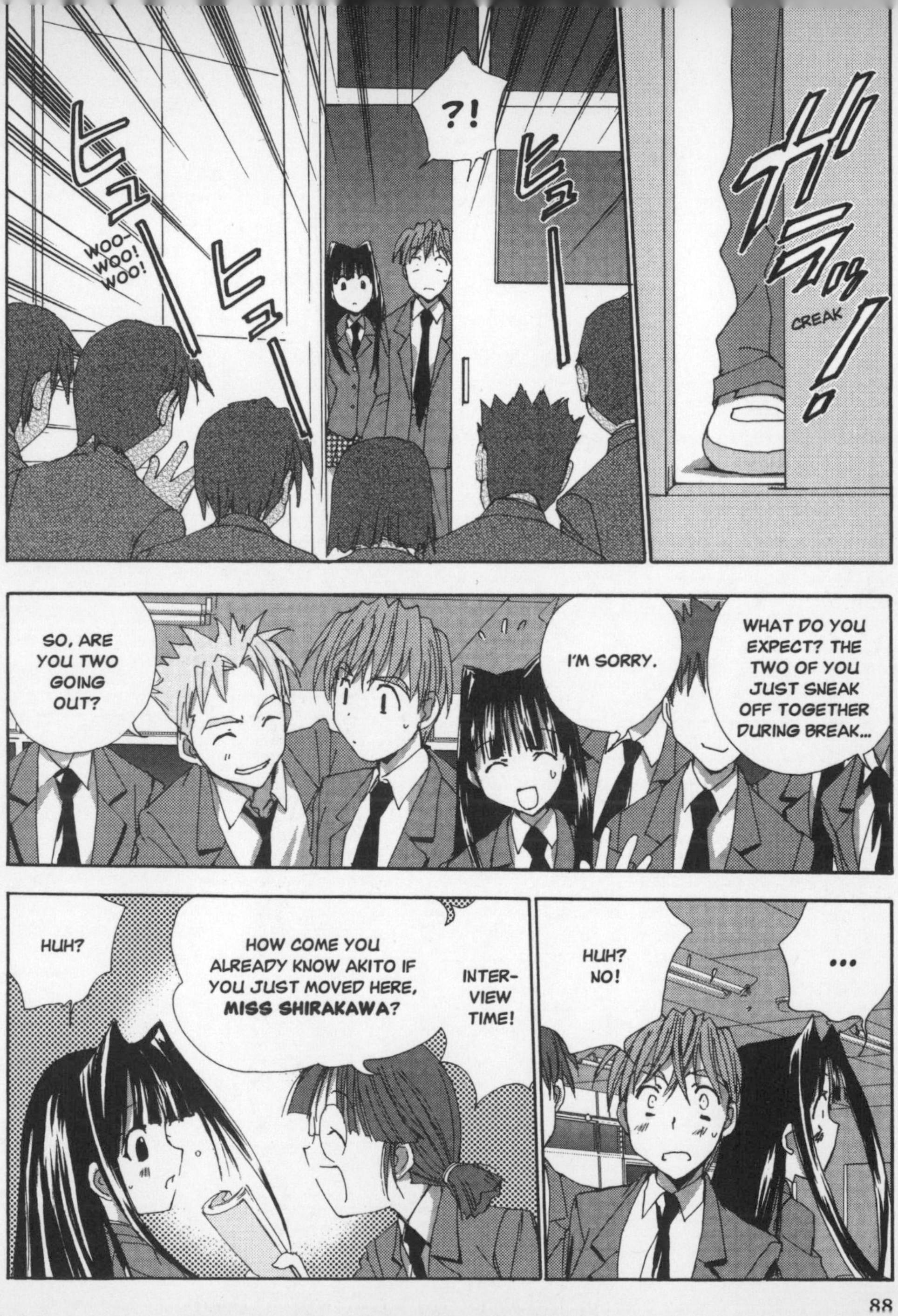
ガラッ!
CREAK
?!
ヒュー
ヒュー
ヒュー
WOO-WOO! WOO!
WHAT DO YOU EXPECT? THE TWO OF YOU JUST SNEAK OFF TOGETHER DURING BREAK...
I'M SORRY.
SO, ARE YOU TWO GOING OUT?
...
HUH? NO!
INTER-VIEW TIME!
HOW COME YOU ALREADY KNOW AKITO IF YOU JUST MOVED HERE, MISS SHIRAKAWA?
HUH?

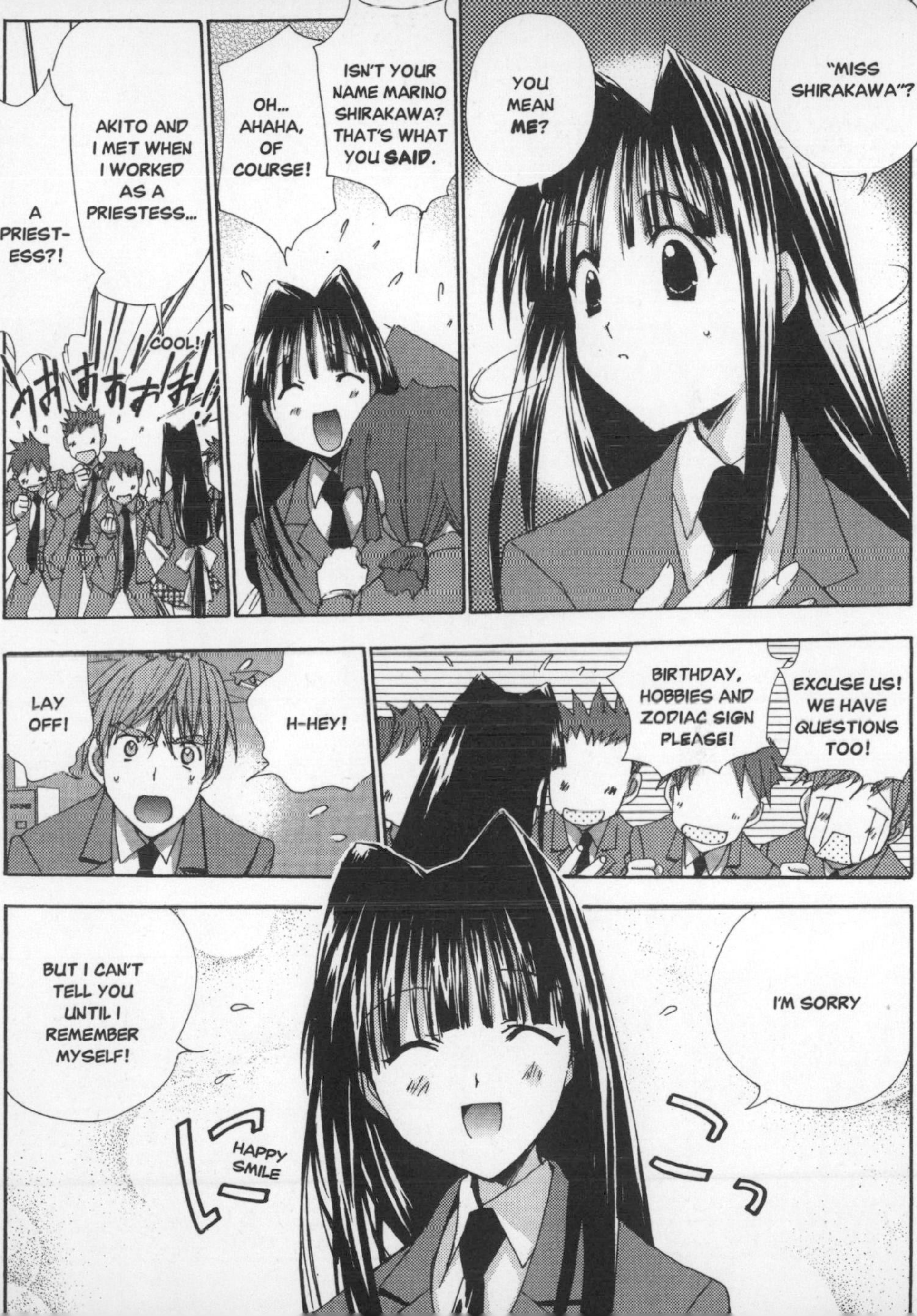
"MISS SHIRAKAWA"?
YOU MEAN ME?
ISN'T YOUR NAME MARINO SHIRAKAWA? THAT'S WHAT YOU SAID.
OH... AHAHA, OF COURSE!
AKITO AND I MET WHEN I WORKED AS A PRIESTESS...
A PRIEST-ESS?!
COOL!
EXCUSE US! WE HAVE QUESTIONS TOO!
BIRTHDAY, HOBBIES AND ZODIAC SIGN PLEASE!
H-HEY!
LAY OFF!
I'M SORRY
BUT I CAN'T TELL YOU UNTIL I REMEMBER MYSELF!
HAPPY SMILE

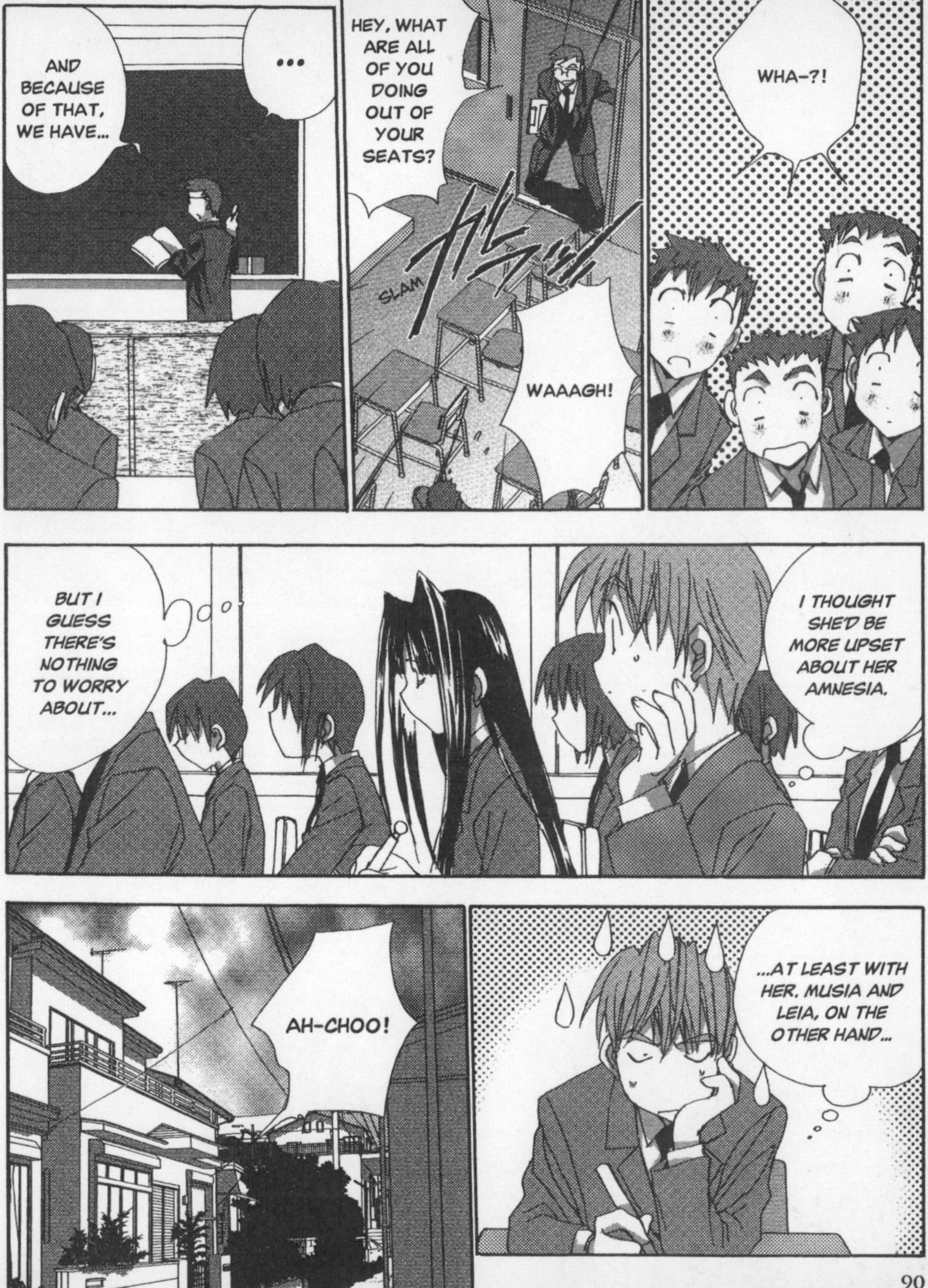
WHA-?!
HEY, WHAT ARE ALL OF YOU DOING OUT OF YOUR SEATS?
SLAM
WAAAGH!
...
AND BECAUSE OF THAT, WE HAVE...
I THOUGHT SHE'D BE MORE UPSET ABOUT HER AMNESIA.
BUT I GUESS THERE'S NOTHING TO WORRY ABOUT...
...AT LEAST WITH HER. MUSIA AND LEIA, ON THE OTHER HAND...
AH-CHOO!

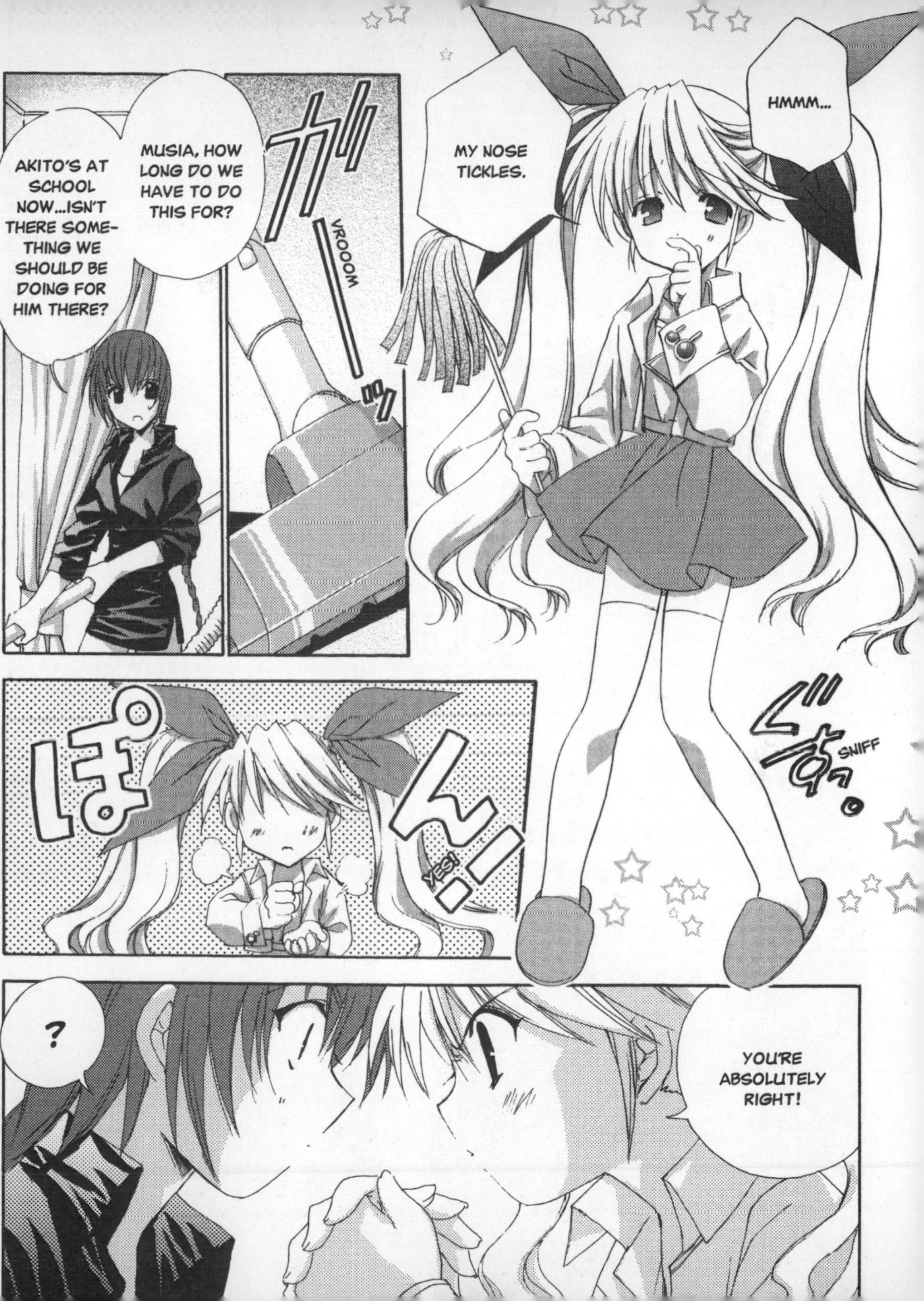
HMMM...
MY NOSE TICKLES.
SNIFF
VROOOM
MUSIA, HOW LONG DO WE HAVE TO DO THIS FOR?
AKITO'S AT SCHOOL NOW...ISN'T THERE SOMETHING WE SHOULD BE DOING FOR HIM THERE?
YES!
YOU'RE ABSOLUTELY RIGHT!
?

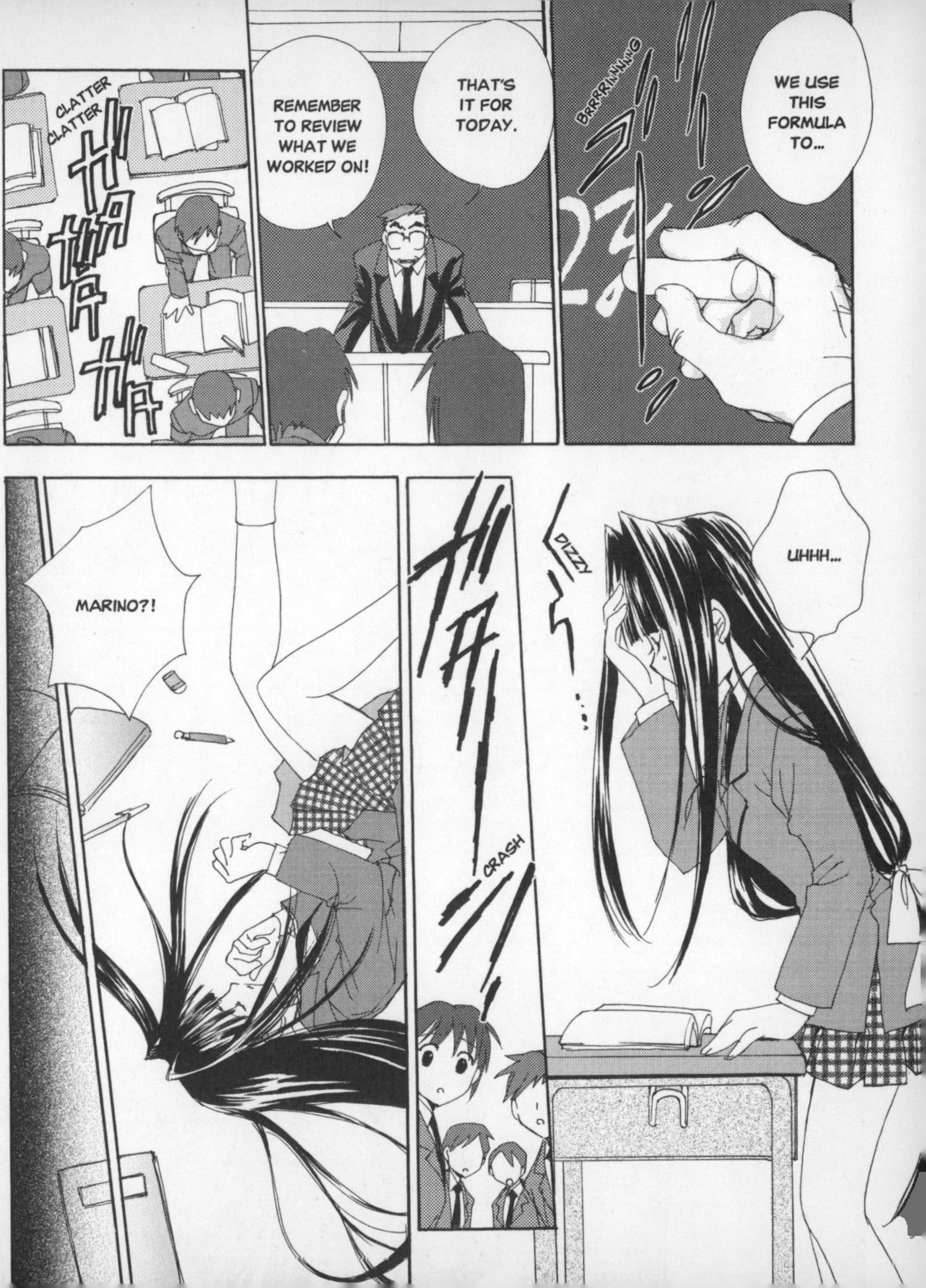
WE USE THIS FORMULA TO...
BRRRRINNNNG
THAT'S IT FOR TODAY.
REMEMBER TO REVIEW WHAT WE WORKED ON!
CLATTER CLATTER
UHHH...
DIZZY
CRASH
MARINO?!

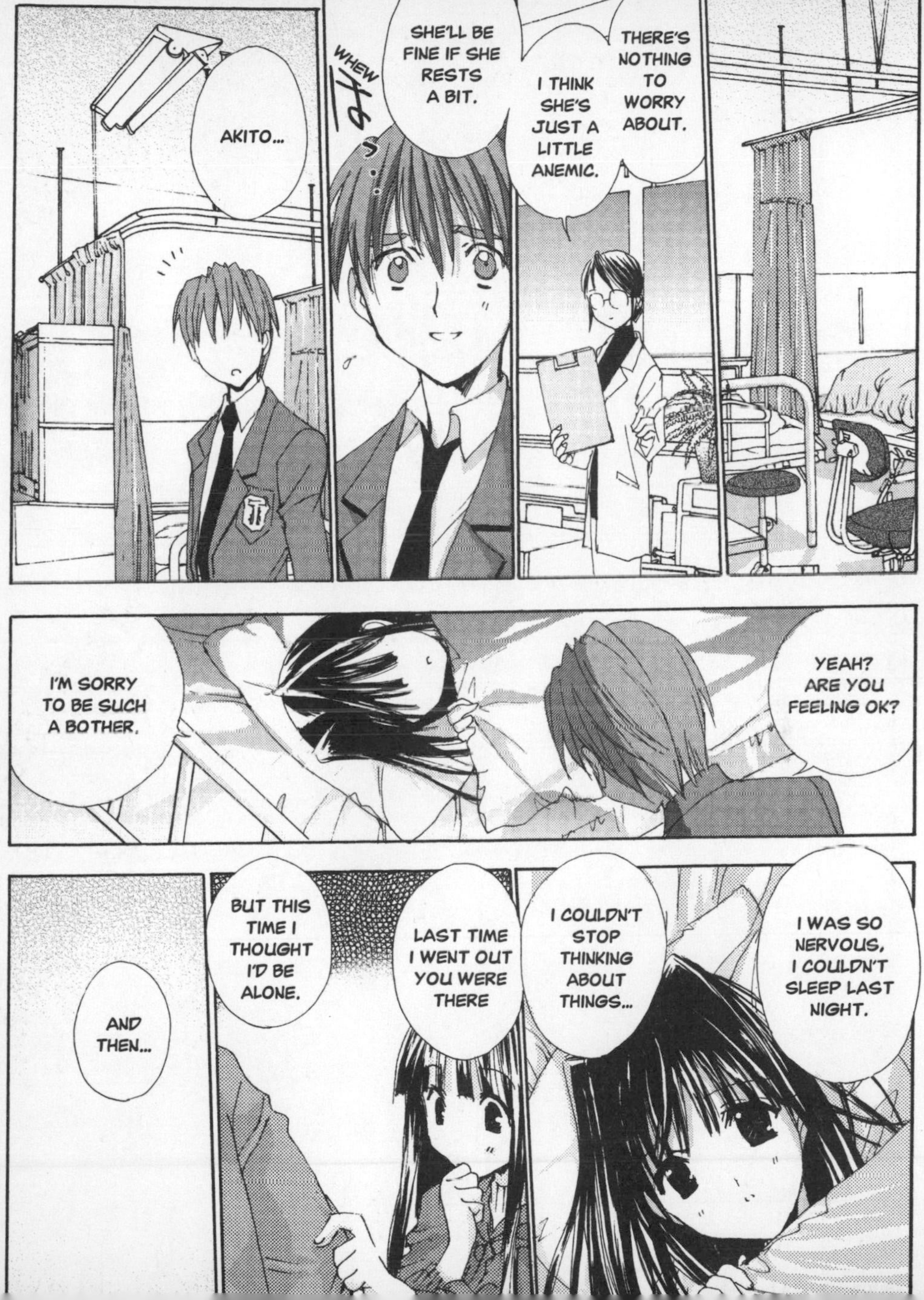
THERE'S NOTHING TO WORRY ABOUT.
I THINK SHE'S JUST A LITTLE ANEMIC.
SHE'LL BE FINE IF SHE RESTS A BIT.
WHEW
AKITO...
YEAH? ARE YOU FEELING OK?
I'M SORRY TO BE SUCH A BOTHER.
I WAS SO NERVOUS, I COULDN'T SLEEP LAST NIGHT.
I COULDN'T STOP THINKING ABOUT THINGS...
LAST TIME I WENT OUT YOU WERE THERE
BUT THIS TIME I THOUGHT I'D BE ALONE.
AND THEN...

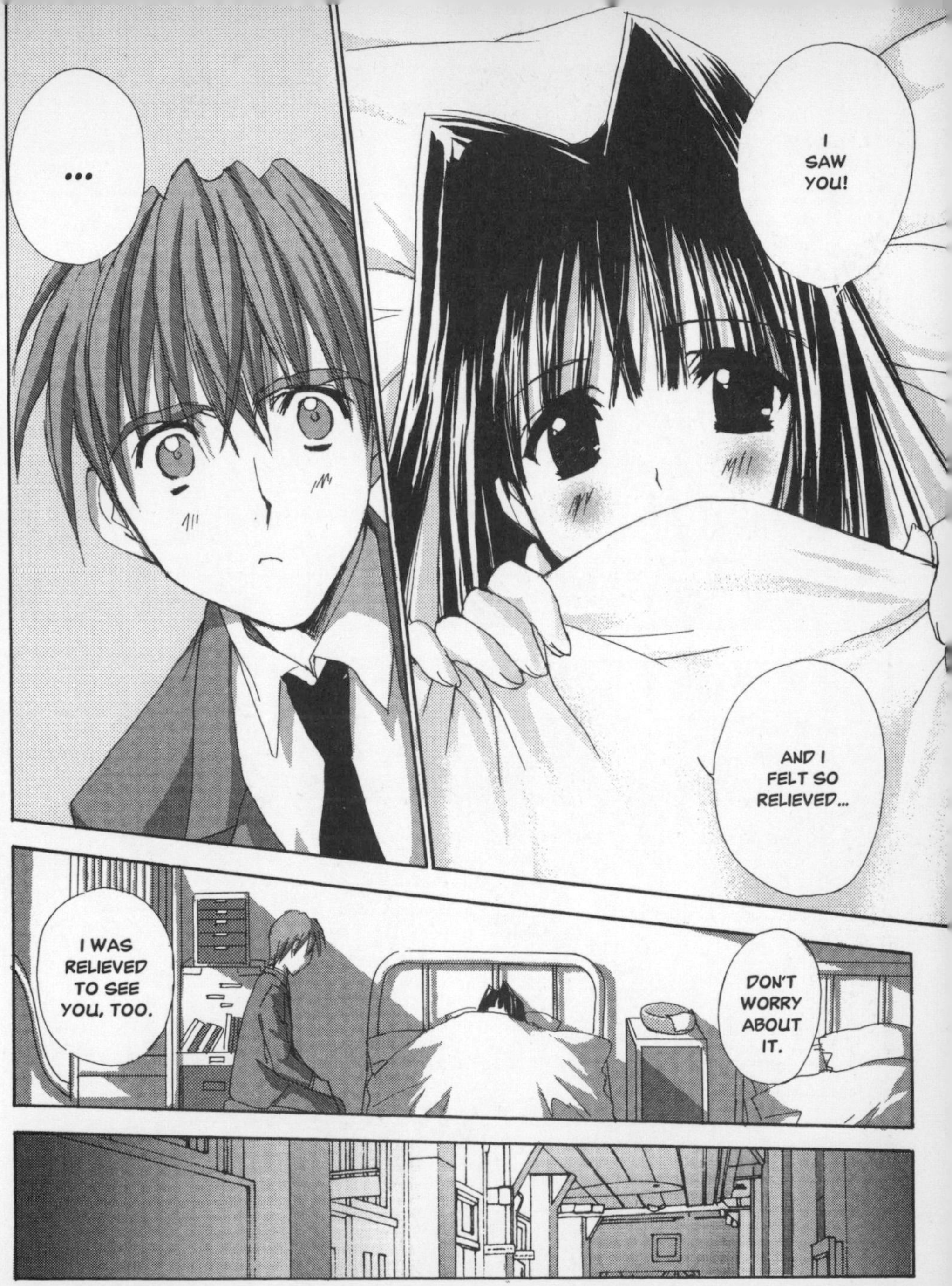
I SAW YOU!
AND I FELT SO RELIEVED...
...
DON'T WORRY ABOUT IT.
I WAS RELIEVED TO SEE YOU, TOO.

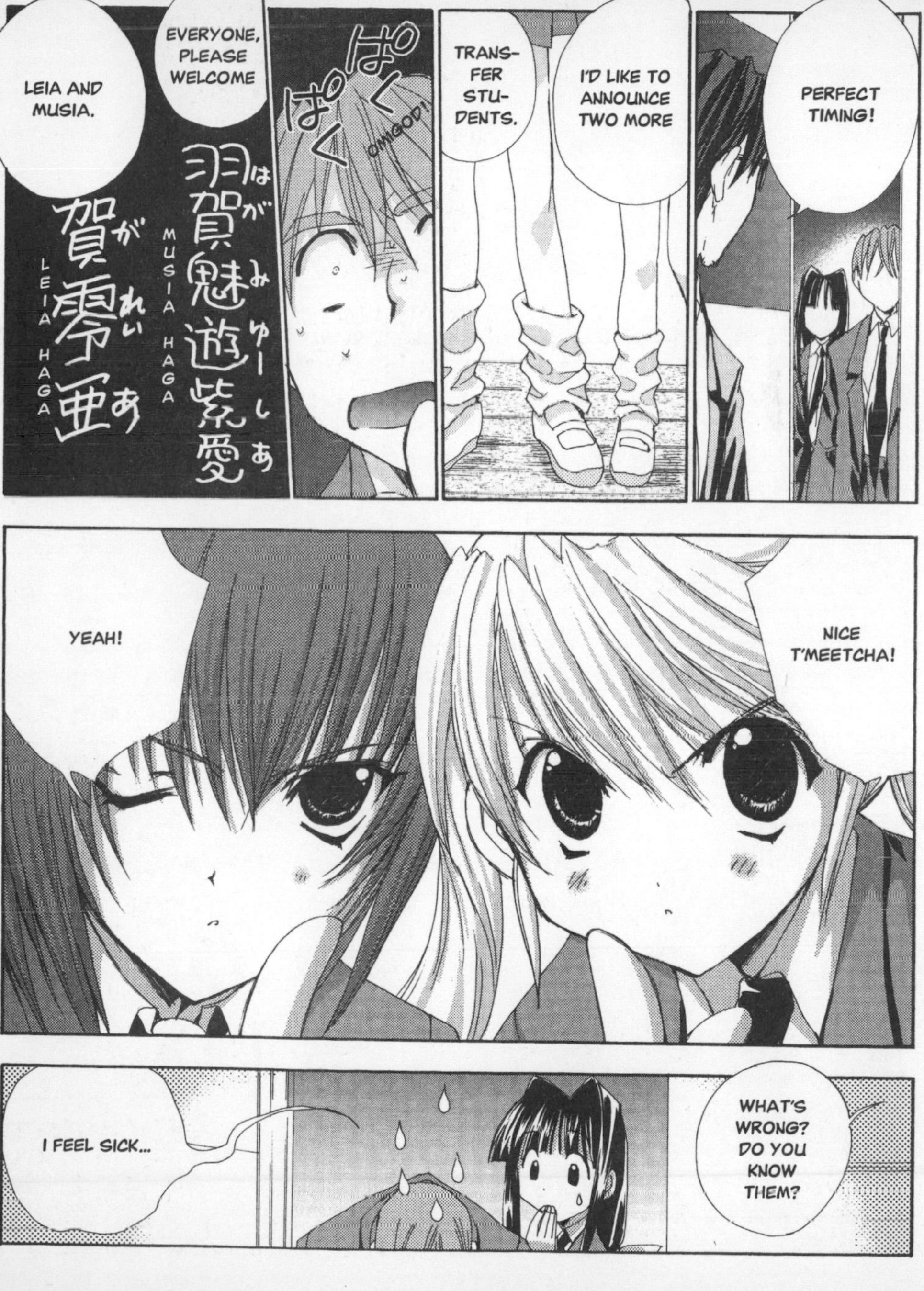

PERFECT TIMING!
I'D LIKE TO ANNOUNCE TWO MORE
TRANS-FER STU-DENTS.
ぱくぱく
OMIGOD!
EVERYONE, PLEASE WELCOME
羽賀魅遊紫愛
MUSIA HAGA
賀零亜
LEIA HAGA
LEIA AND MUSIA.
NICE T'MEETCHA!
YEAH!
WHAT'S WRONG? DO YOU KNOW THEM?
I FEEL SICK...

SCENE 7

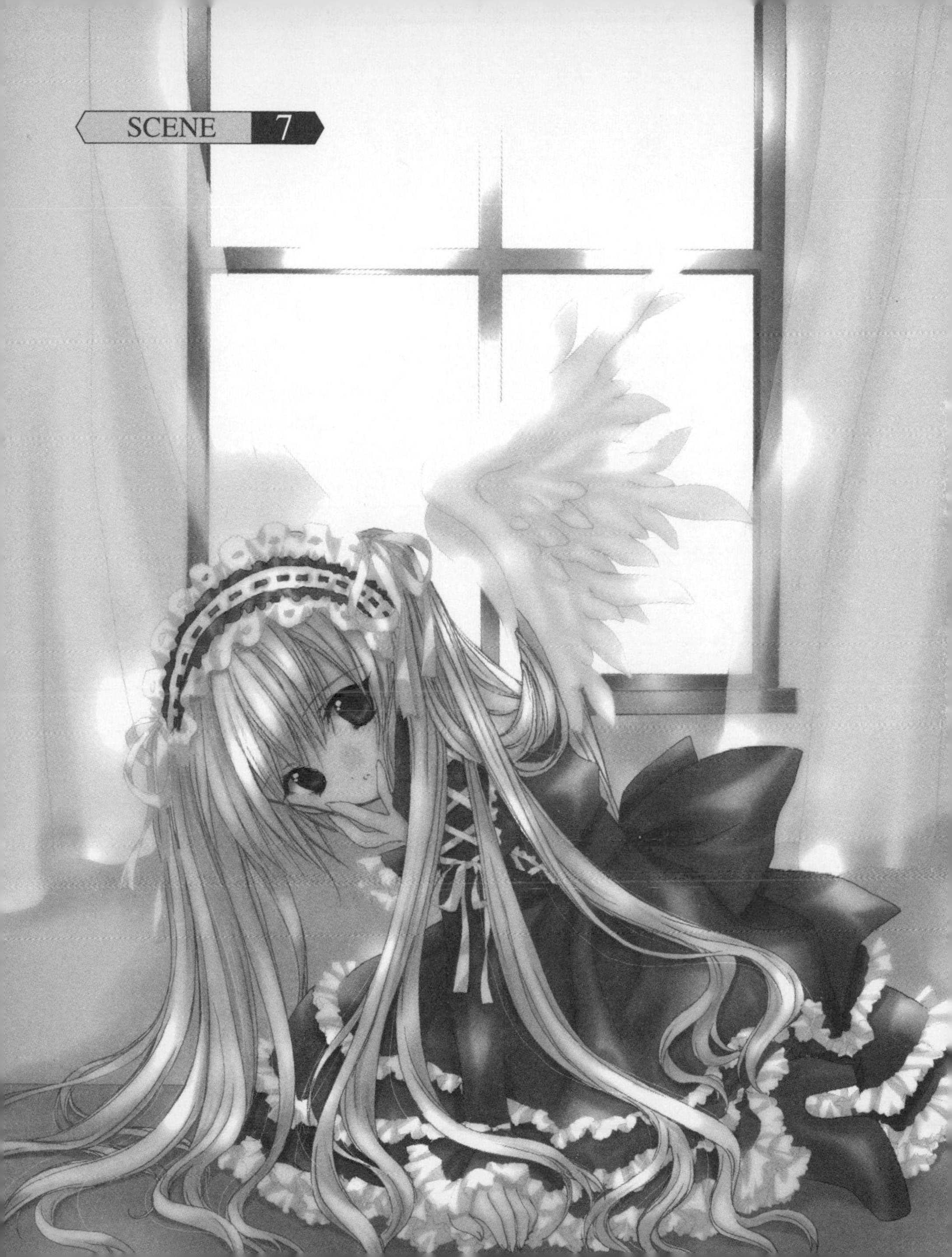

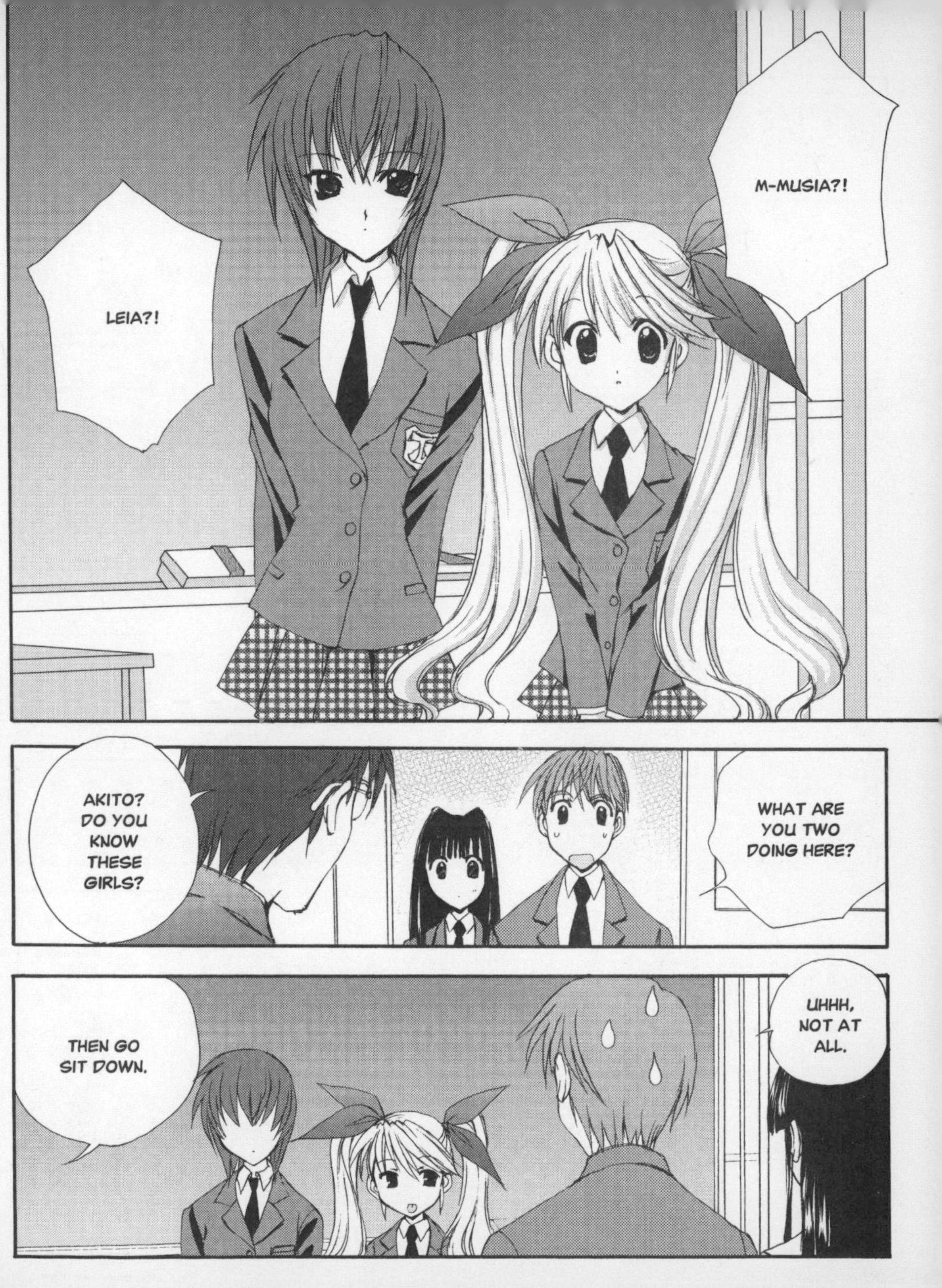
M-MUSIA?!
LEIA?!
WHAT ARE YOU TWO DOING HERE?
AKITO? DO YOU KNOW THESE GIRLS?
UHHH, NOT AT ALL.
THEN GO SIT DOWN.

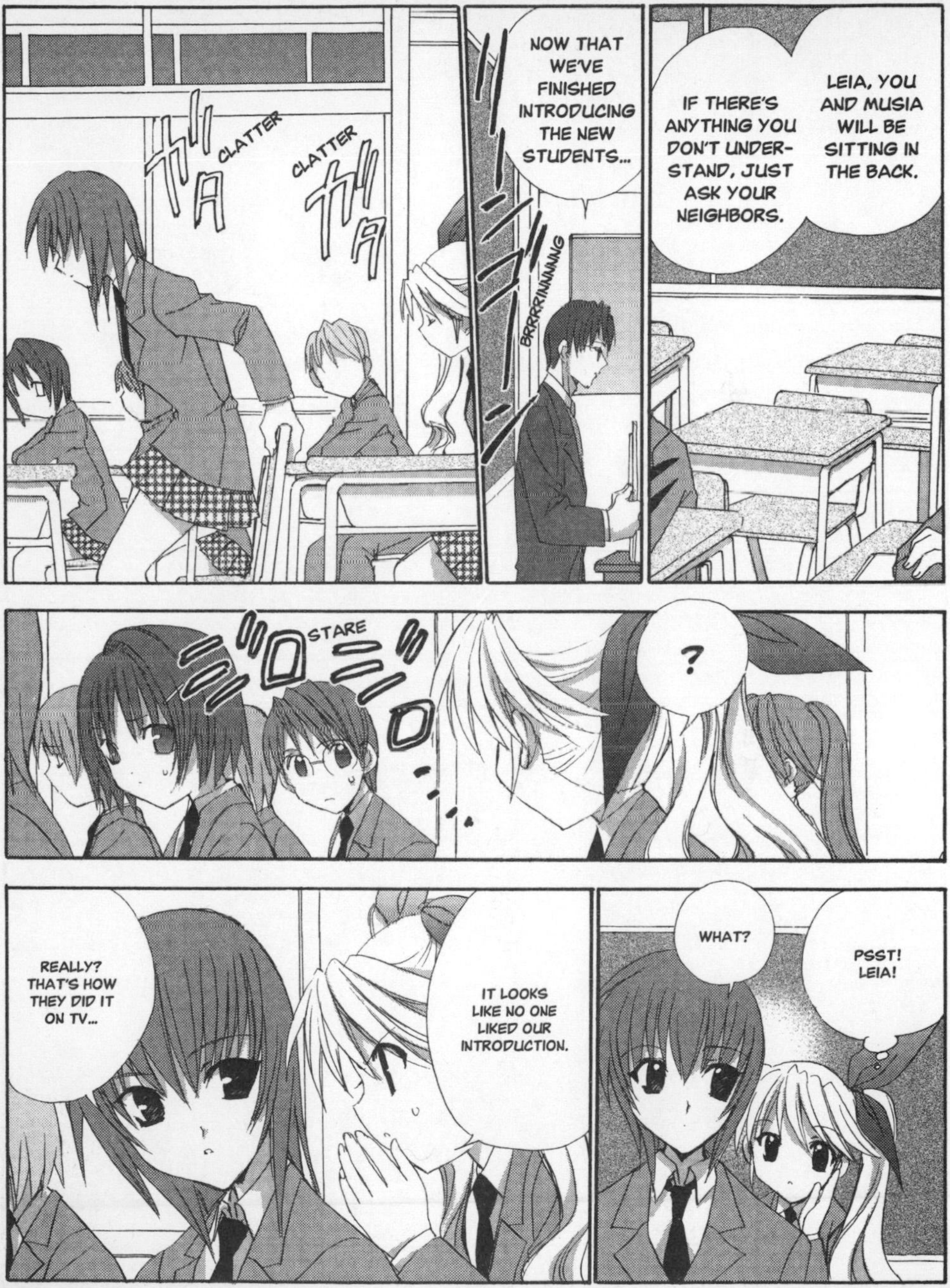
LEIA, YOU AND MUSIA WILL BE SITTING IN THE BACK.
IF THERE'S ANYTHING YOU DON'T UNDER-STAND, JUST ASK YOUR NEIGHBORS.
NOW THAT WE'VE FINISHED INTRODUCING THE NEW STUDENTS...
BRRRINNNNNG
CLATTER
CLATTER
?
STARE
PSST! LEIA!
WHAT?
IT LOOKS LIKE NO ONE LIKED OUR INTRODUCTION.
REALLY? THAT'S HOW THEY DID IT ON TV...

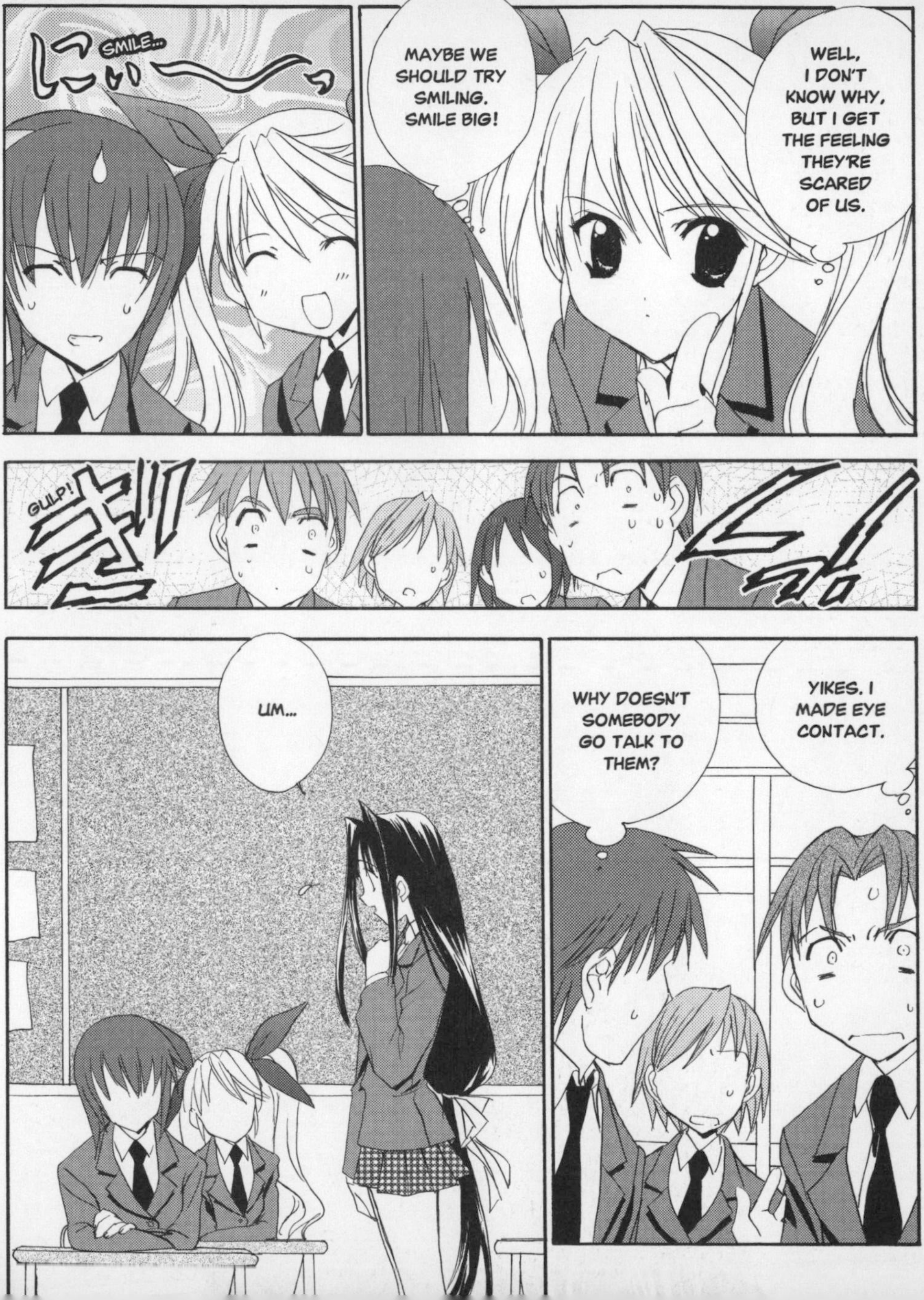

WELL, I DON'T KNOW WHY, BUT I GET THE FEELING THEY'RE SCARED OF US.
MAYBE WE SHOULD TRY SMILING. SMILE BIG!
SMILE...
にっこ〜〜〜っ
しーん
きょ
GULP!
YIKES. I MADE EYE CONTACT.
WHY DOESN'T SOMEBODY GO TALK TO THEM?
UM...

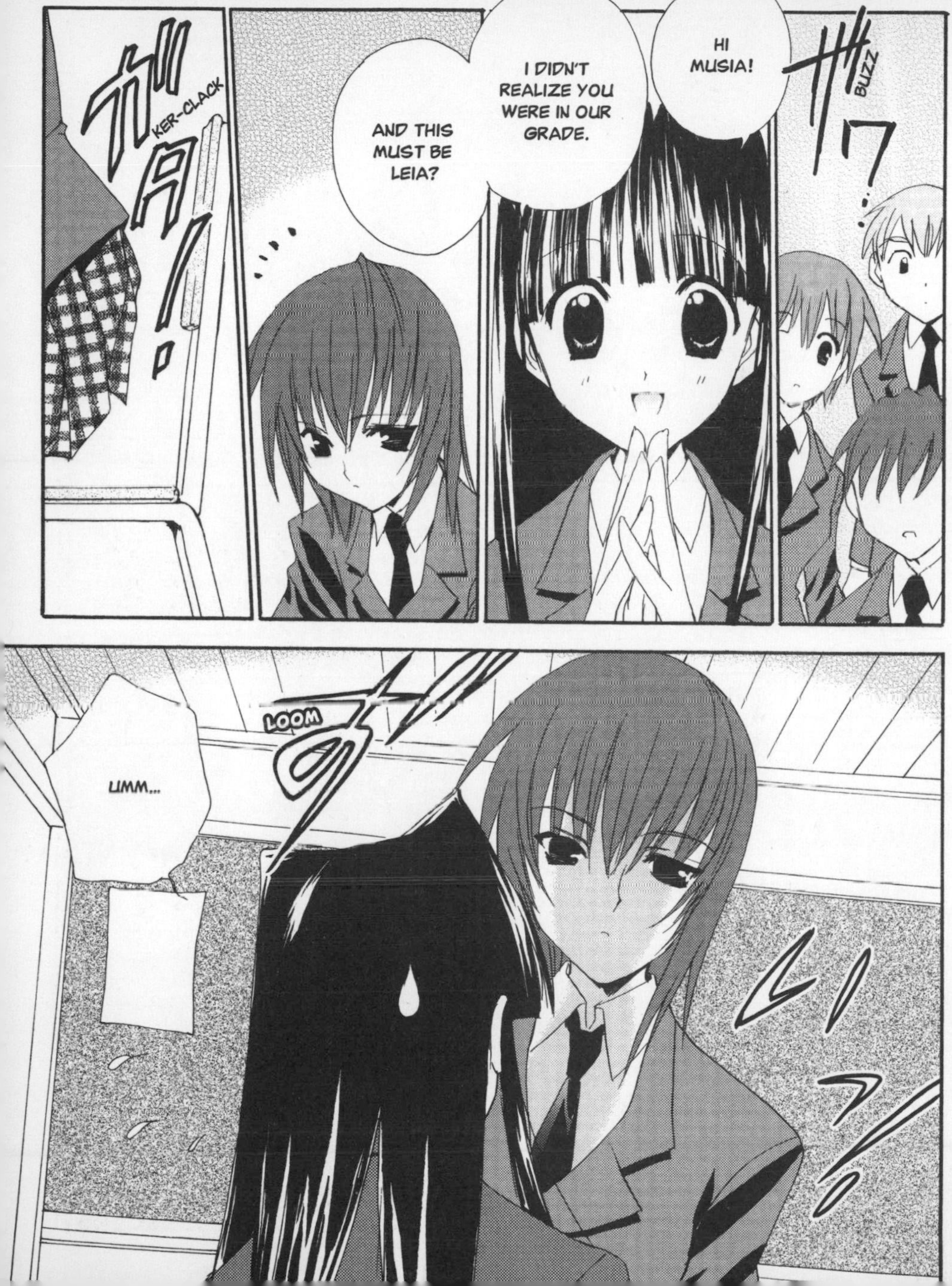
BUZZ
HI MUSIA!
I DIDN'T REALIZE YOU WERE IN OUR GRADE.
AND THIS MUST BE LEIA?
KER-CLACK
LOOM
UMM...

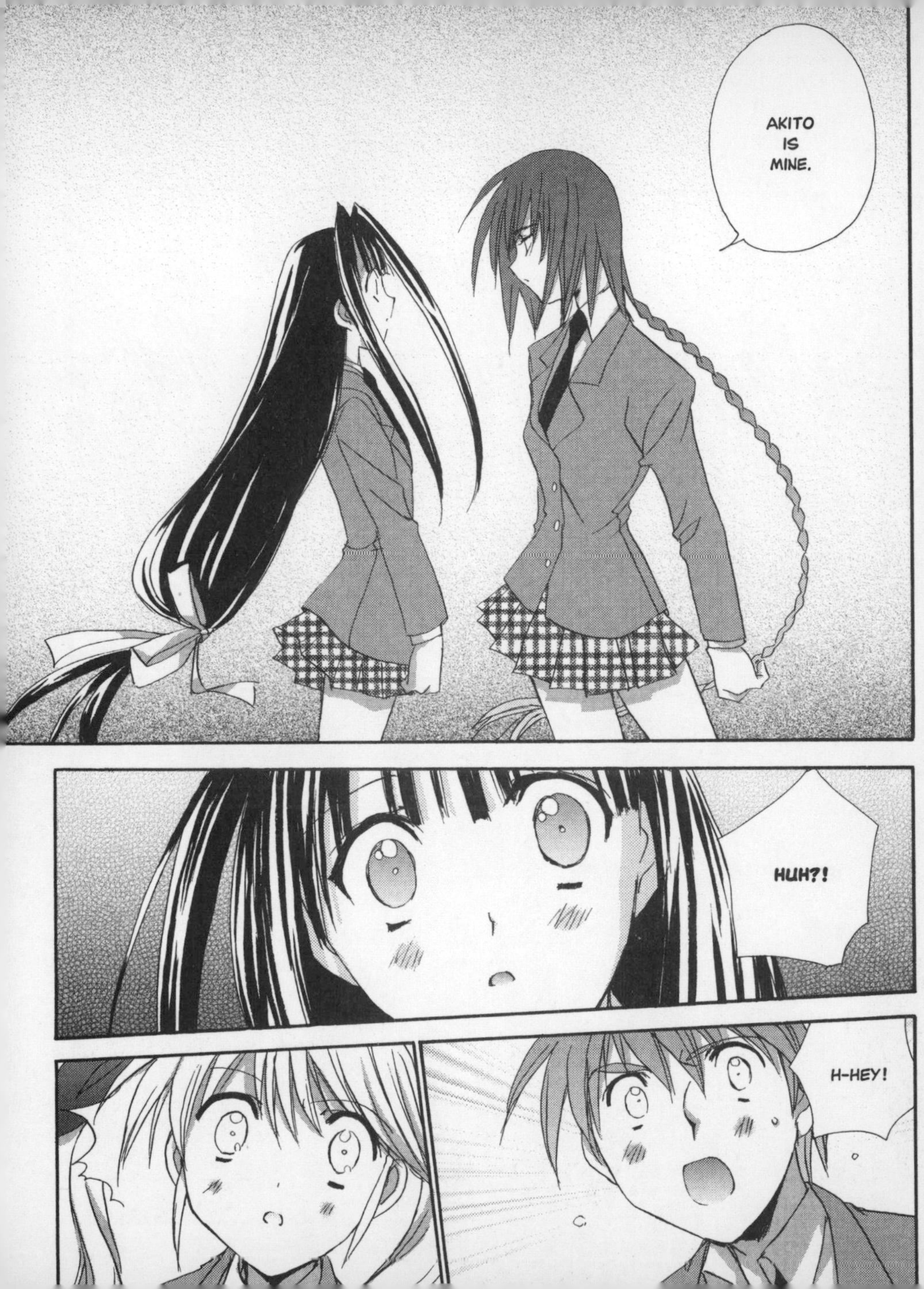
AKITO IS MINE.
HUH?!
H-HEY!

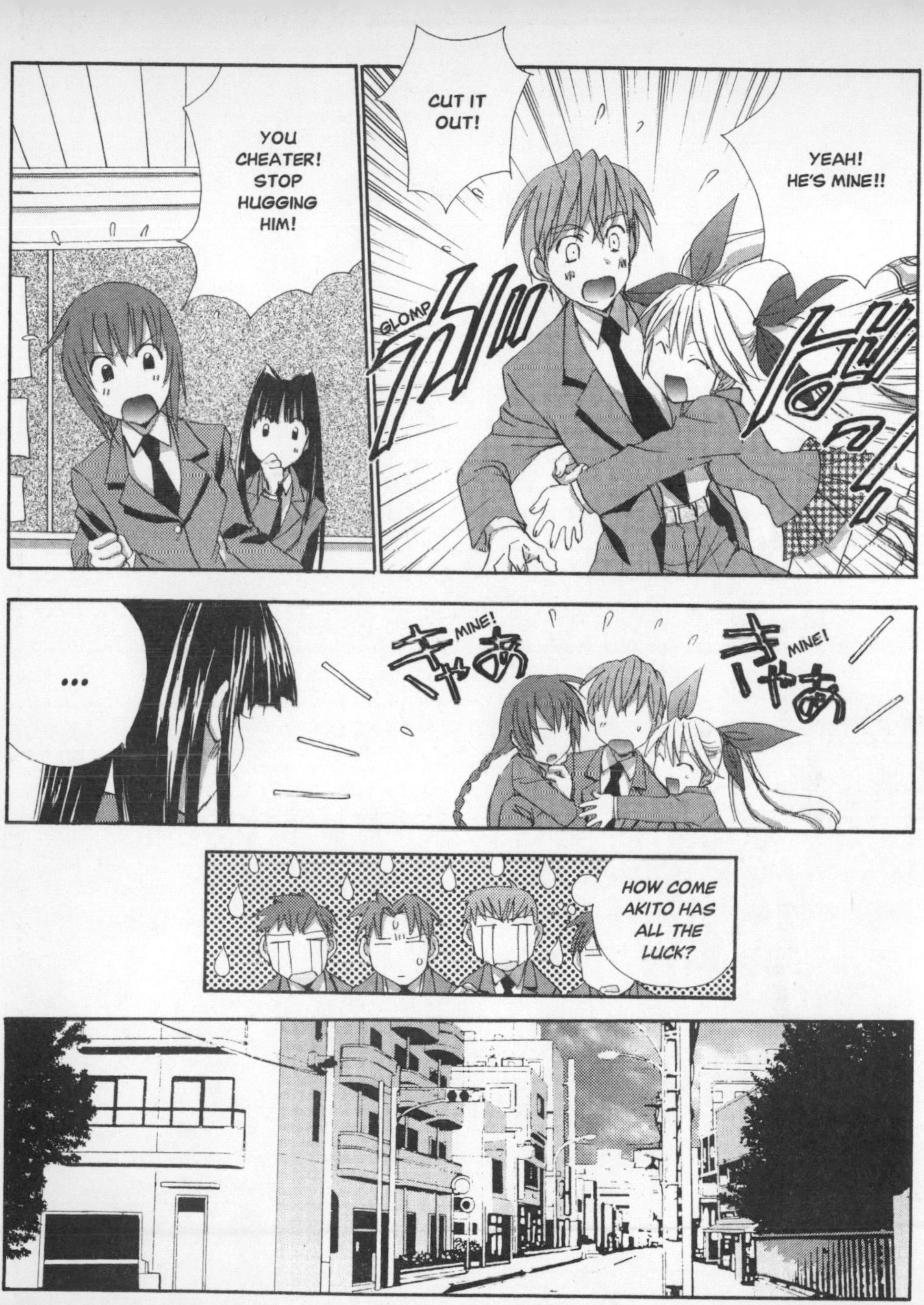
YEAH! HE'S MINE!!
CUT IT OUT!
GLOMP
YOU CHEATER! STOP HUGGING HIM!
MINE!
MINE!
...
HOW COME AKITO HAS ALL THE LUCK?

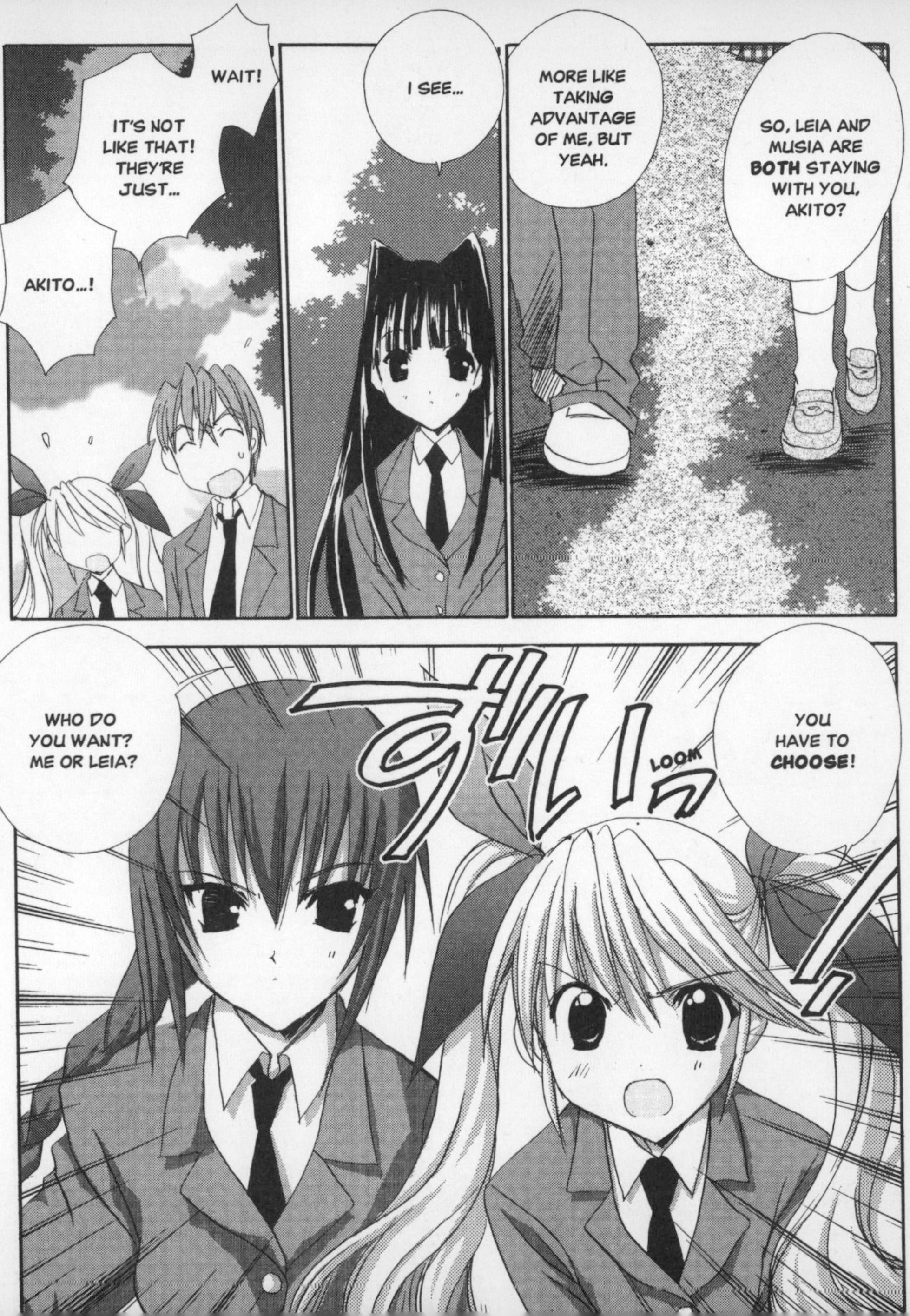
SO, LEIA AND MUSIA ARE BOTH STAYING WITH YOU, AKITO?
MORE LIKE TAKING ADVANTAGE OF ME, BUT YEAH.
I SEE...
WAIT!
IT'S NOT LIKE THAT! THEY'RE JUST...
AKITO...!
YOU HAVE TO CHOOSE!
LOOM
WHO DO YOU WANT? ME OR LEIA?

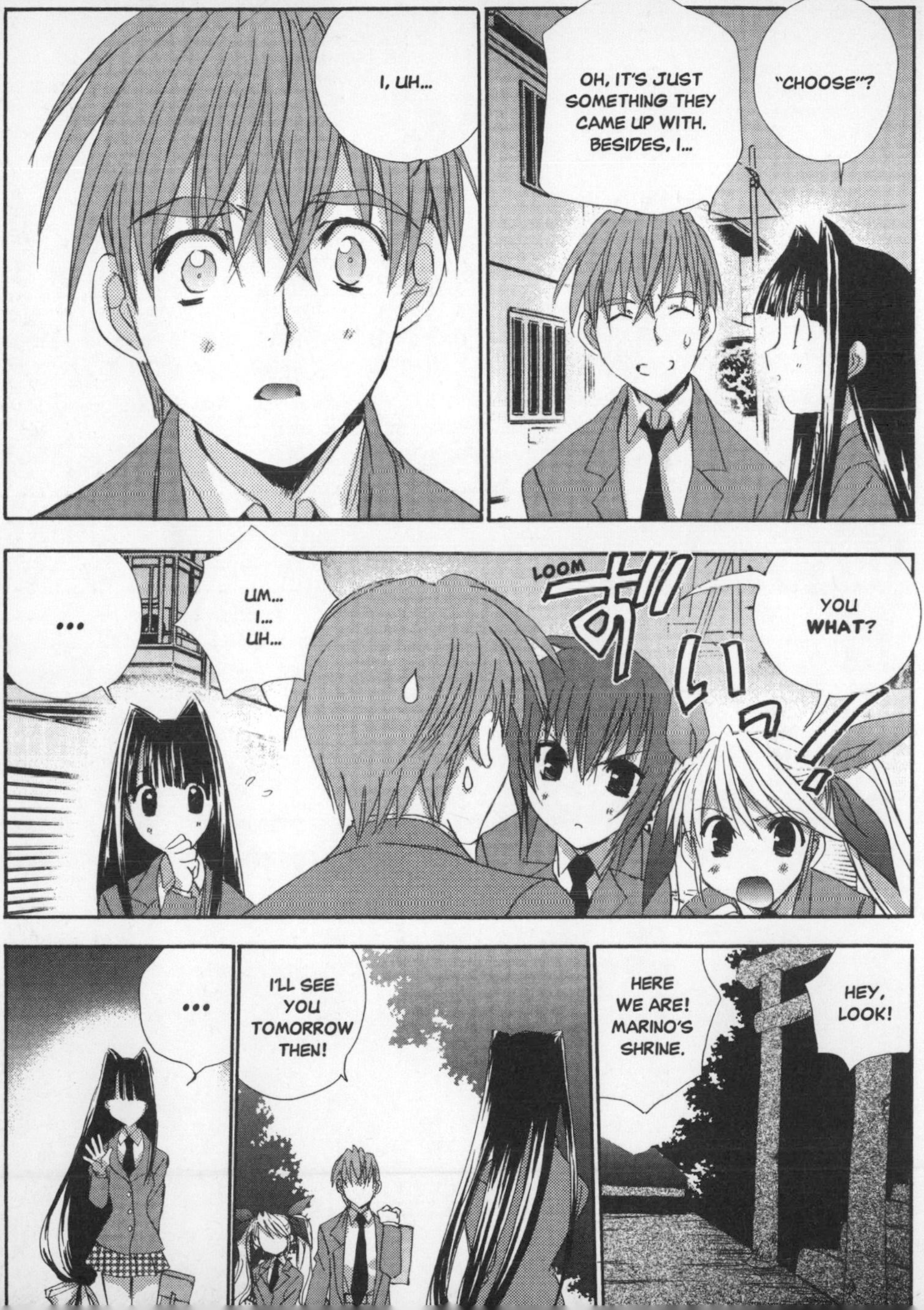
"CHOOSE"?
OH, IT'S JUST SOMETHING THEY CAME UP WITH. BESIDES, I...
I, UH...
YOU WHAT?
LOOM
UM... I... UH...
...
HEY, LOOK!
HERE WE ARE! MARINO'S SHRINE.
I'LL SEE YOU TOMORROW THEN!
...

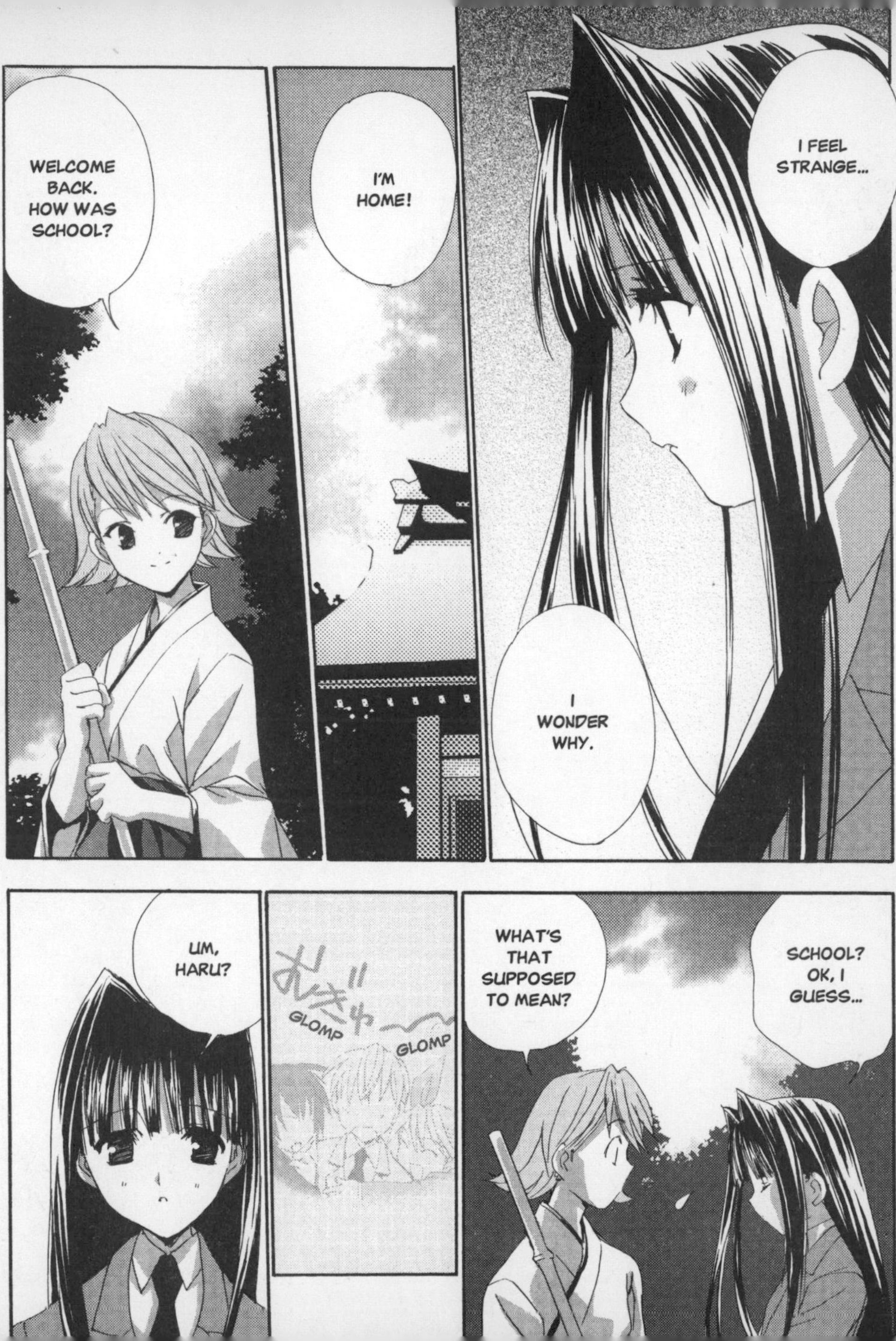
I FEEL STRANGE...
I WONDER WHY.
I'M HOME!
WELCOME BACK. HOW WAS SCHOOL?
SCHOOL? OK, I GUESS...
WHAT'S THAT SUPPOSED TO MEAN?
GLOMP
GLOMP
UM, HARU?

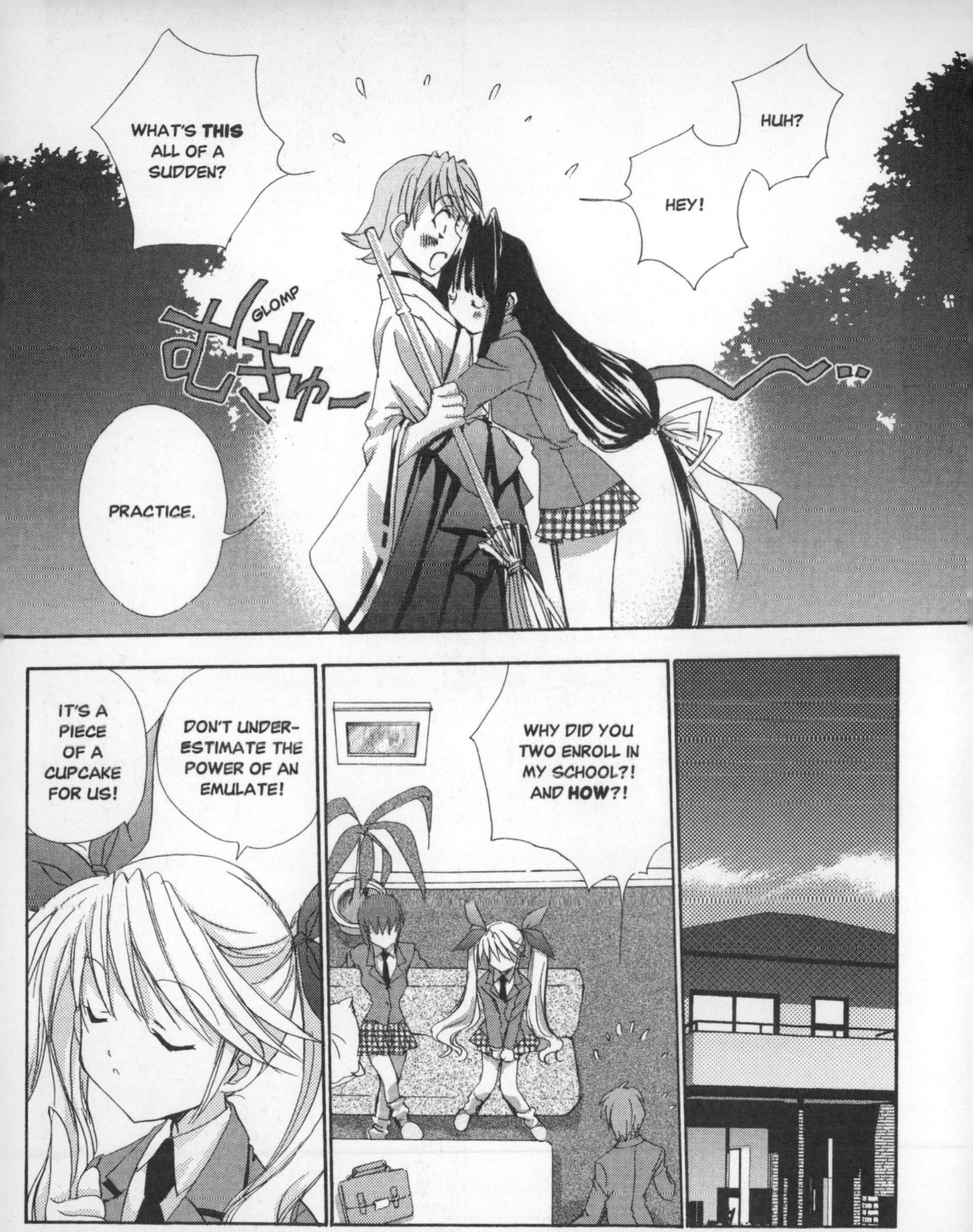
HUH?
HEY!
WHAT'S THIS ALL OF A SUDDEN?
GLOMP
むぎゅー
PRACTICE.
WHY DID YOU TWO ENROLL IN MY SCHOOL?! AND HOW?!
DON'T UNDER-ESTIMATE THE POWER OF AN EMULATE!
IT'S A PIECE OF A CUPCAKE FOR US!

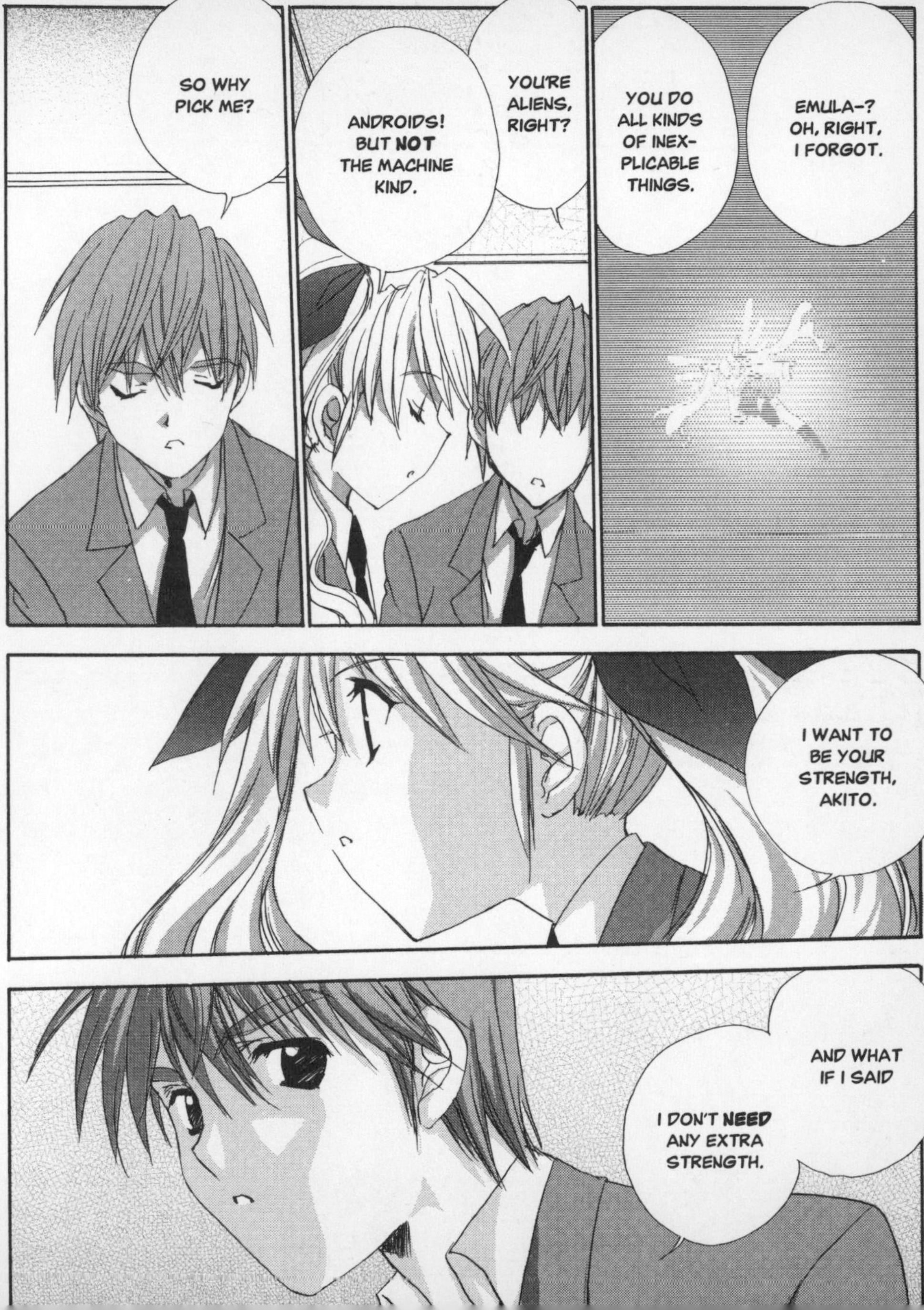
SO WHY PICK ME?
YOU'RE ALIENS, RIGHT?
ANDROIDS! BUT NOT THE MACHINE KIND.
YOU DO ALL KINDS OF INEX-PLICABLE THINGS.
EMULA-? OH, RIGHT, I FORGOT.
I WANT TO BE YOUR STRENGTH, AKITO.
AND WHAT IF I SAID
I DON'T NEED ANY EXTRA STRENGTH.

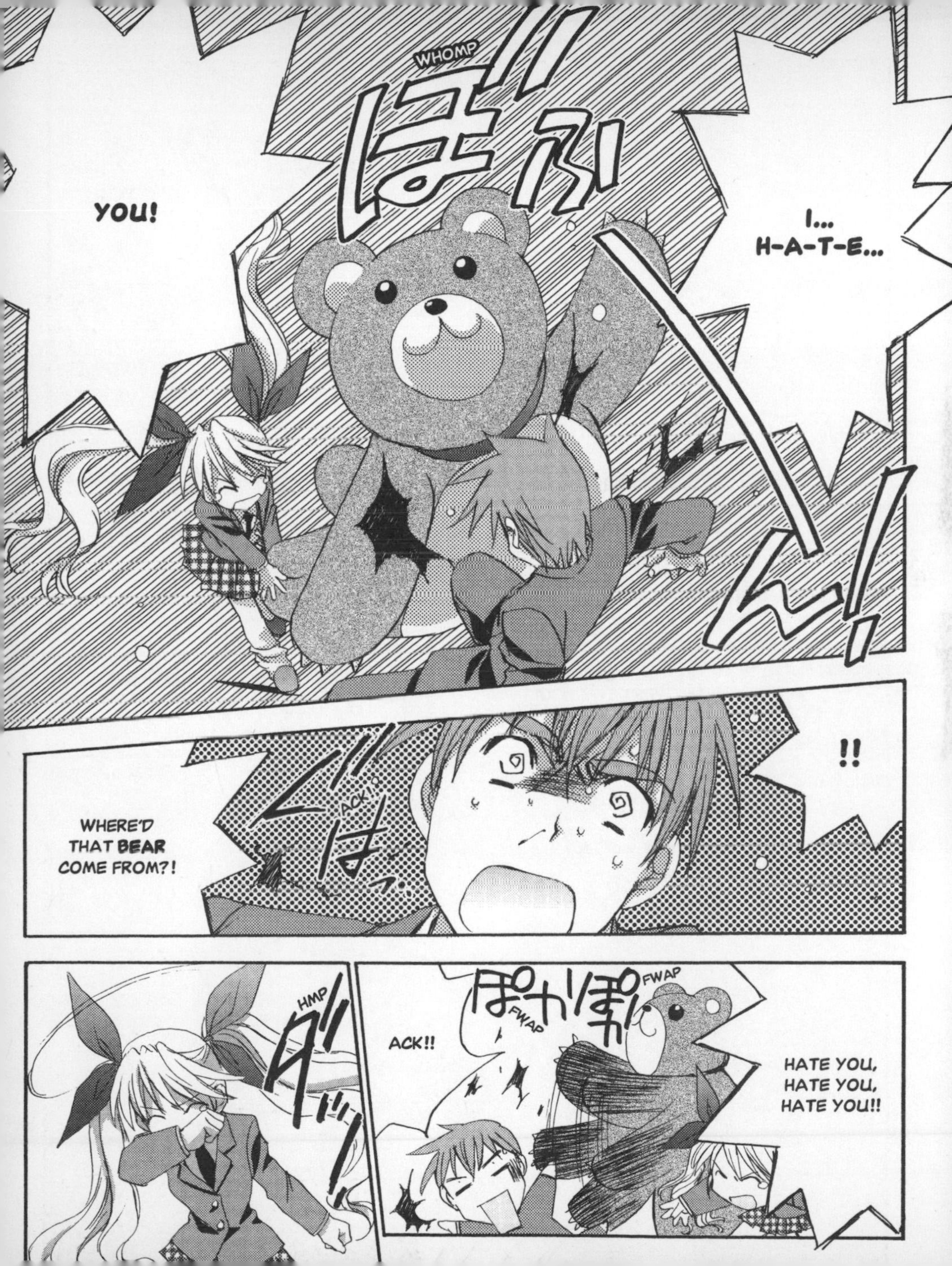
I... H-A-T-E...
WHOMP
YOU!
!!
ACK!
WHERE'D THAT BEAR COME FROM?!
HATE YOU, HATE YOU, HATE YOU!!
FWAP
FWAP
ACK!!
HMP

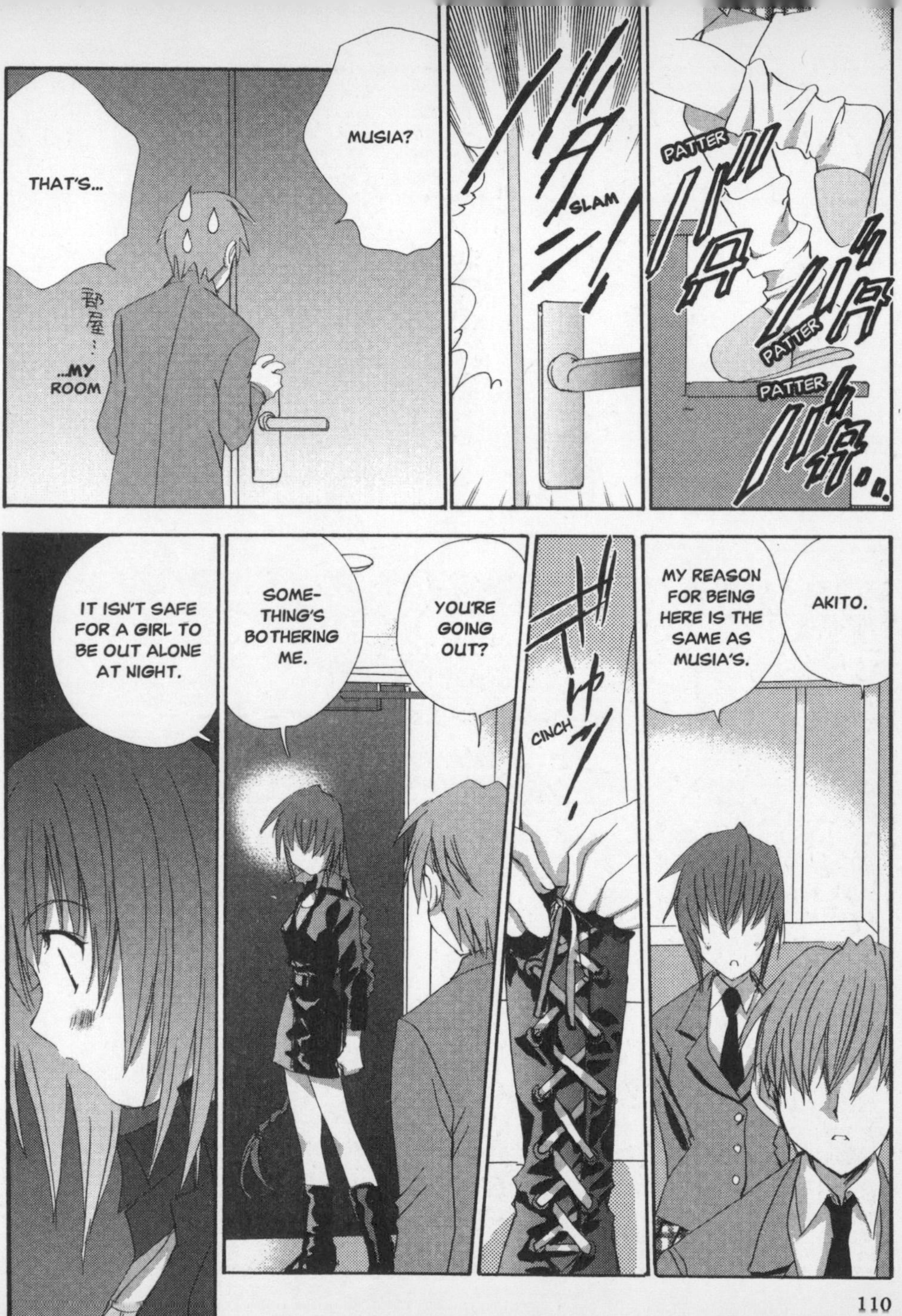
PATTER
PATTER
PATTER
SLAM
MUSIA?
THAT'S...
部屋…
...MY ROOM
AKITO.
MY REASON FOR BEING HERE IS THE SAME AS MUSIA'S.
CINCH
YOU'RE GOING OUT?
SOME-THING'S BOTHERING ME.
IT ISN'T SAFE FOR A GIRL TO BE OUT ALONE AT NIGHT.

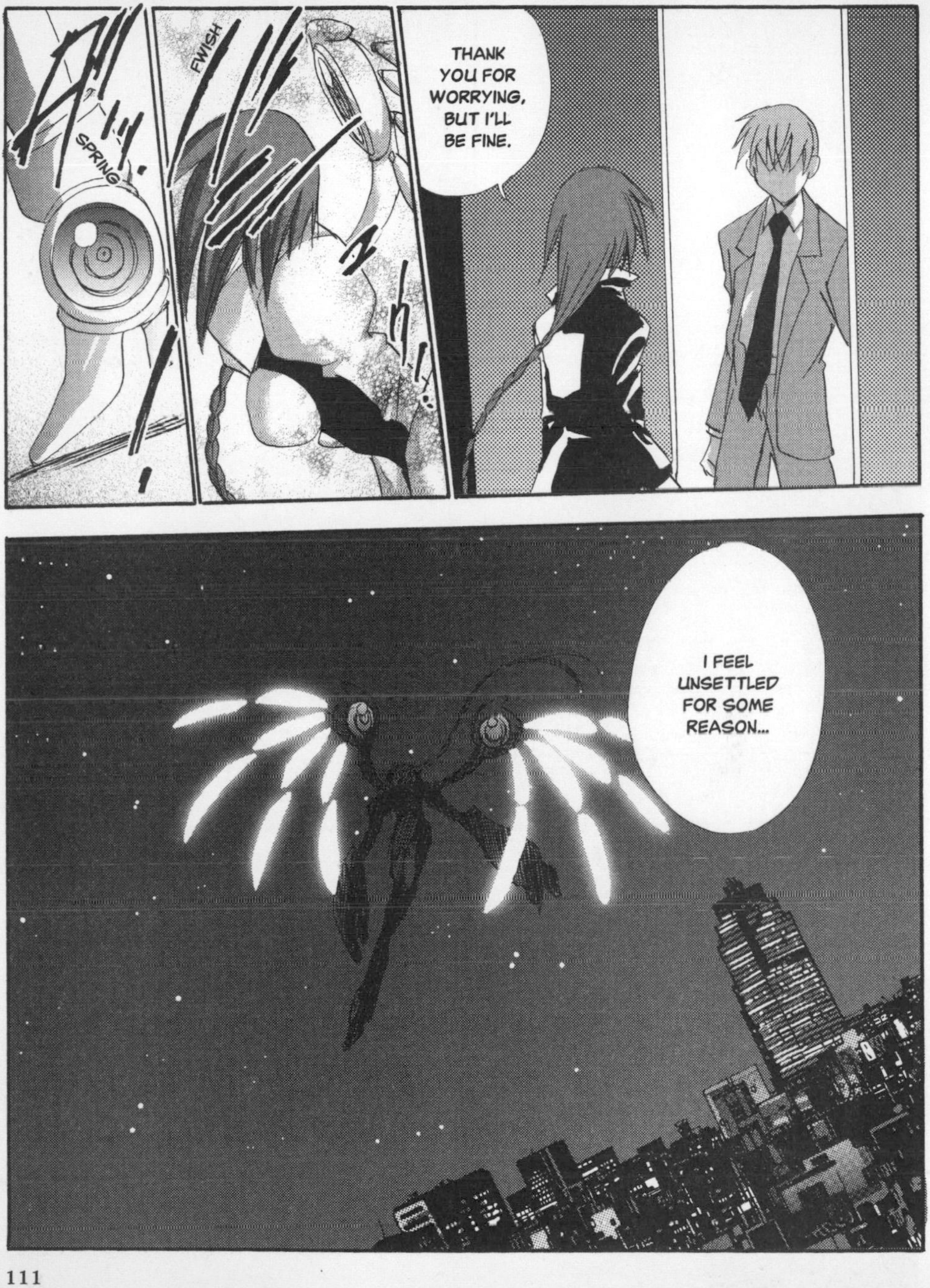
THANK YOU FOR WORRYING, BUT I'LL BE FINE.
FWISH
SPRING
I FEEL UNSETTLED FOR SOME REASON...

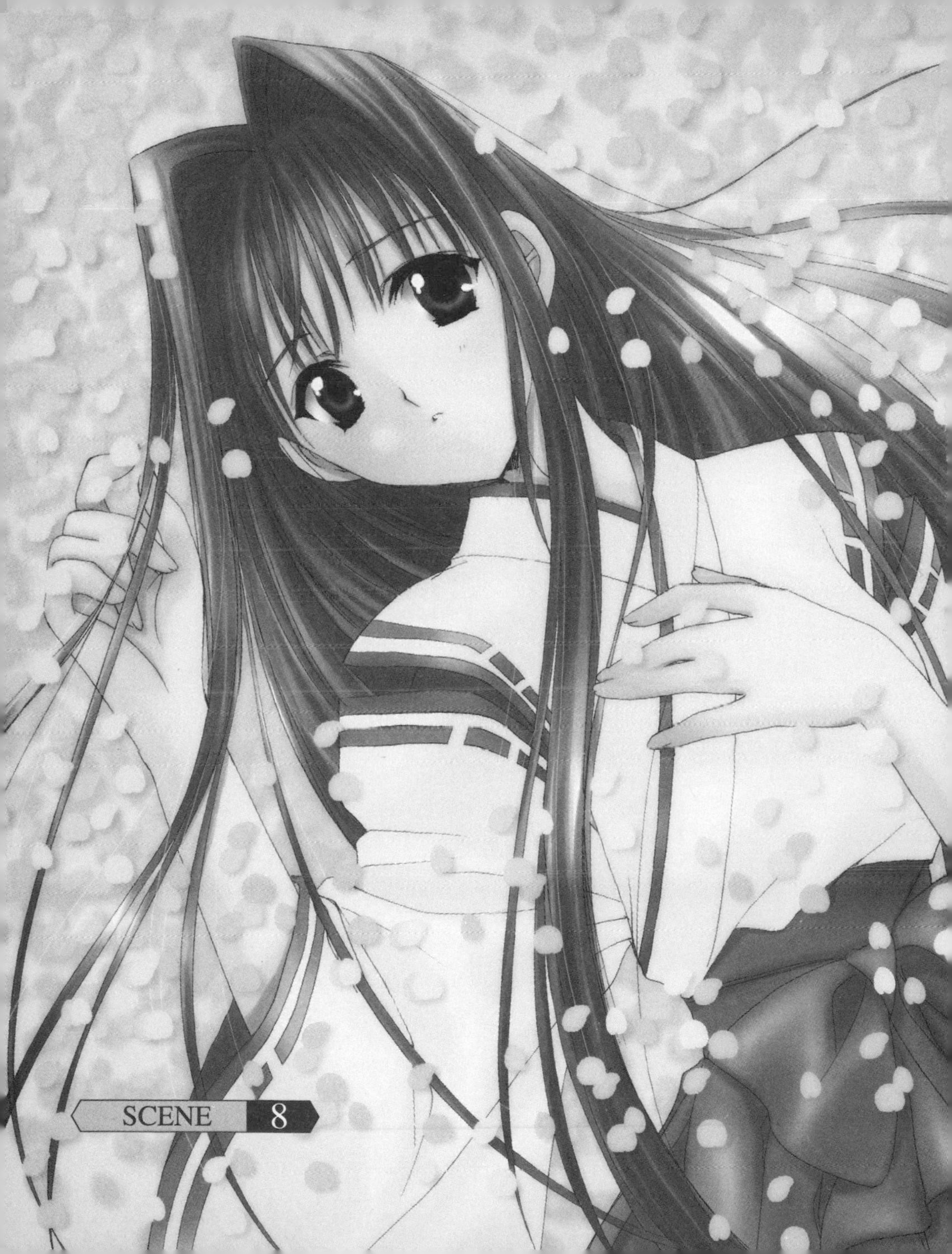
SCENE 8

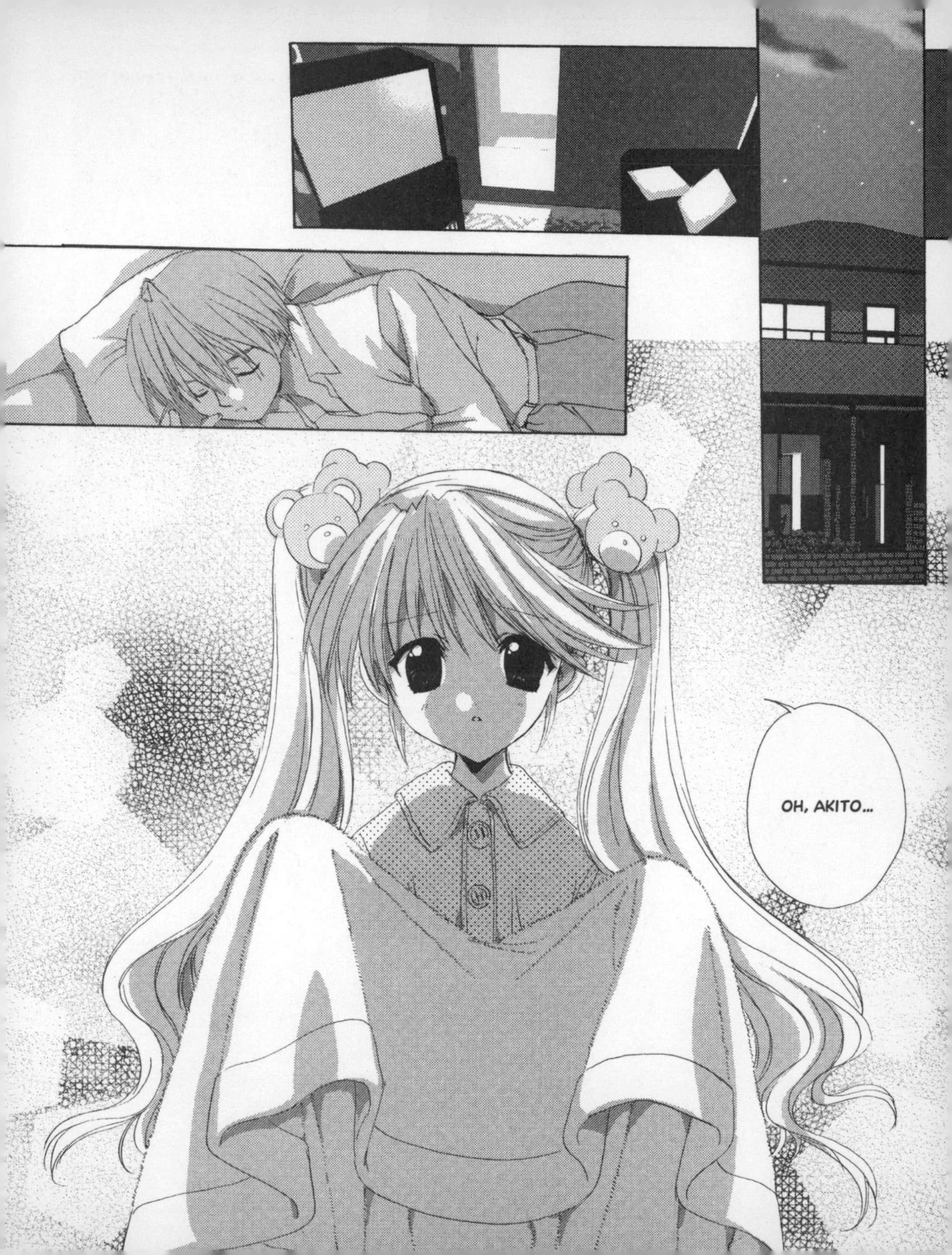
OH, AKITO...

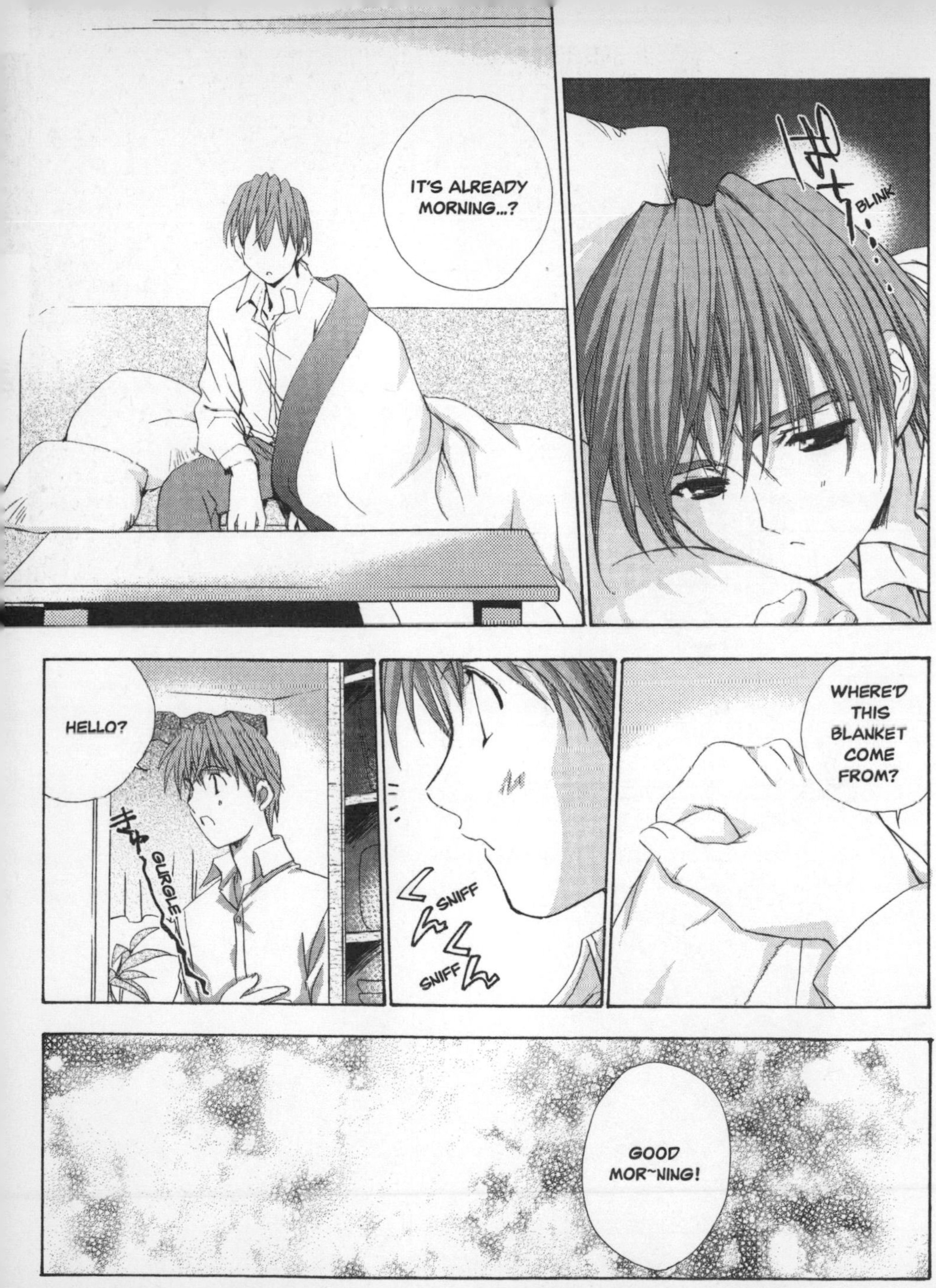
BLINK
IT'S ALREADY MORNING...?
WHERE'D THIS BLANKET COME FROM?
SNIFF
SNIFF
HELLO?
GURGLE
GOOD MOR~NING!

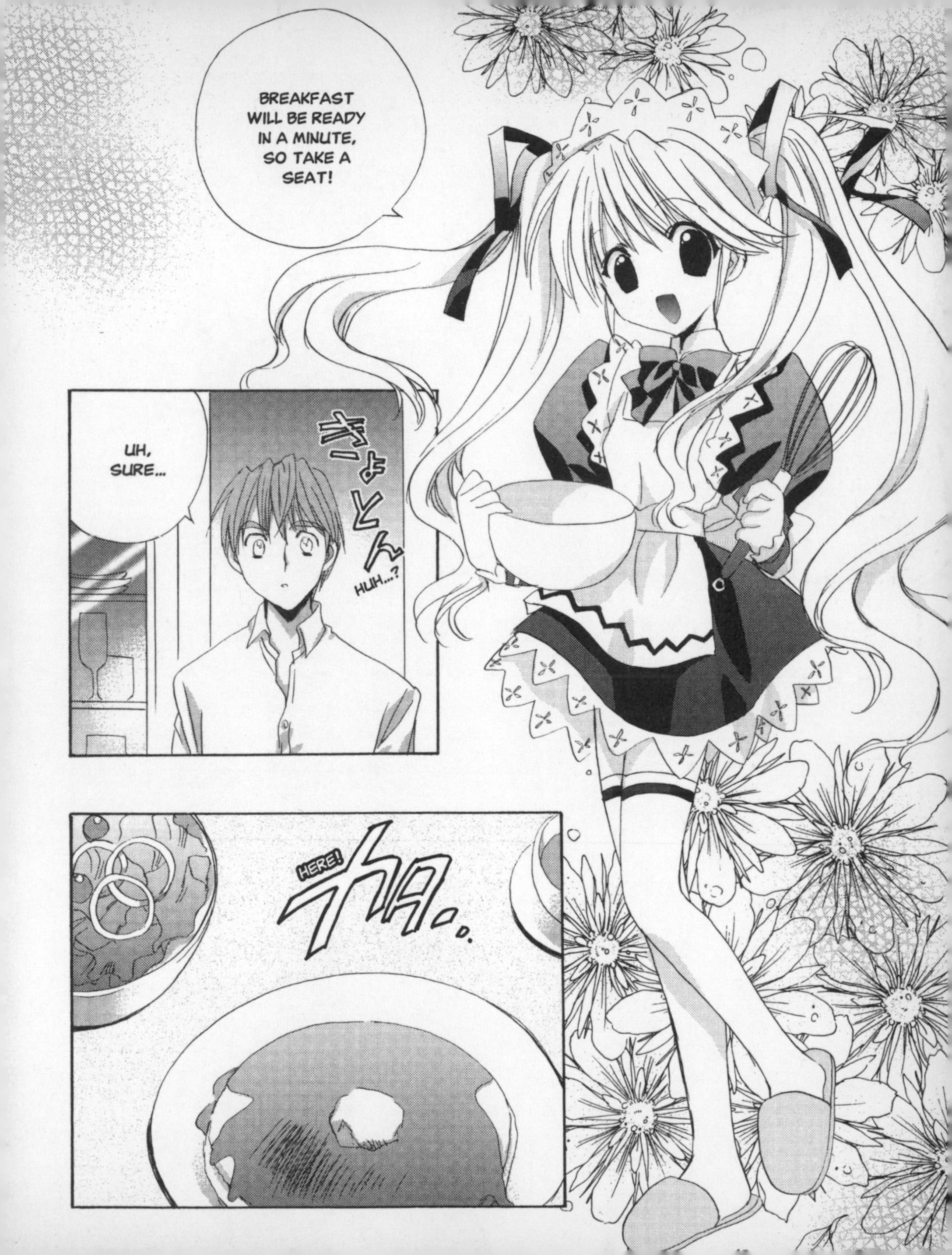
BREAKFAST WILL BE READY IN A MINUTE, SO TAKE A SEAT!
UH, SURE...
きょとん
HUH...?
HERE!

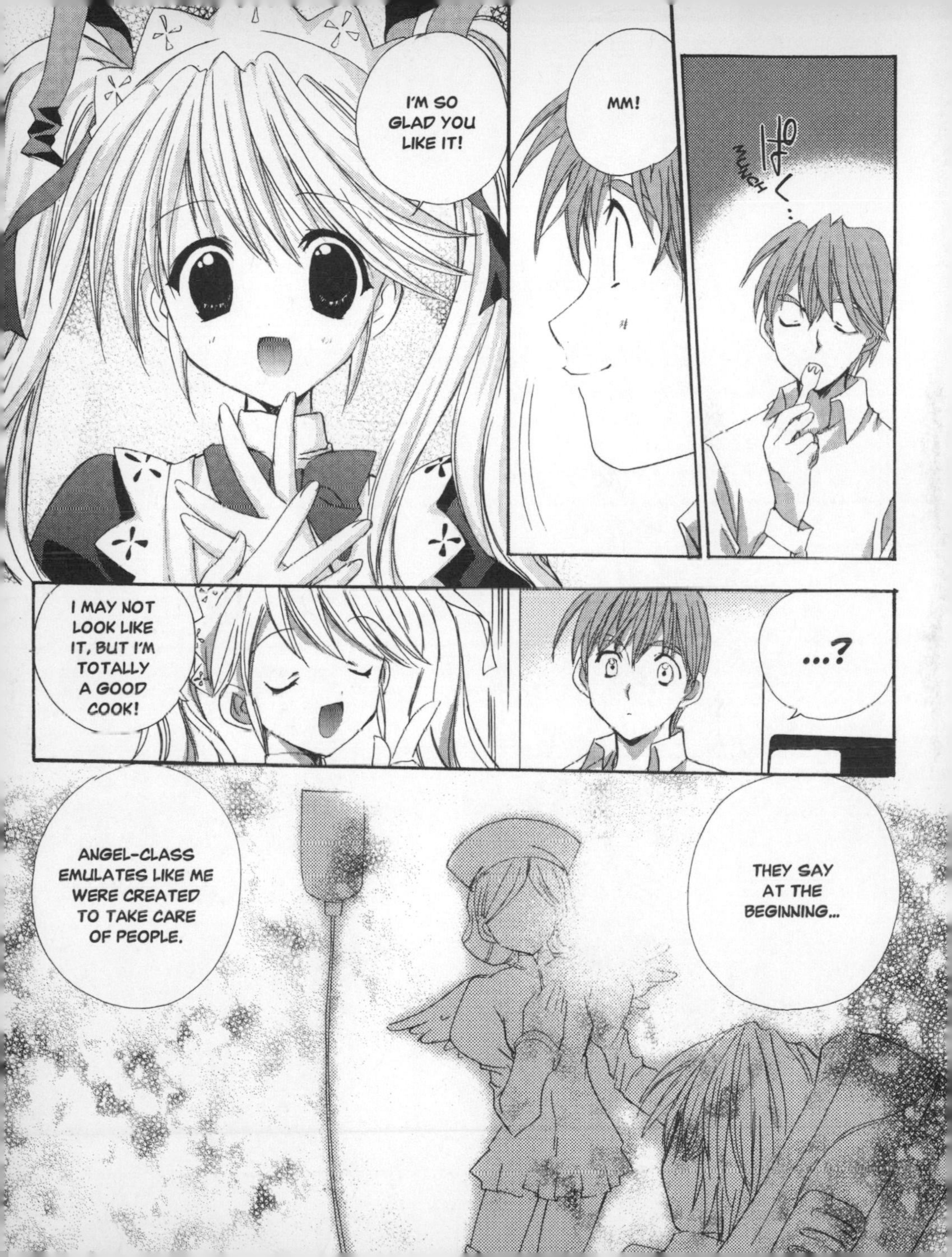
MUNCH
MM!
I'M SO GLAD YOU LIKE IT!
...?
I MAY NOT LOOK LIKE IT, BUT I'M TOTALLY A GOOD COOK!
THEY SAY AT THE BEGINNING...
ANGEL-CLASS EMULATES LIKE ME WERE CREATED TO TAKE CARE OF PEOPLE.

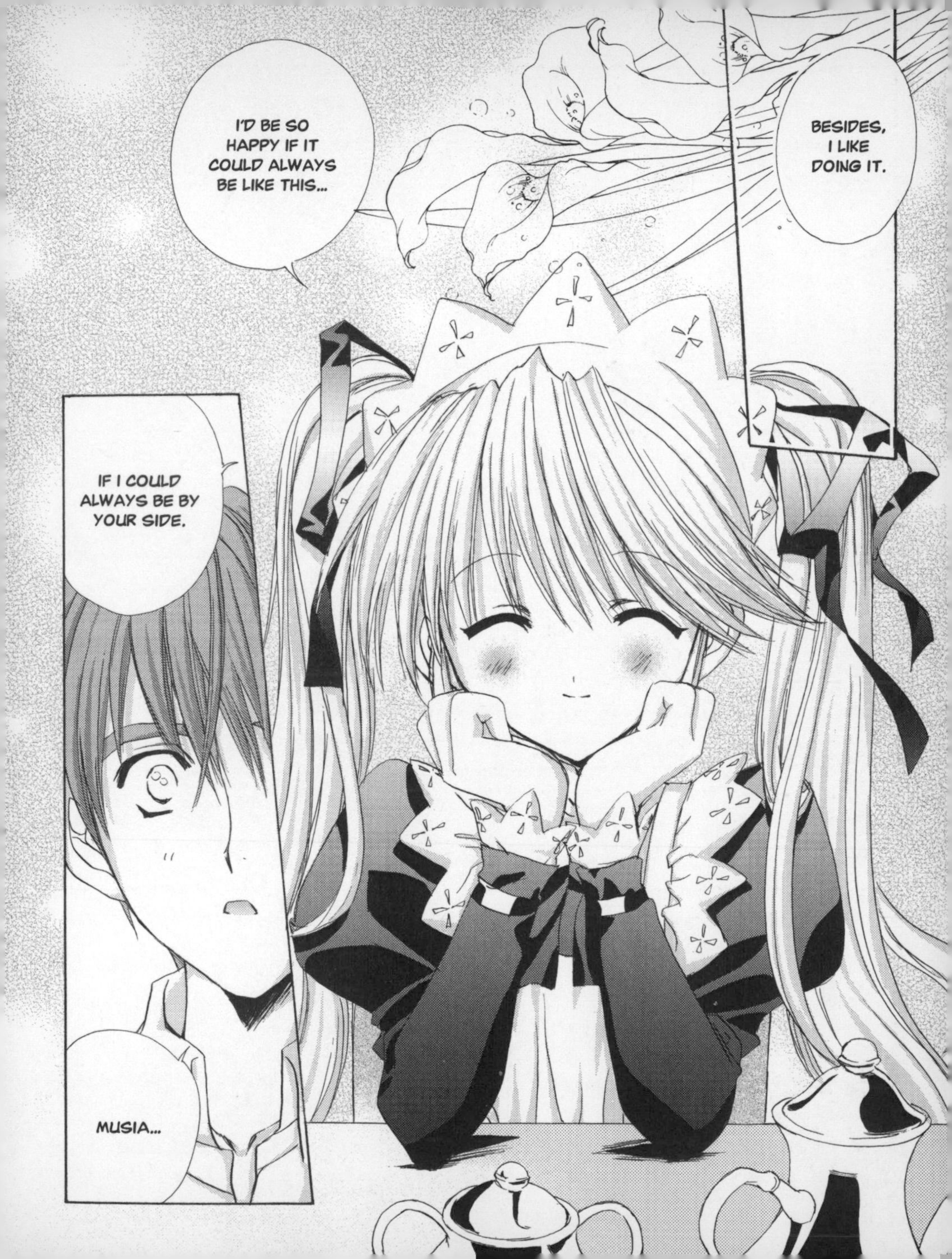
BESIDES, I LIKE DOING IT.
I'D BE SO HAPPY IF IT COULD ALWAYS BE LIKE THIS...
IF I COULD ALWAYS BE BY YOUR SIDE.
MUSIA...

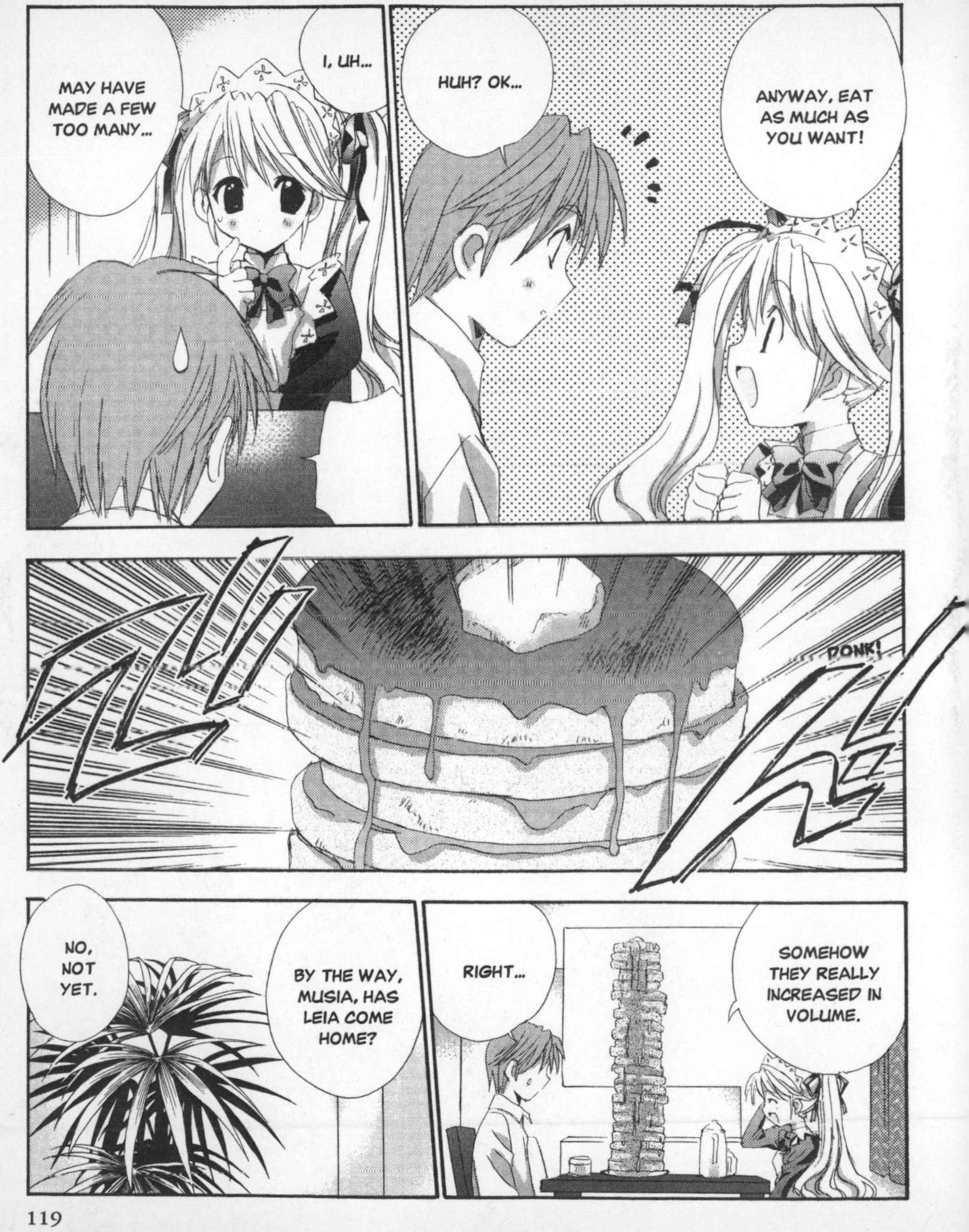
I, UH...
MAY HAVE MADE A FEW TOO MANY...
ANYWAY, EAT AS MUCH AS YOU WANT!
HUH? OK...
DONK!
SOMEHOW THEY REALLY INCREASED IN VOLUME.
RIGHT...
BY THE WAY, MUSIA, HAS LEIA COME HOME?
NO, NOT YET.

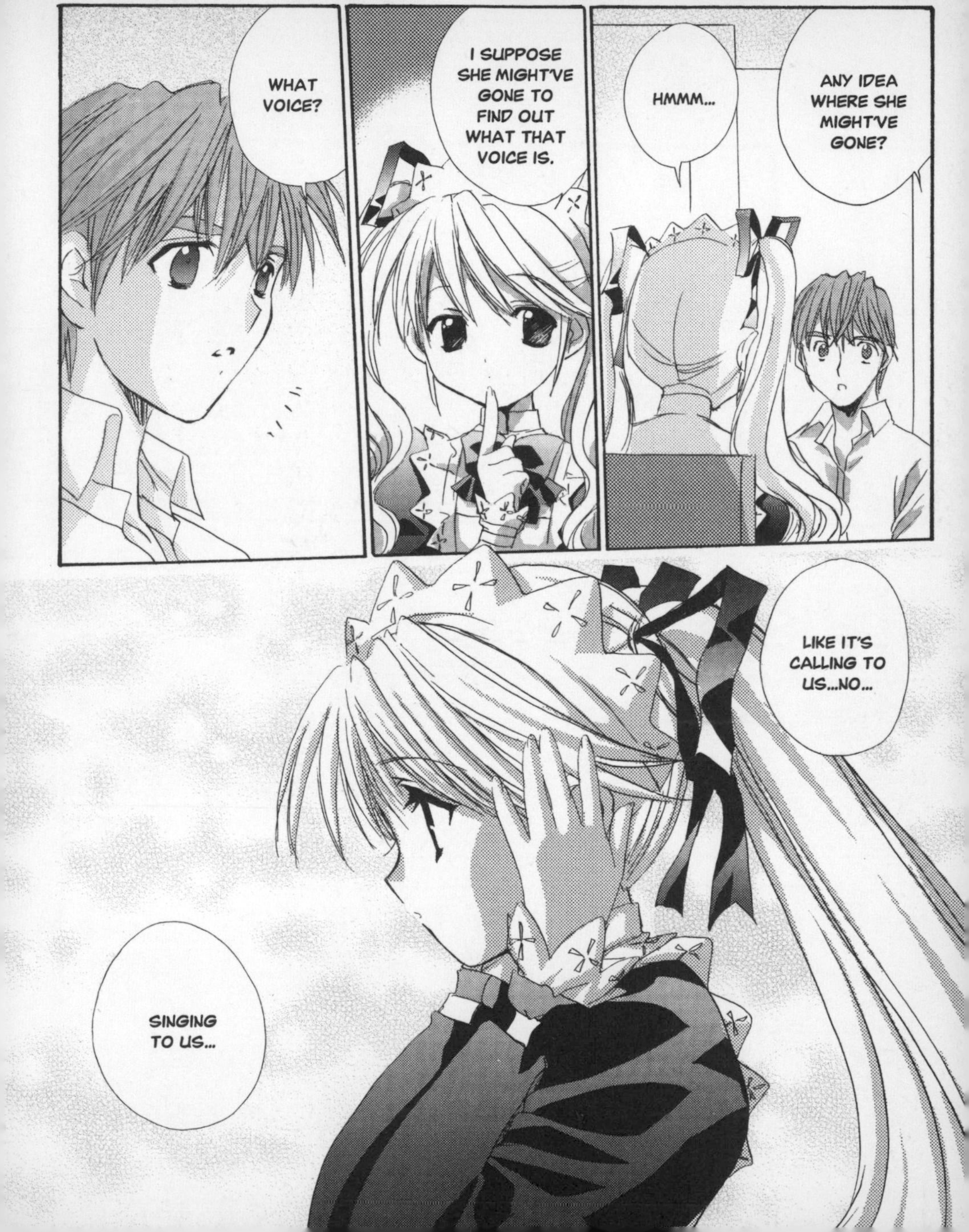
ANY IDEA WHERE SHE MIGHT'VE GONE?
HMMM...
I SUPPOSE SHE MIGHT'VE GONE TO FIND OUT WHAT THAT VOICE IS.
WHAT VOICE?
LIKE IT'S CALLING TO US...NO...
SINGING TO US...

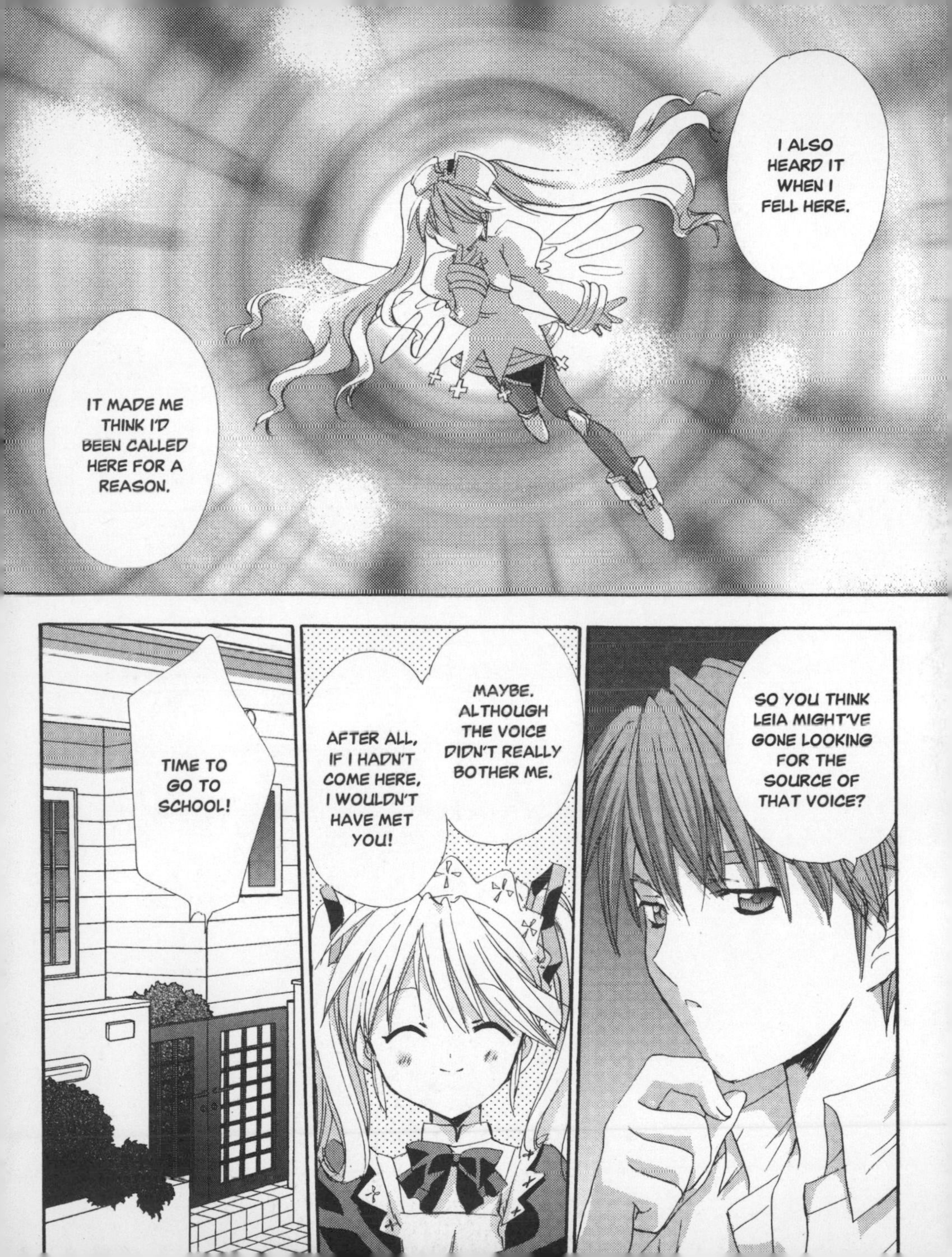
I ALSO HEARD IT WHEN I FELL HERE.
IT MADE ME THINK I'D BEEN CALLED HERE FOR A REASON.
SO YOU THINK LEIA MIGHT'VE GONE LOOKING FOR THE SOURCE OF THAT VOICE?
MAYBE. ALTHOUGH THE VOICE DIDN'T REALLY BOTHER ME.
AFTER ALL, IF I HADN'T COME HERE, I WOULDN'T HAVE MET YOU!
TIME TO GO TO SCHOOL!

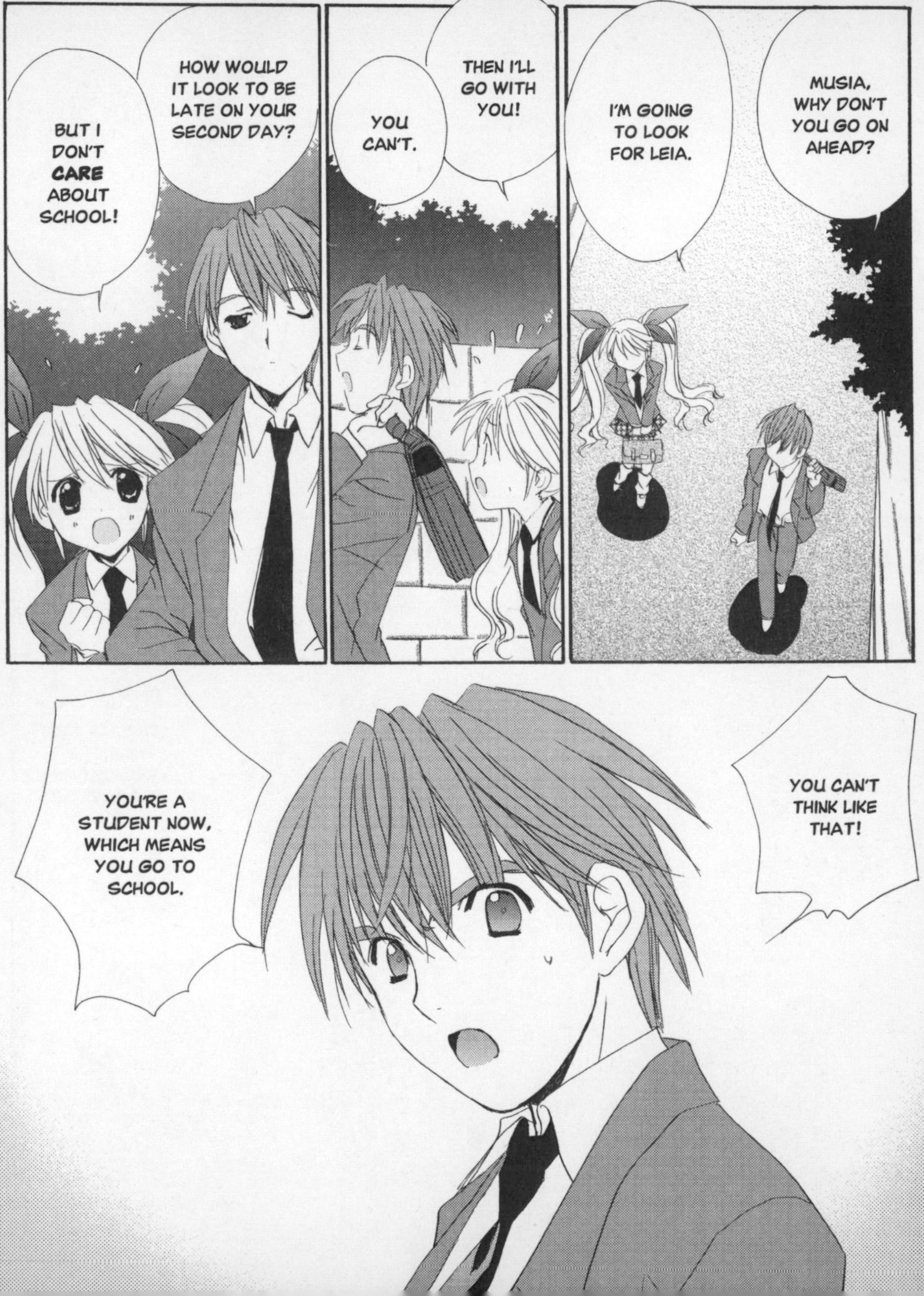
MUSIA, WHY DON'T YOU GO ON AHEAD?
I'M GOING TO LOOK FOR LEIA.
THEN I'LL GO WITH YOU!
YOU CAN'T.
HOW WOULD IT LOOK TO BE LATE ON YOUR SECOND DAY?
BUT I DON'T CARE ABOUT SCHOOL!
YOU CAN'T THINK LIKE THAT!
YOU'RE A STUDENT NOW, WHICH MEANS YOU GO TO SCHOOL.

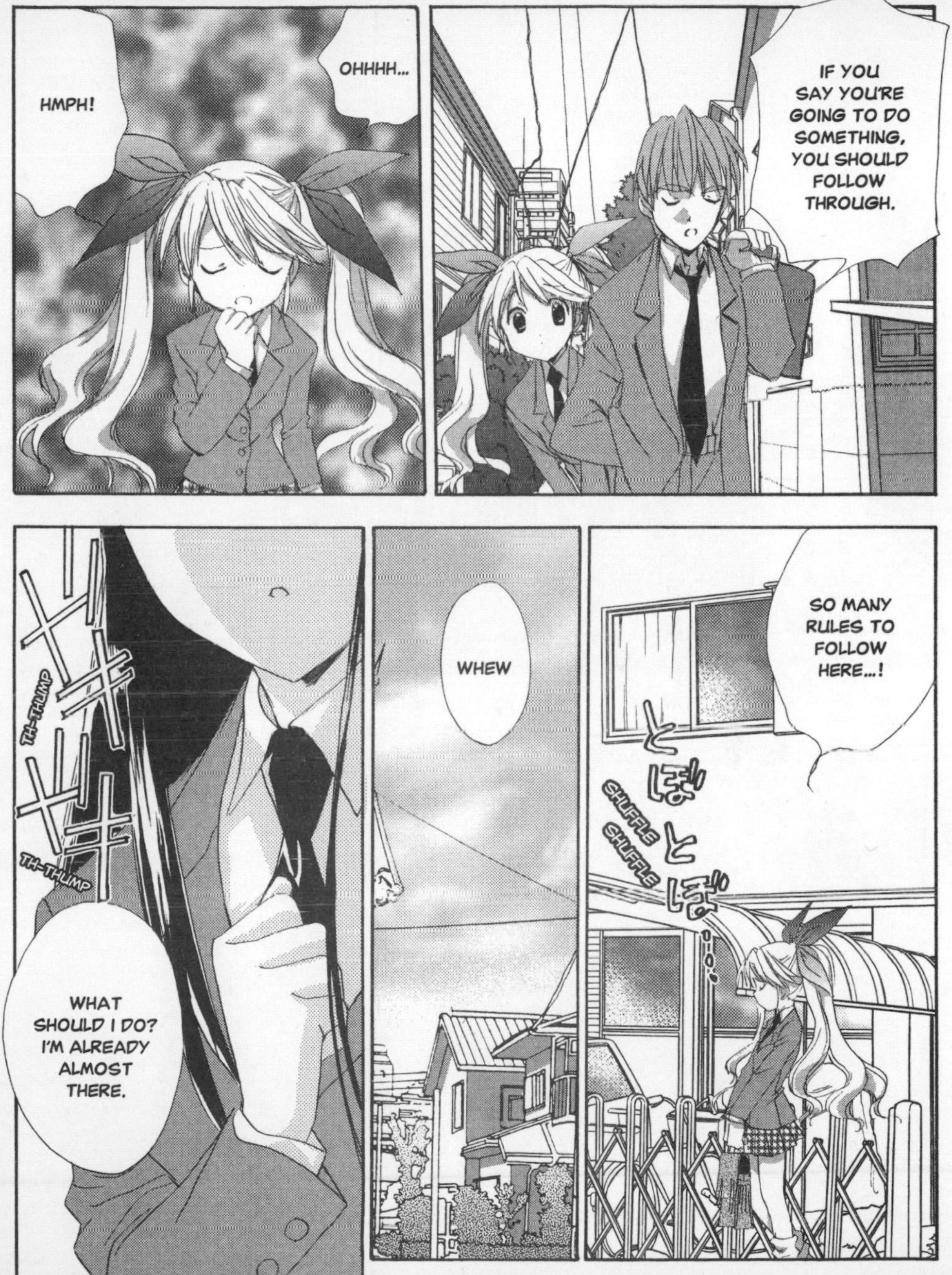
IF YOU SAY YOU'RE GOING TO DO SOMETHING, YOU SHOULD FOLLOW THROUGH.
OHHHH...
HMPH!
SO MANY RULES TO FOLLOW HERE...!
とぼとぼ
SHUFFLE SHUFFLE
WHEW
TH-THUMP
TH-THUMP
WHAT SHOULD I DO? I'M ALREADY ALMOST THERE.

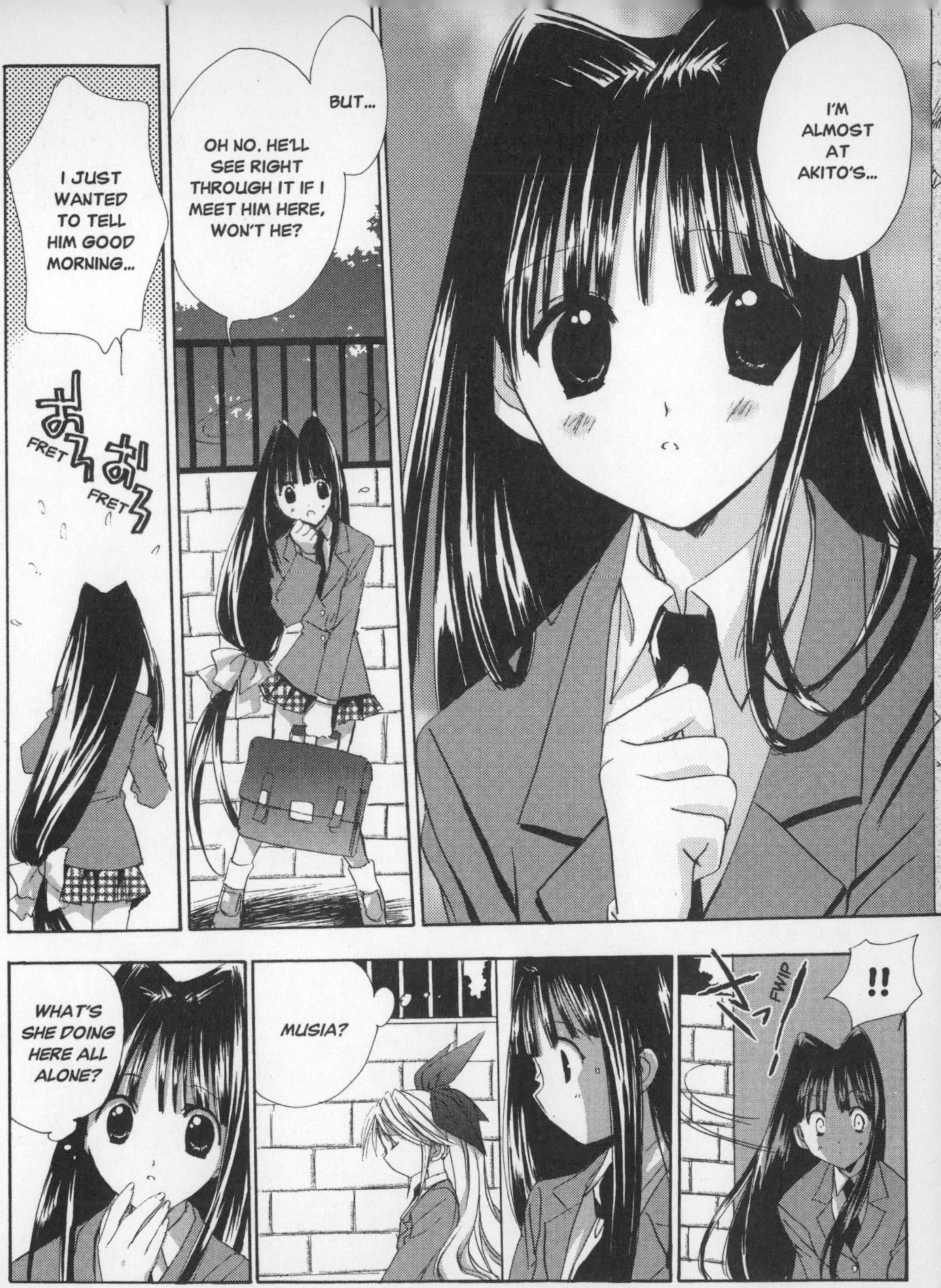
I'M ALMOST AT AKITO'S...
BUT...
OH NO. HE'LL SEE RIGHT THROUGH IT IF I MEET HIM HERE, WON'T HE?
I JUST WANTED TO TELL HIM GOOD MORNING...
FRET FRET
!!
FWIP
MUSIA?
WHAT'S SHE DOING HERE ALL ALONE?

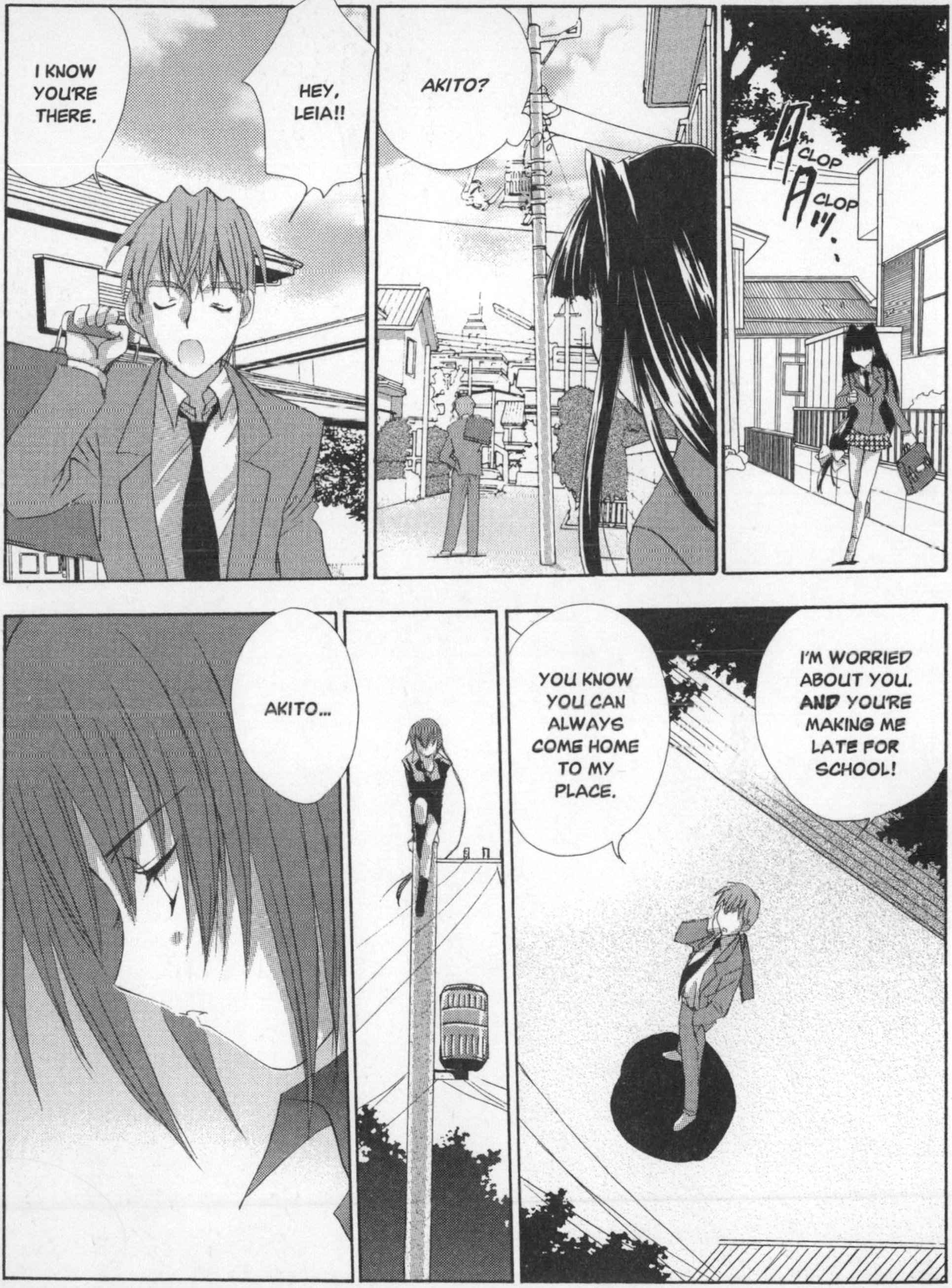
CLOP
CLOP
AKITO?
HEY, LEIA!!
I KNOW YOU'RE THERE.
I'M WORRIED ABOUT YOU. AND YOU'RE MAKING ME LATE FOR SCHOOL!
YOU KNOW YOU CAN ALWAYS COME HOME TO MY PLACE.
AKITO...

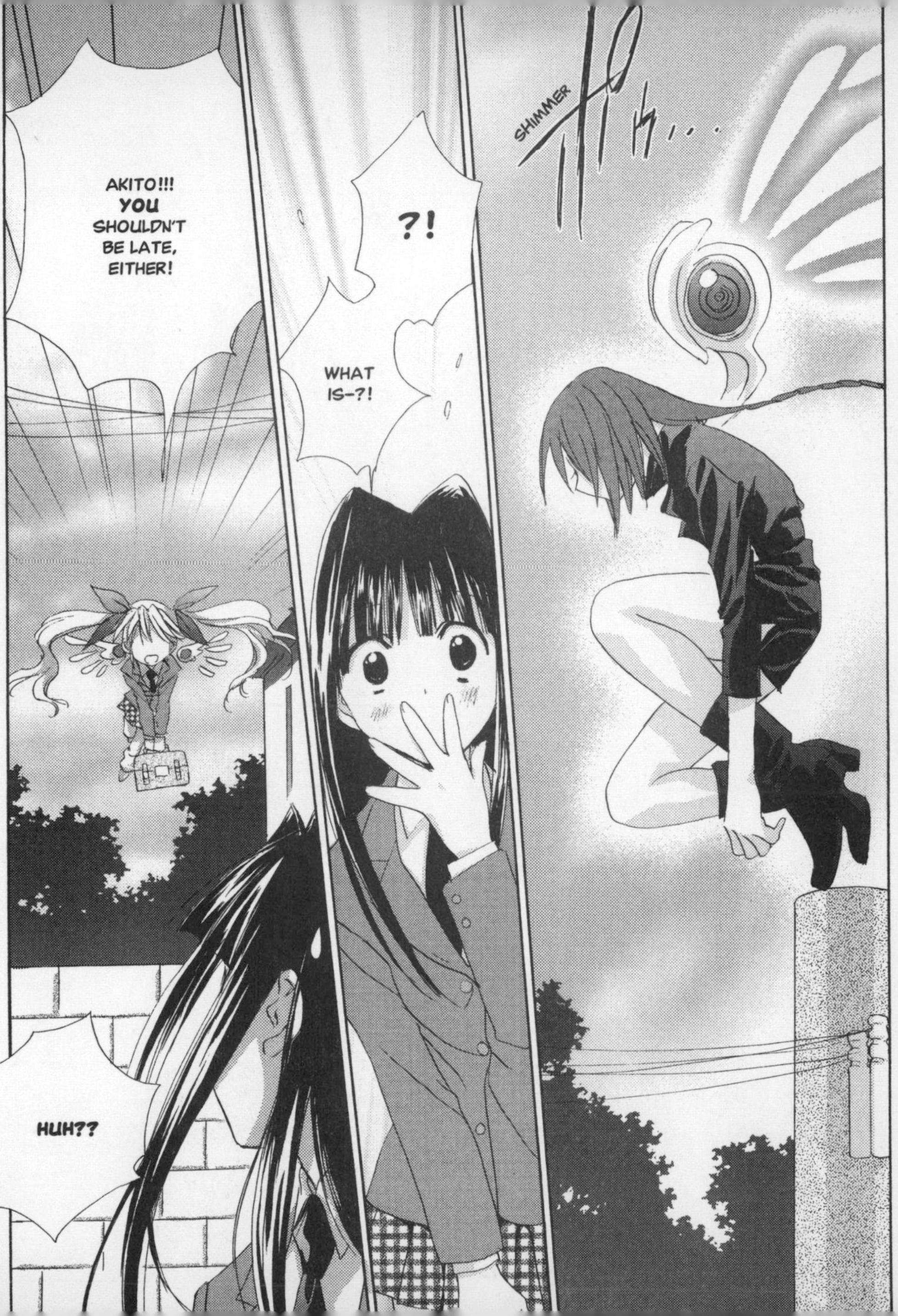
SHIMMER
?!
WHAT IS-?!
AKITO!!! YOU SHOULDN'T BE LATE, EITHER!
HUH??

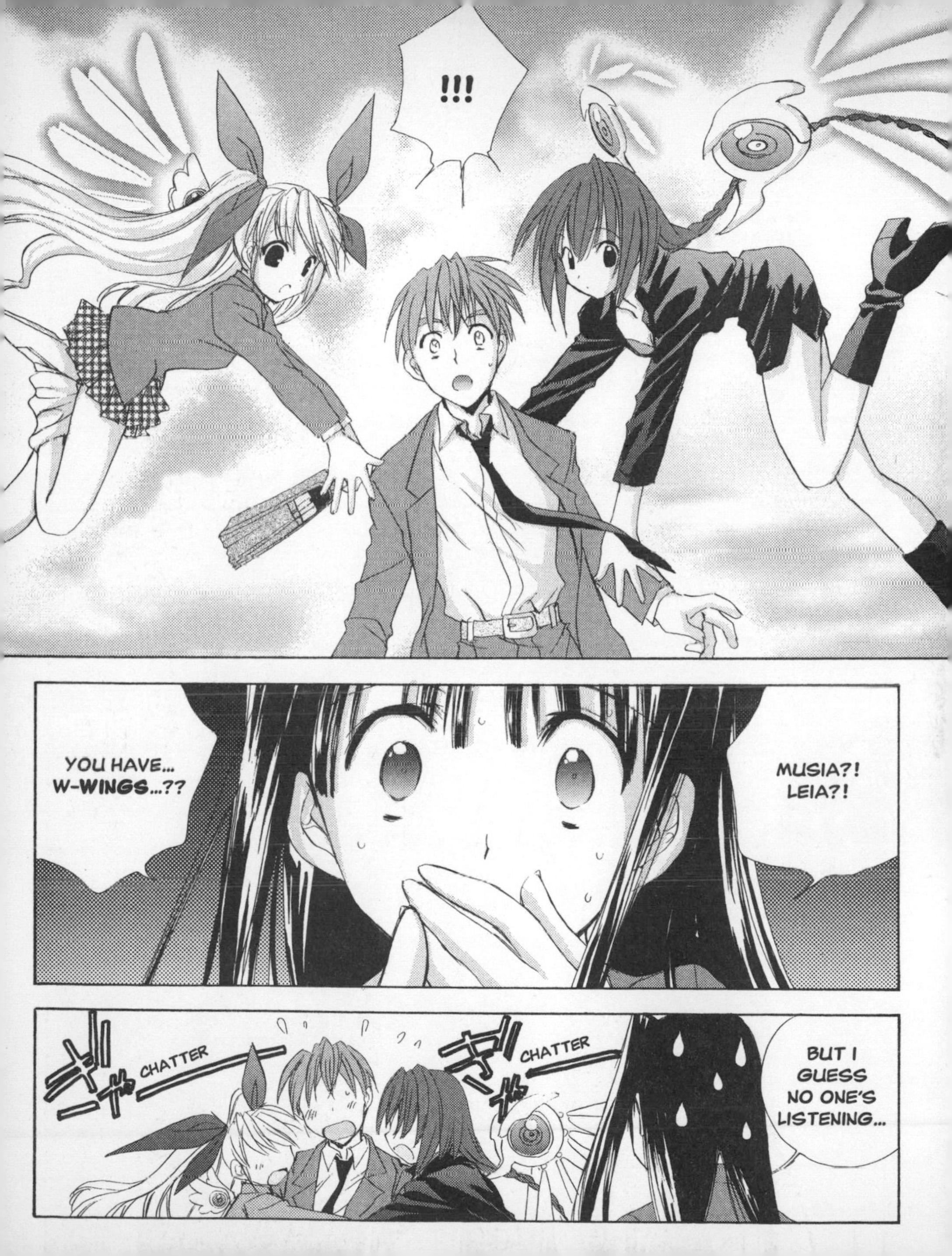
!!!
MUSIA?! LEIA?!
YOU HAVE... W-WINGS...??
BUT I GUESS NO ONE'S LISTENING...
CHATTER
CHATTER

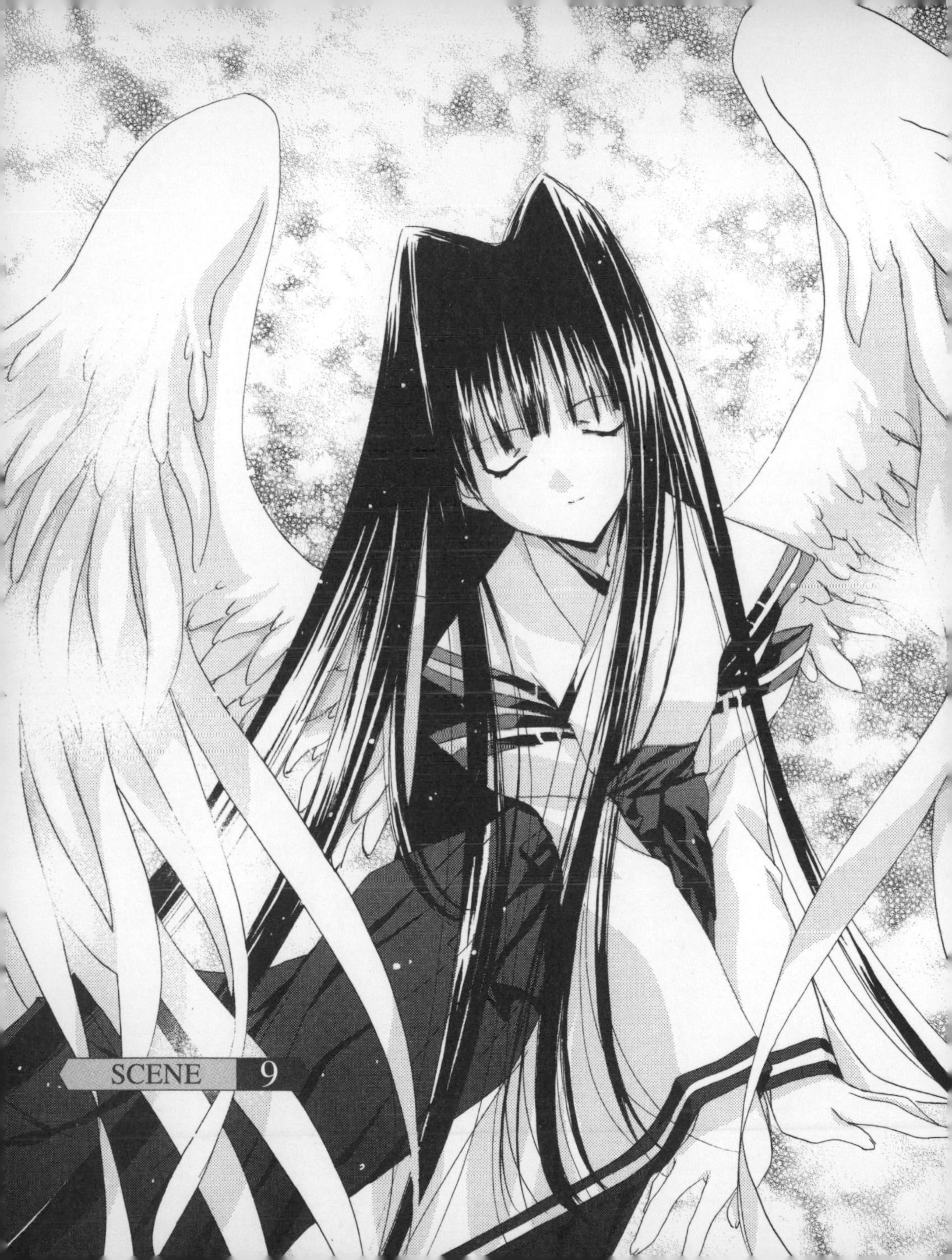
SCENE 9

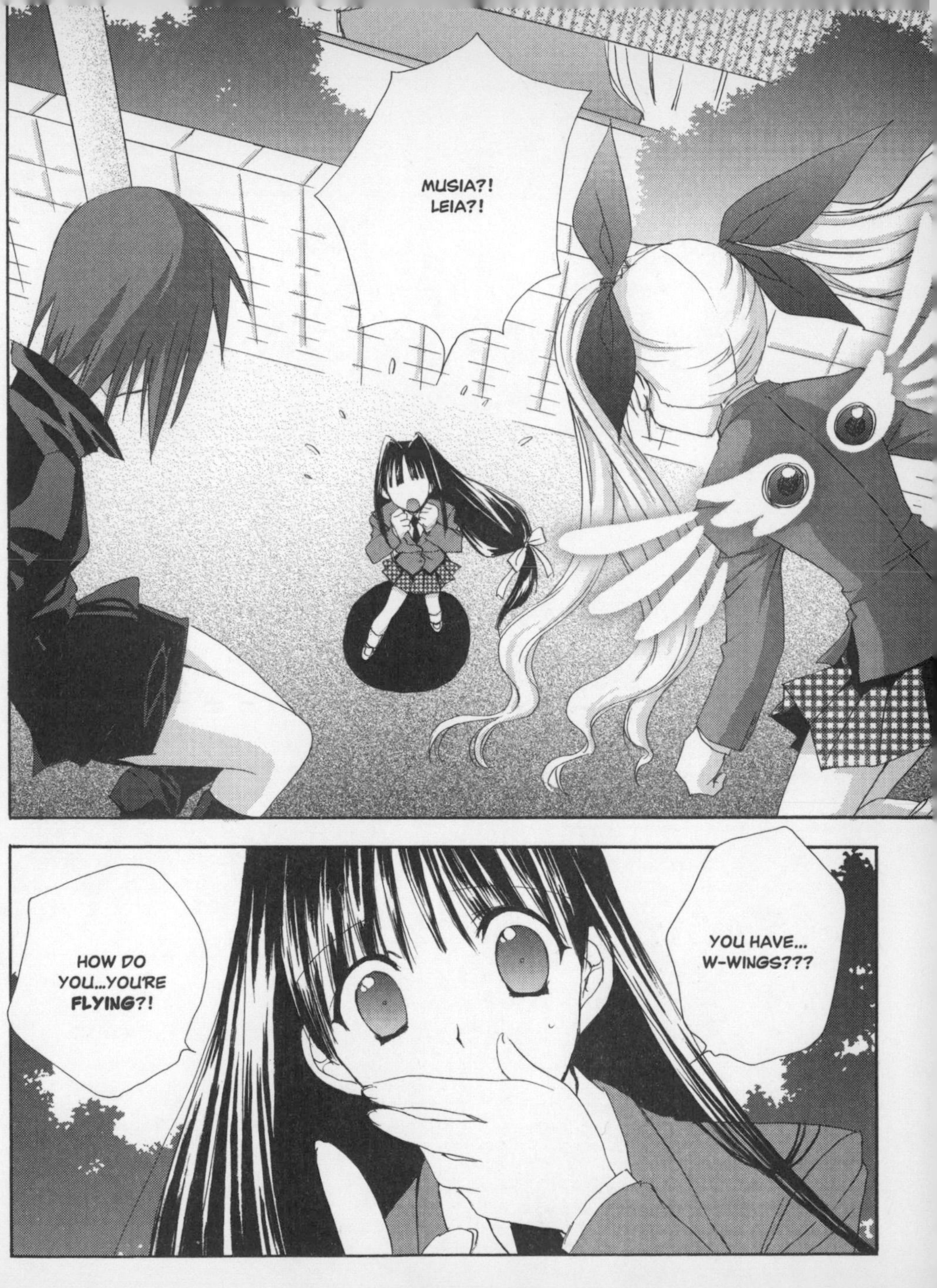
MUSIA?!
LEIA?!
YOU HAVE... W-WINGS???
HOW DO YOU...YOU'RE **FLYING**?!

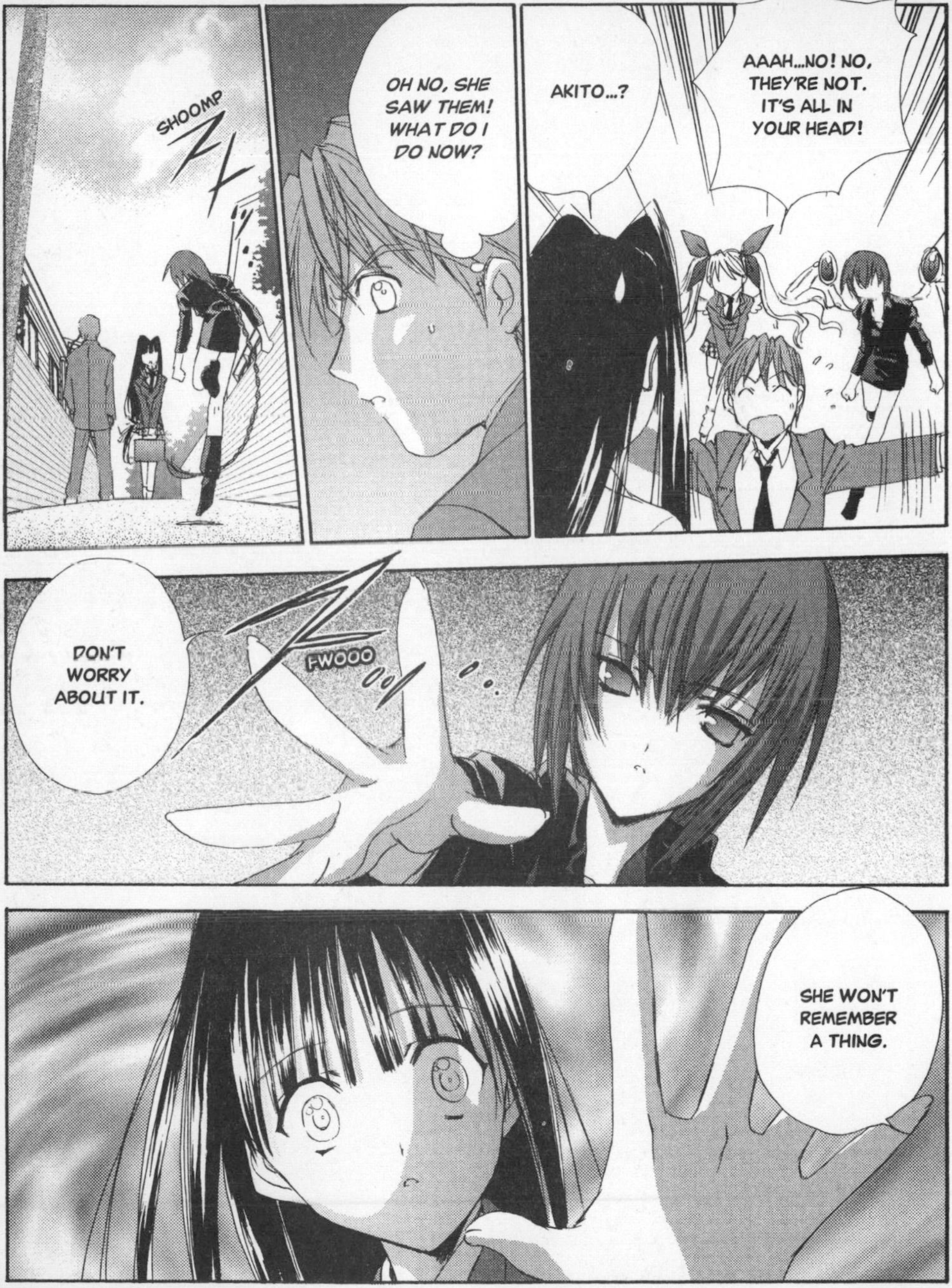
SHOOMP
OH NO, SHE SAW THEM! WHAT DO I DO NOW?
AKITO...?
AAAH...NO! NO, THEY'RE NOT. IT'S ALL IN YOUR HEAD!
DON'T WORRY ABOUT IT.
FWOOO
SHE WON'T REMEMBER A THING.

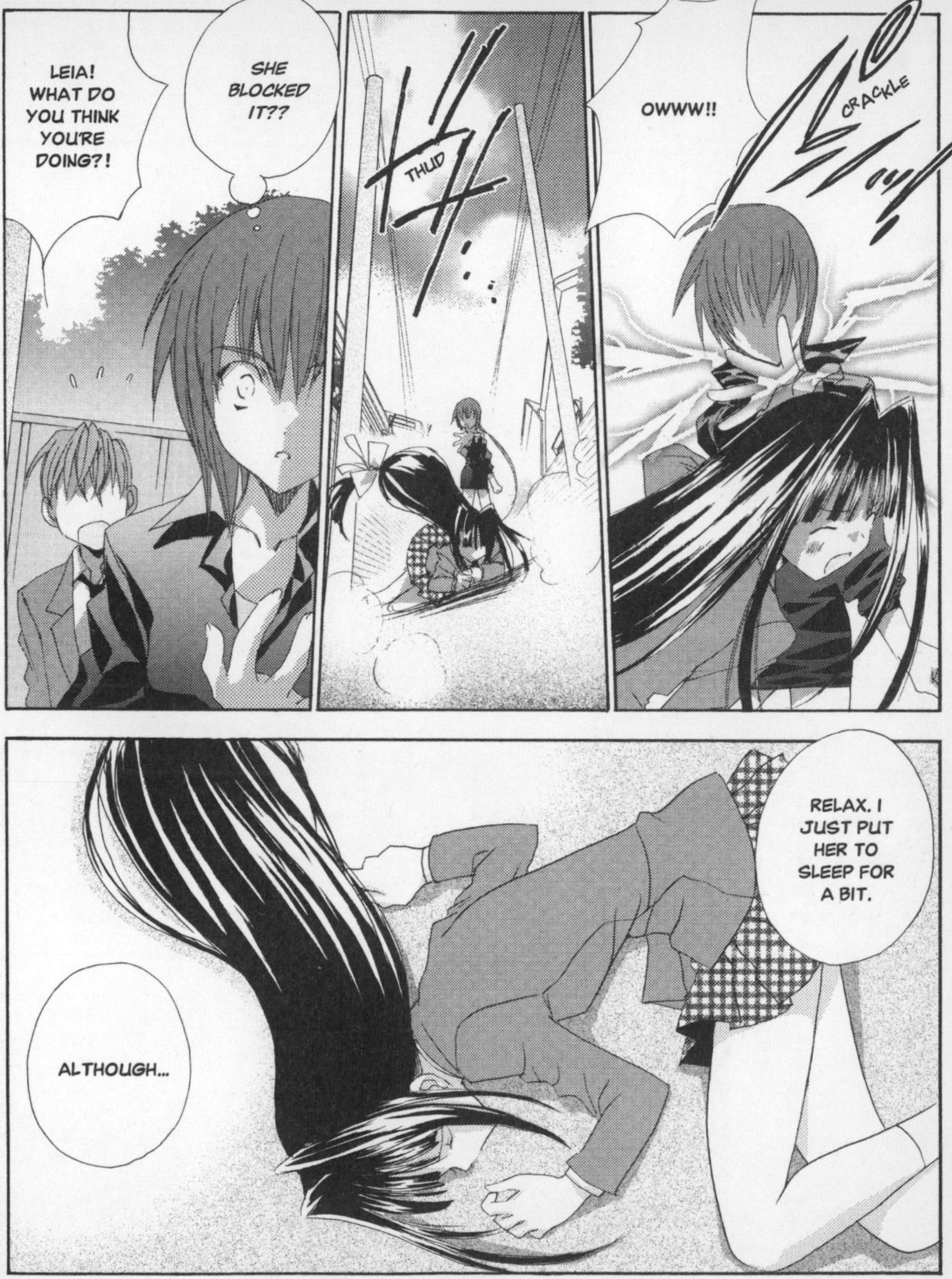
LEIA! WHAT DO YOU THINK YOU'RE DOING?!
SHE BLOCKED IT??
THUD
OWWW!!
CRACKLE
RELAX. I JUST PUT HER TO SLEEP FOR A BIT.
ALTHOUGH...

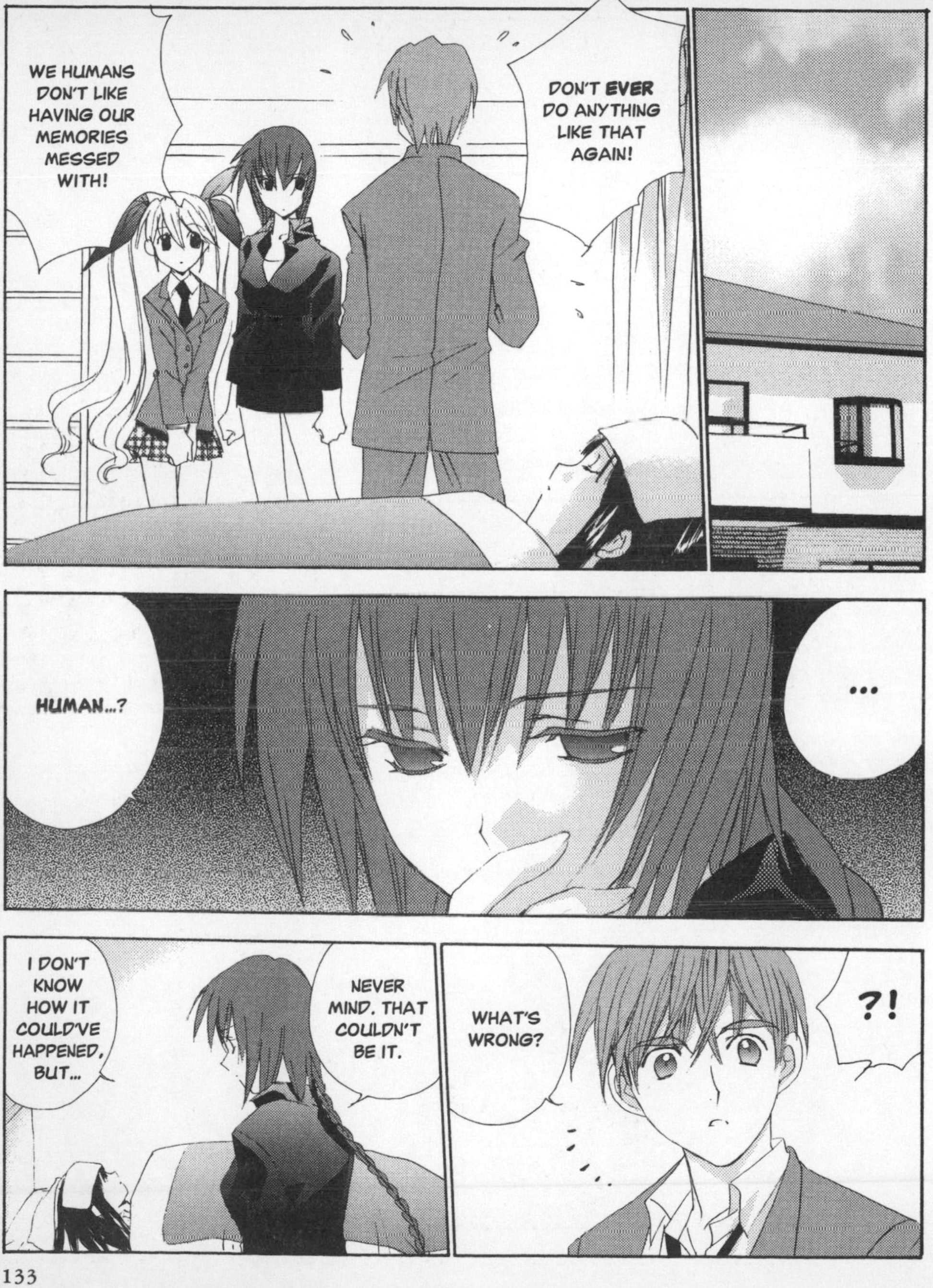
DON'T EVER DO ANYTHING LIKE THAT AGAIN!
WE HUMANS DON'T LIKE HAVING OUR MEMORIES MESSED WITH!
...
HUMAN...?
?!
WHAT'S WRONG?
NEVER MIND. THAT COULDN'T BE IT.
I DON'T KNOW HOW IT COULD'VE HAPPENED, BUT...

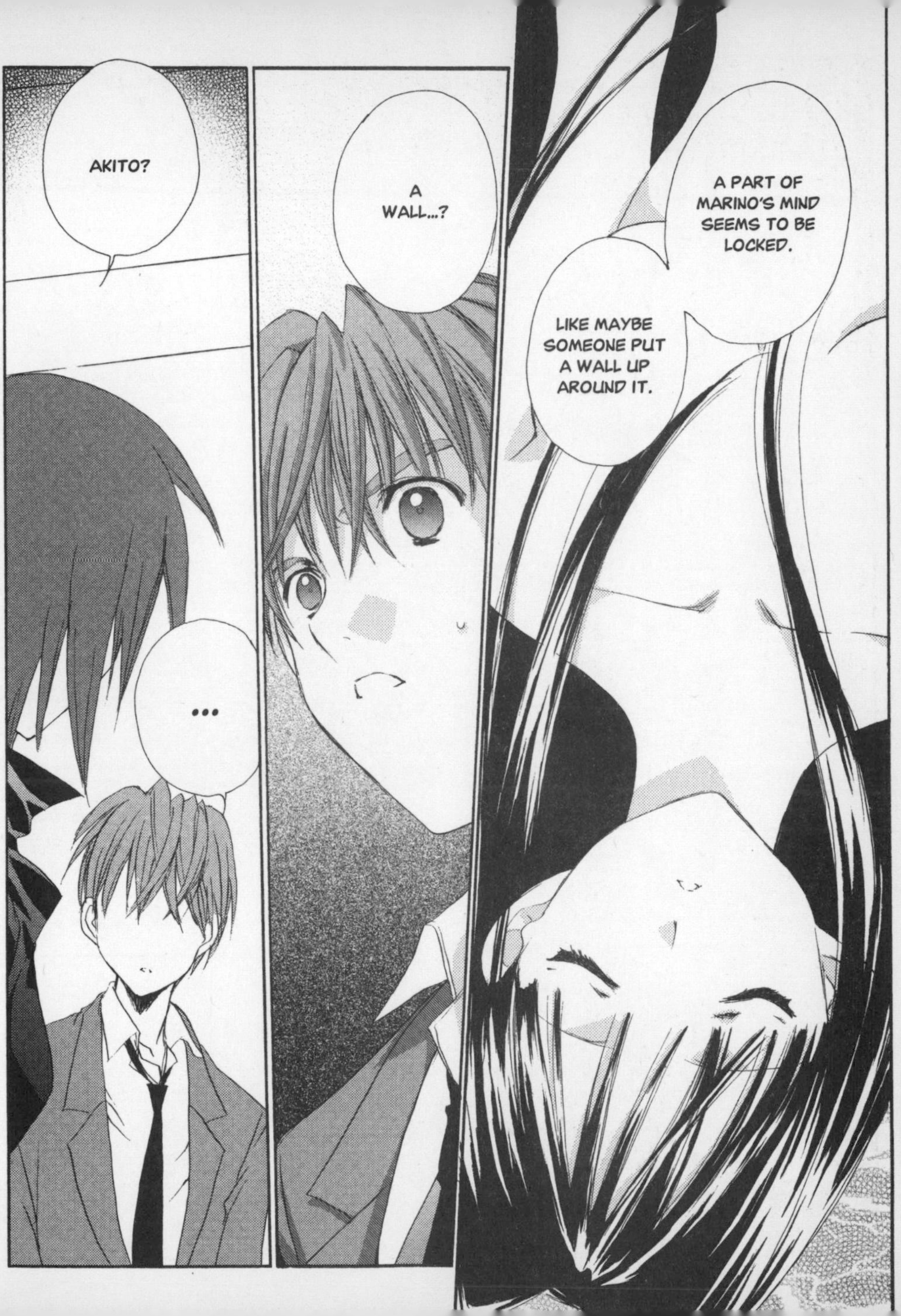
A PART OF MARINO'S MIND SEEMS TO BE LOCKED.
LIKE MAYBE SOMEONE PUT A WALL UP AROUND IT.
A WALL...?
AKITO?
...

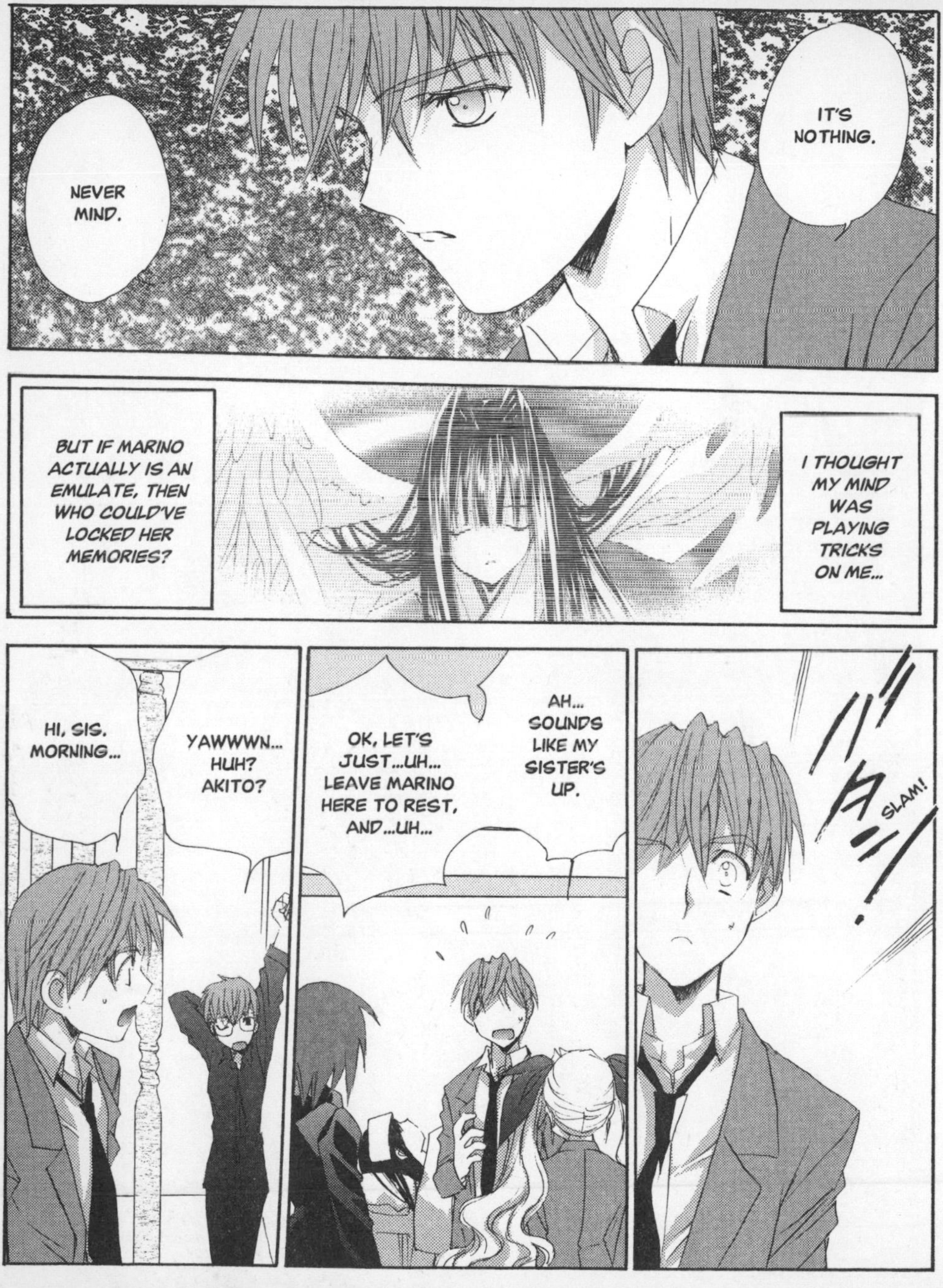
IT'S NOTHING.
NEVER MIND.
I THOUGHT MY MIND WAS PLAYING TRICKS ON ME...
BUT IF MARINO ACTUALLY IS AN EMULATE, THEN WHO COULD'VE LOCKED HER MEMORIES?
SLAM!
AH... SOUNDS LIKE MY SISTER'S UP.
OK, LET'S JUST...UH... LEAVE MARINO HERE TO REST, AND...UH...
YAWWWN... HUH? AKITO?
HI, SIS. MORNING...

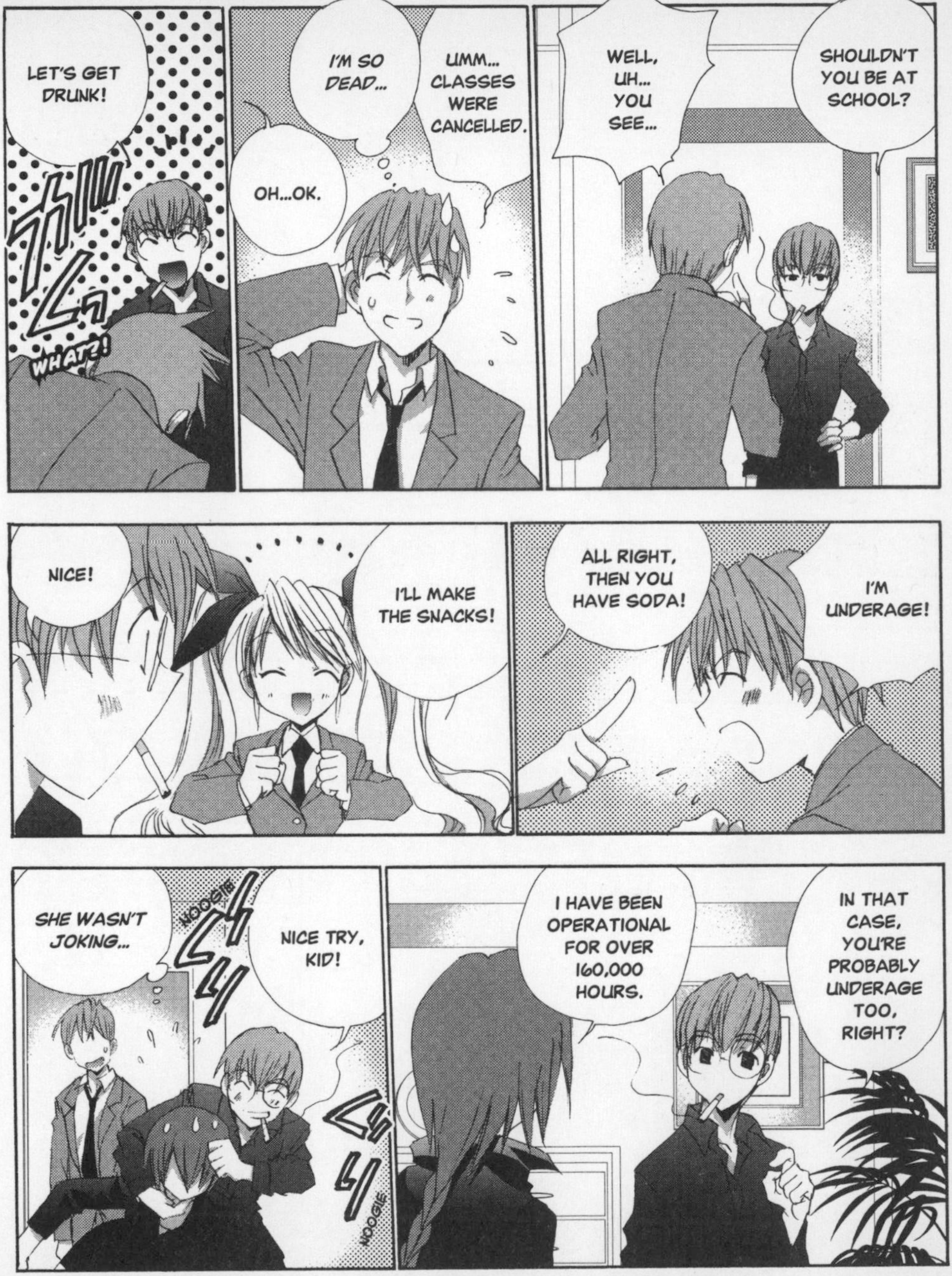
SHOULDN'T YOU BE AT SCHOOL?
WELL, UH... YOU SEE...
UMM... CLASSES WERE CANCELLED.
I'M SO DEAD...
OH...OK.
LET'S GET DRUNK!
WHAT?!
I'M UNDERAGE!
ALL RIGHT, THEN YOU HAVE SODA!
I'LL MAKE THE SNACKS!
NICE!
IN THAT CASE, YOU'RE PROBABLY UNDERAGE TOO, RIGHT?
I HAVE BEEN OPERATIONAL FOR OVER 160,000 HOURS.
NICE TRY, KID!
NOOGIE
NOOGIE
SHE WASN'T JOKING...

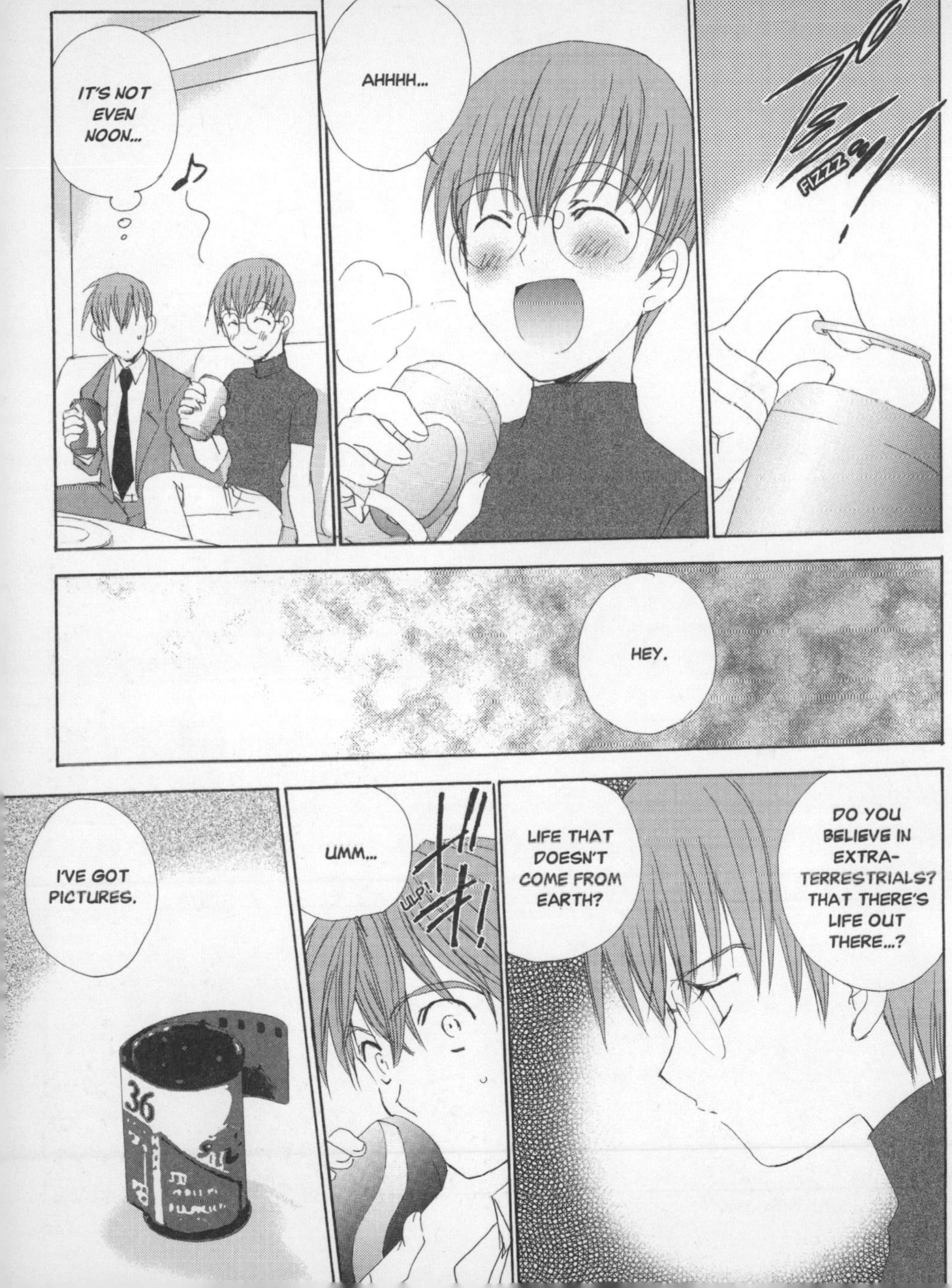
FIZZZ
AHHHH...
IT'S NOT EVEN NOON...
HEY.
DO YOU BELIEVE IN EXTRA-TERRESTRIALS? THAT THERE'S LIFE OUT THERE...?
LIFE THAT DOESN'T COME FROM EARTH?
ULP!
UMM...
I'VE GOT PICTURES.
36

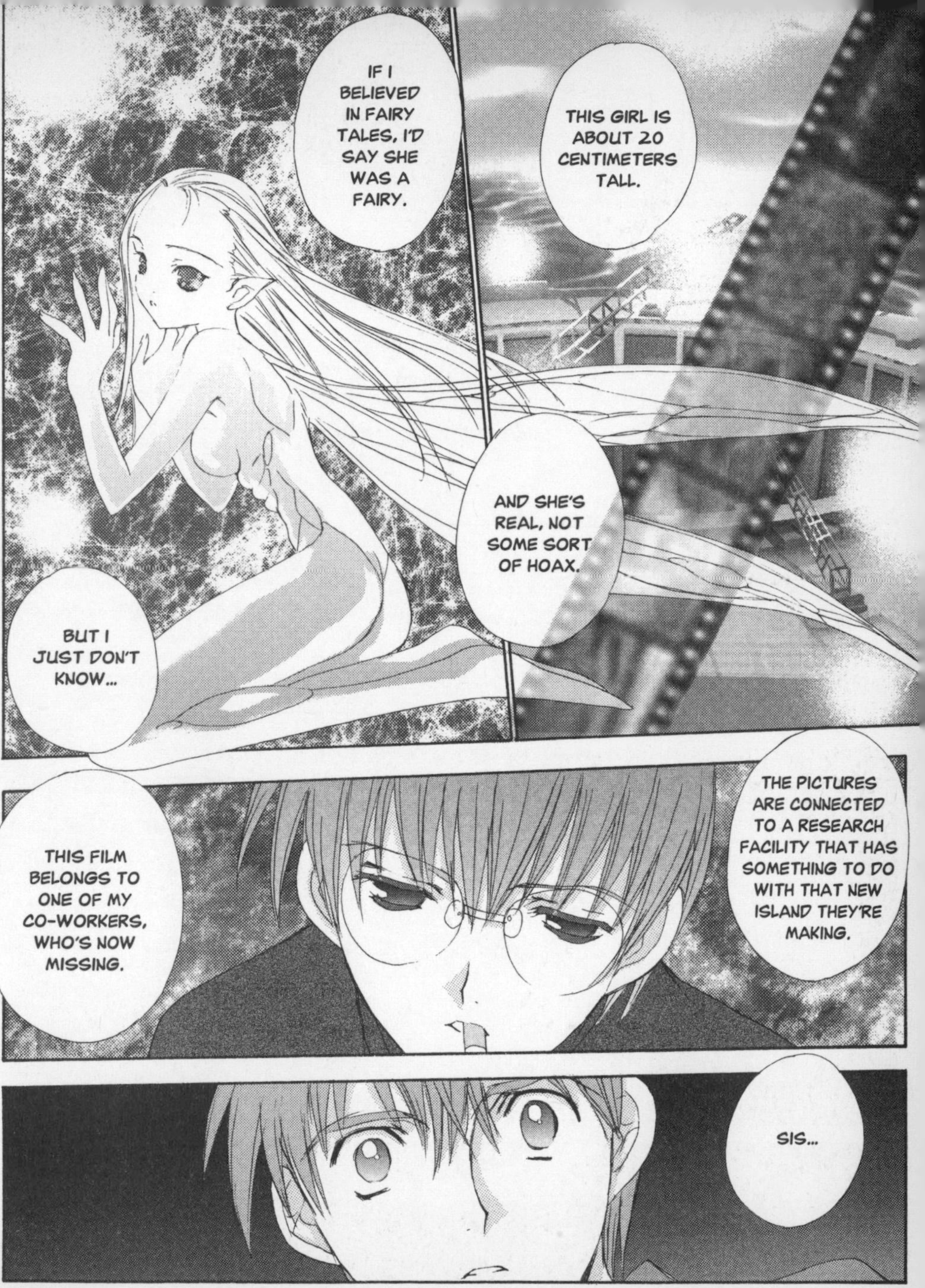
THIS GIRL IS ABOUT 20 CENTIMETERS TALL.
IF I BELIEVED IN FAIRY TALES, I'D SAY SHE WAS A FAIRY.
AND SHE'S REAL, NOT SOME SORT OF HOAX.
BUT I JUST DON'T KNOW...
THE PICTURES ARE CONNECTED TO A RESEARCH FACILITY THAT HAS SOMETHING TO DO WITH THAT NEW ISLAND THEY'RE MAKING.
THIS FILM BELONGS TO ONE OF MY CO-WORKERS, WHO'S NOW MISSING.
SIS...

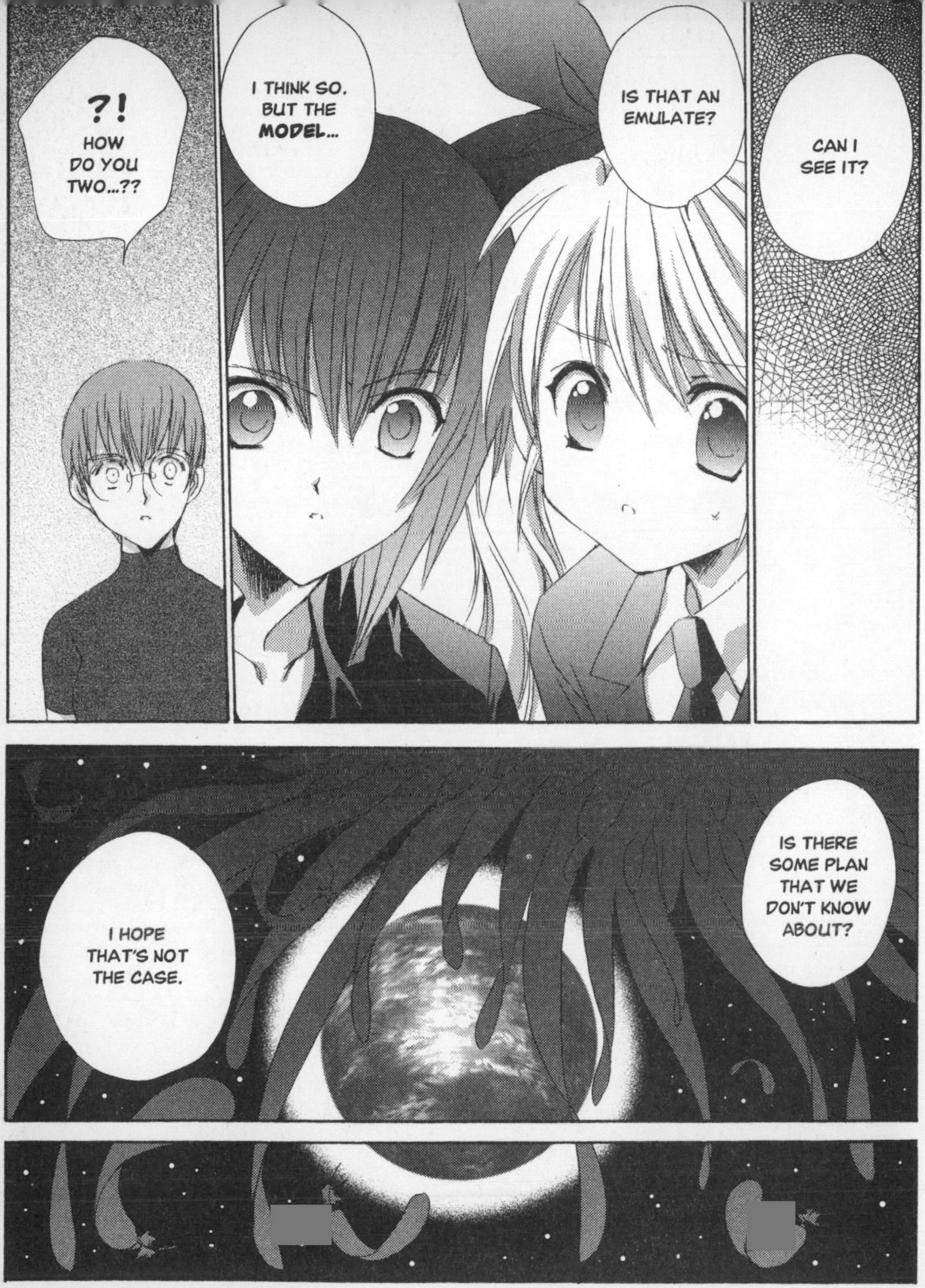
CAN I SEE IT?
IS THAT AN EMULATE?
I THINK SO. BUT THE MODEL...
?! HOW DO YOU TWO...??
IS THERE SOME PLAN THAT WE DON'T KNOW ABOUT?
I HOPE THAT'S NOT THE CASE.

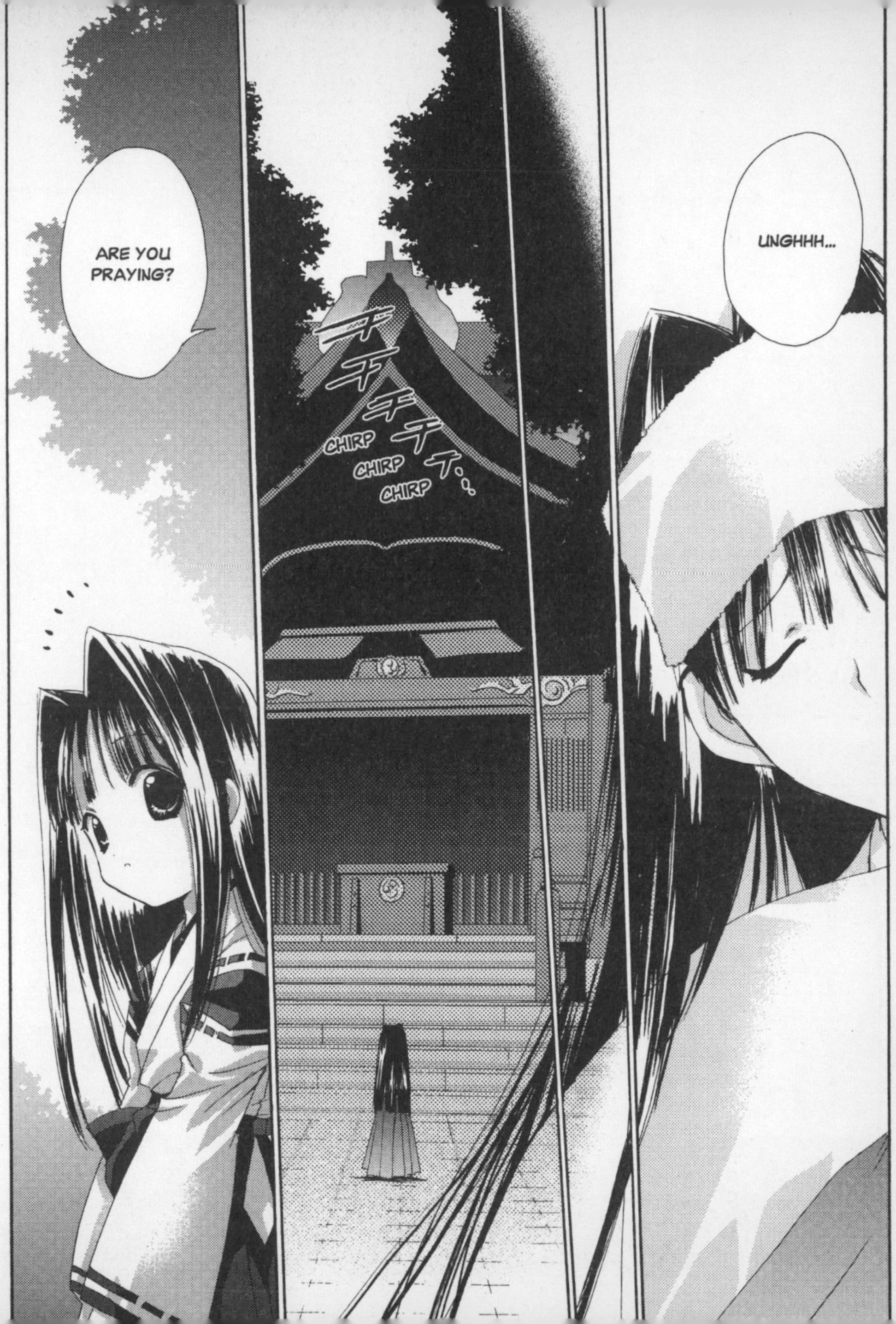
UNGHHH...
チチチ...
CHIRP
CHIRP
CHIRP
ARE YOU PRAYING?

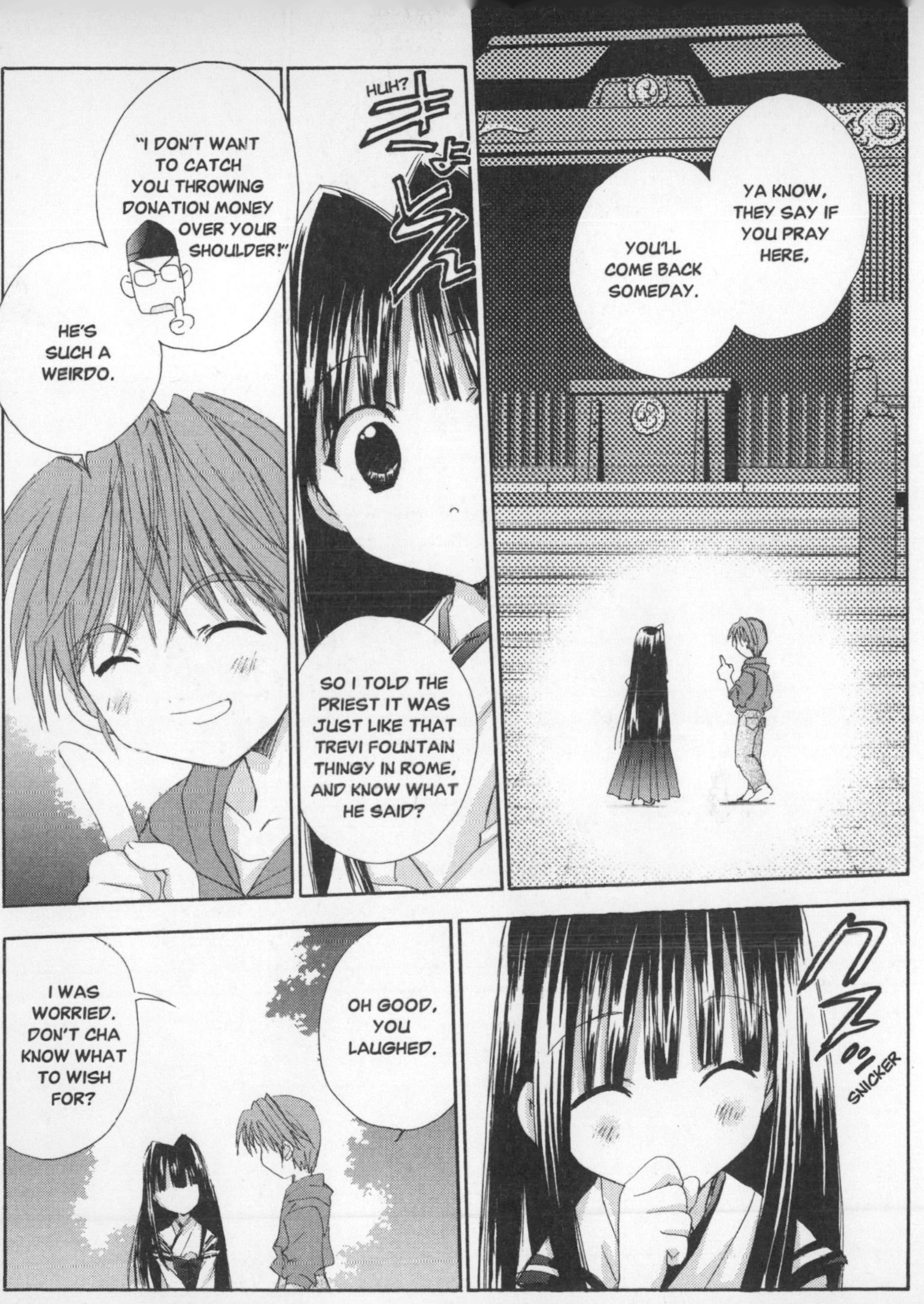
YA KNOW, THEY SAY IF YOU PRAY HERE,
YOU'LL COME BACK SOMEDAY.
HUH?
SO I TOLD THE PRIEST IT WAS JUST LIKE THAT TREVI FOUNTAIN THINGY IN ROME, AND KNOW WHAT HE SAID?
"I DON'T WANT TO CATCH YOU THROWING DONATION MONEY OVER YOUR SHOULDER!"
HE'S SUCH A WEIRDO.
SNICKER
OH GOOD, YOU LAUGHED.
I WAS WORRIED. DON'T CHA KNOW WHAT TO WISH FOR?

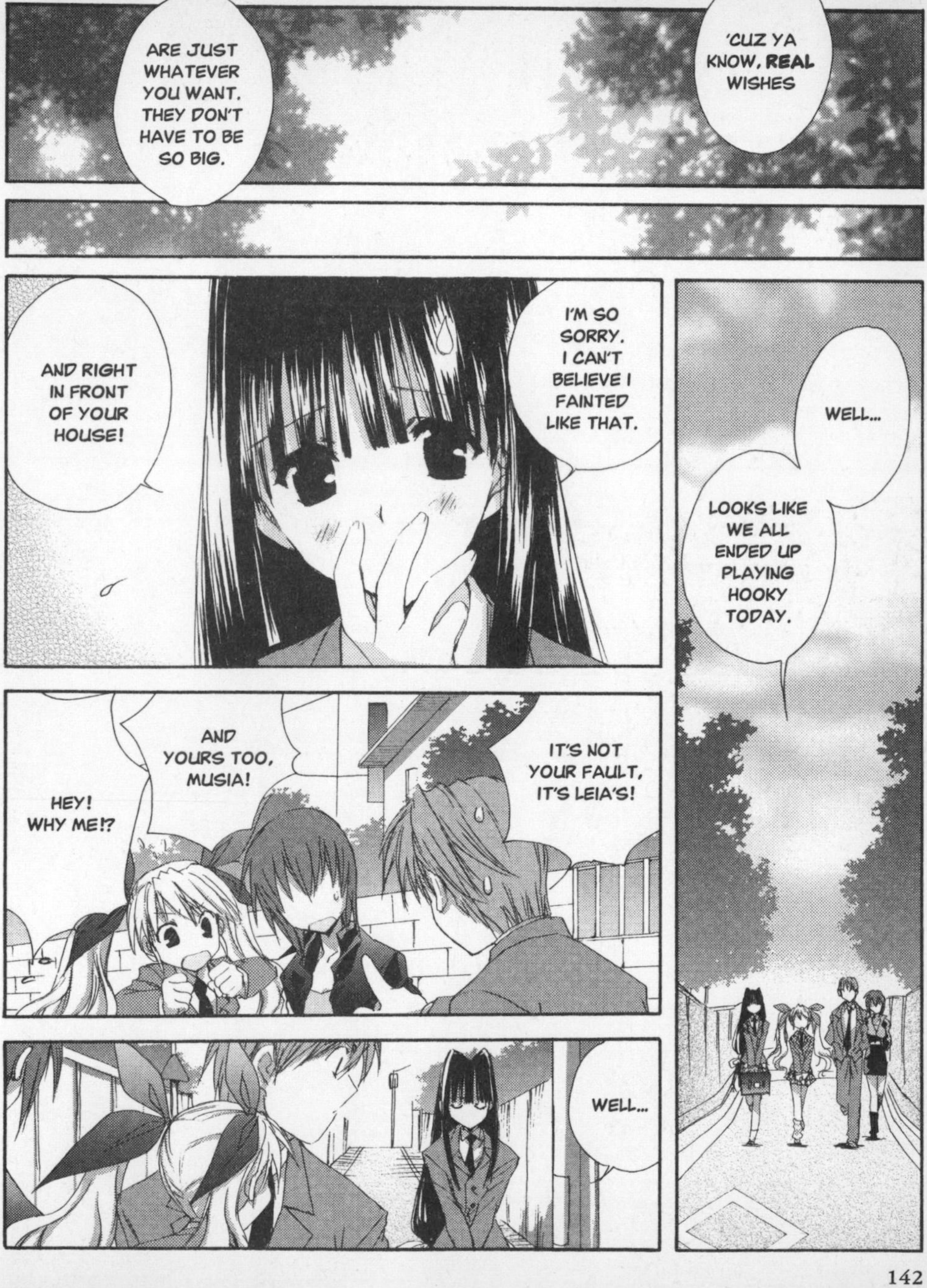
'CUZ YA KNOW, REAL WISHES
ARE JUST WHATEVER YOU WANT. THEY DON'T HAVE TO BE SO BIG.
WELL...
LOOKS LIKE WE ALL ENDED UP PLAYING HOOKY TODAY.
I'M SO SORRY. I CAN'T BELIEVE I FAINTED LIKE THAT.
AND RIGHT IN FRONT OF YOUR HOUSE!
IT'S NOT YOUR FAULT, IT'S LEIA'S!
AND YOURS TOO, MUSIA!
HEY! WHY ME!?
WELL...

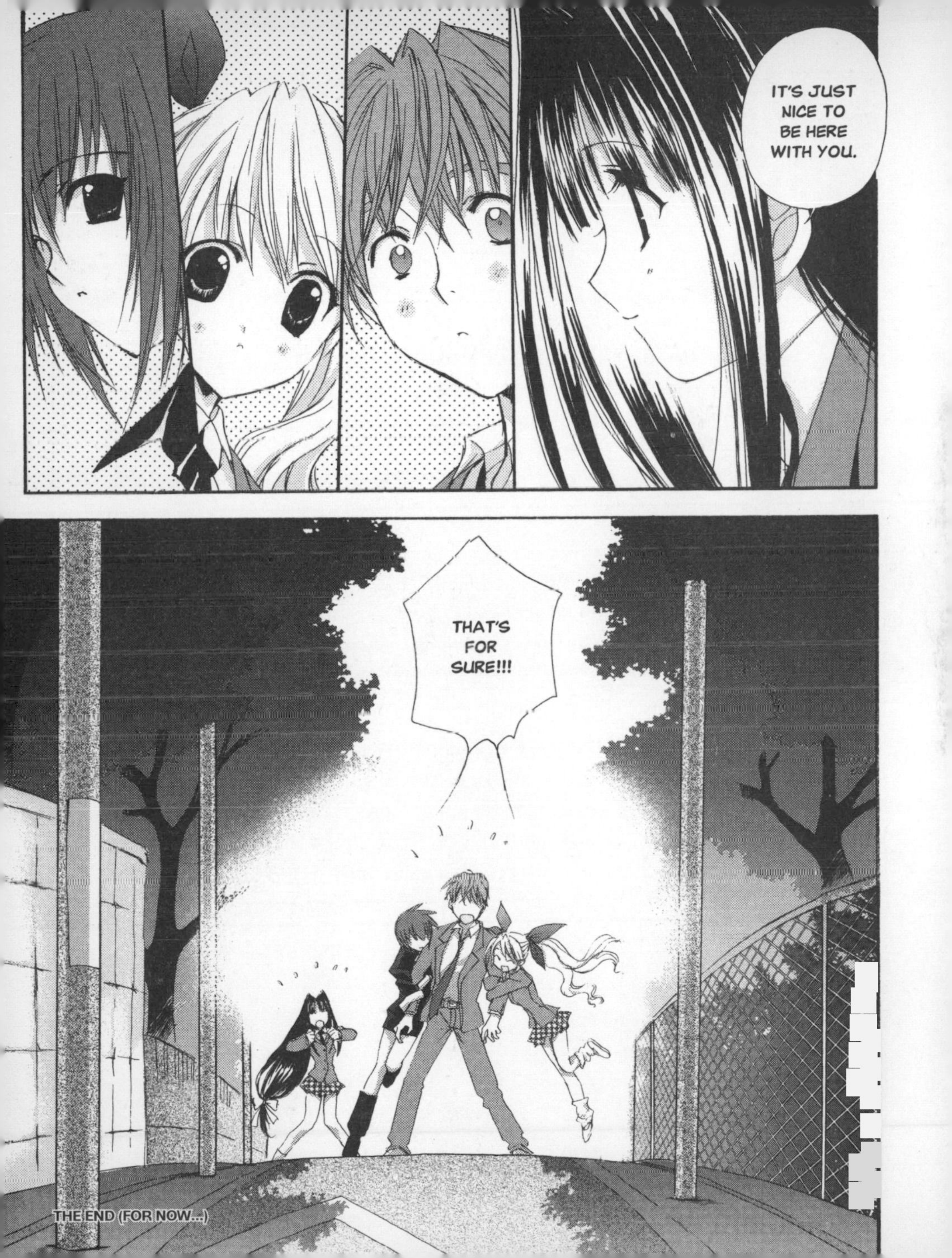
IT'S JUST NICE TO BE HERE WITH YOU.
THAT'S FOR SURE!!!
THE END (FOR NOW...)

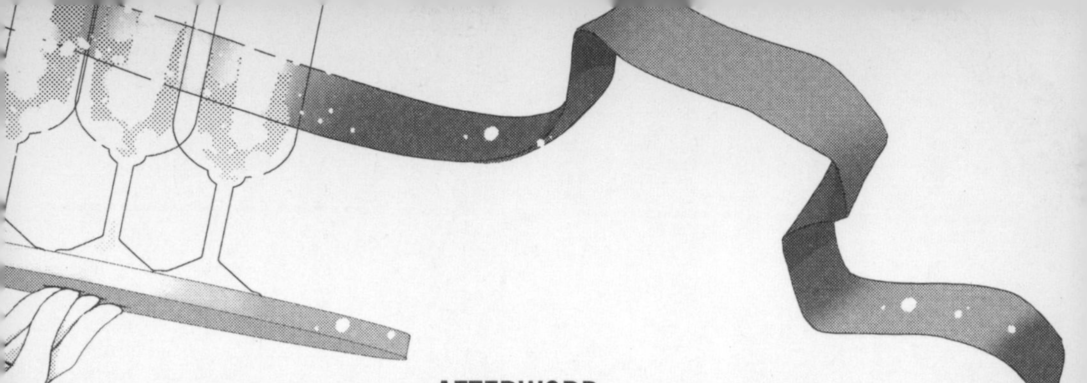

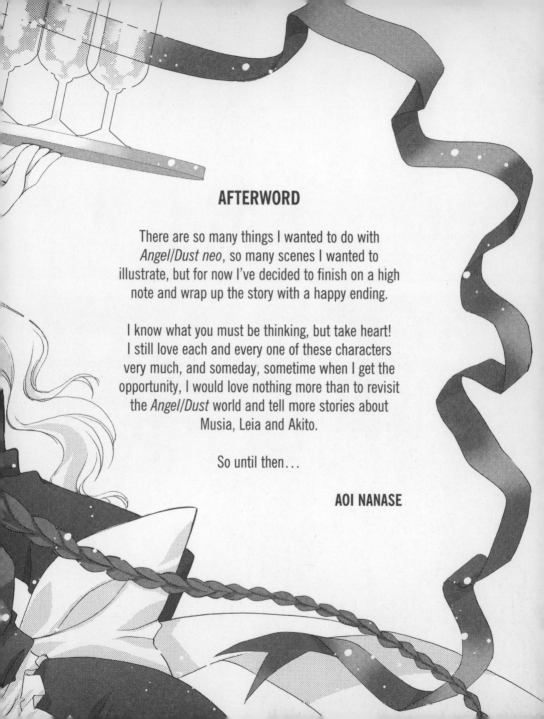

AFTERWORD

There are so many things I wanted to do with *Angel/Dust neo*, so many scenes I wanted to illustrate, but for now I've decided to finish on a high note and wrap up the story with a happy ending.

I know what you must be thinking, but take heart! I still love each and every one of these characters very much, and someday, sometime when I get the opportunity, I would love nothing more than to revisit the *Angel/Dust* world and tell more stories about Musia, Leia and Akito.

So until then…

AOI NANASE

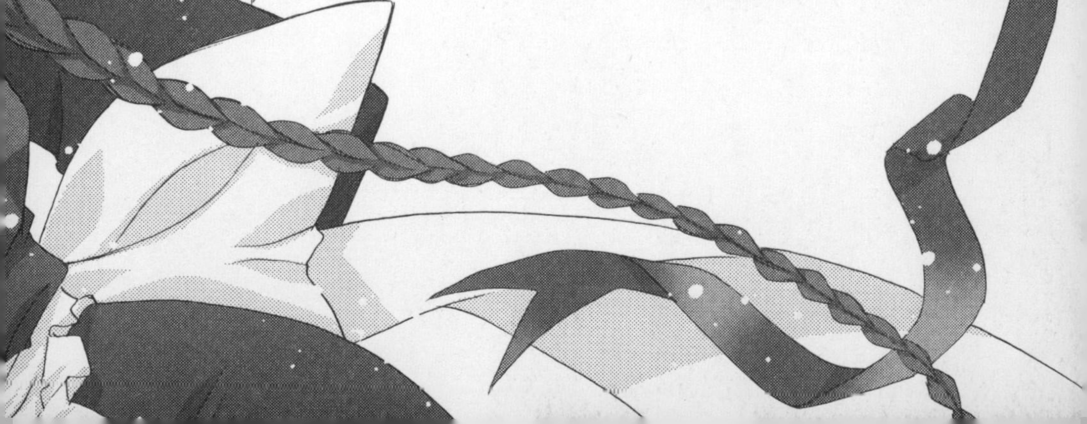

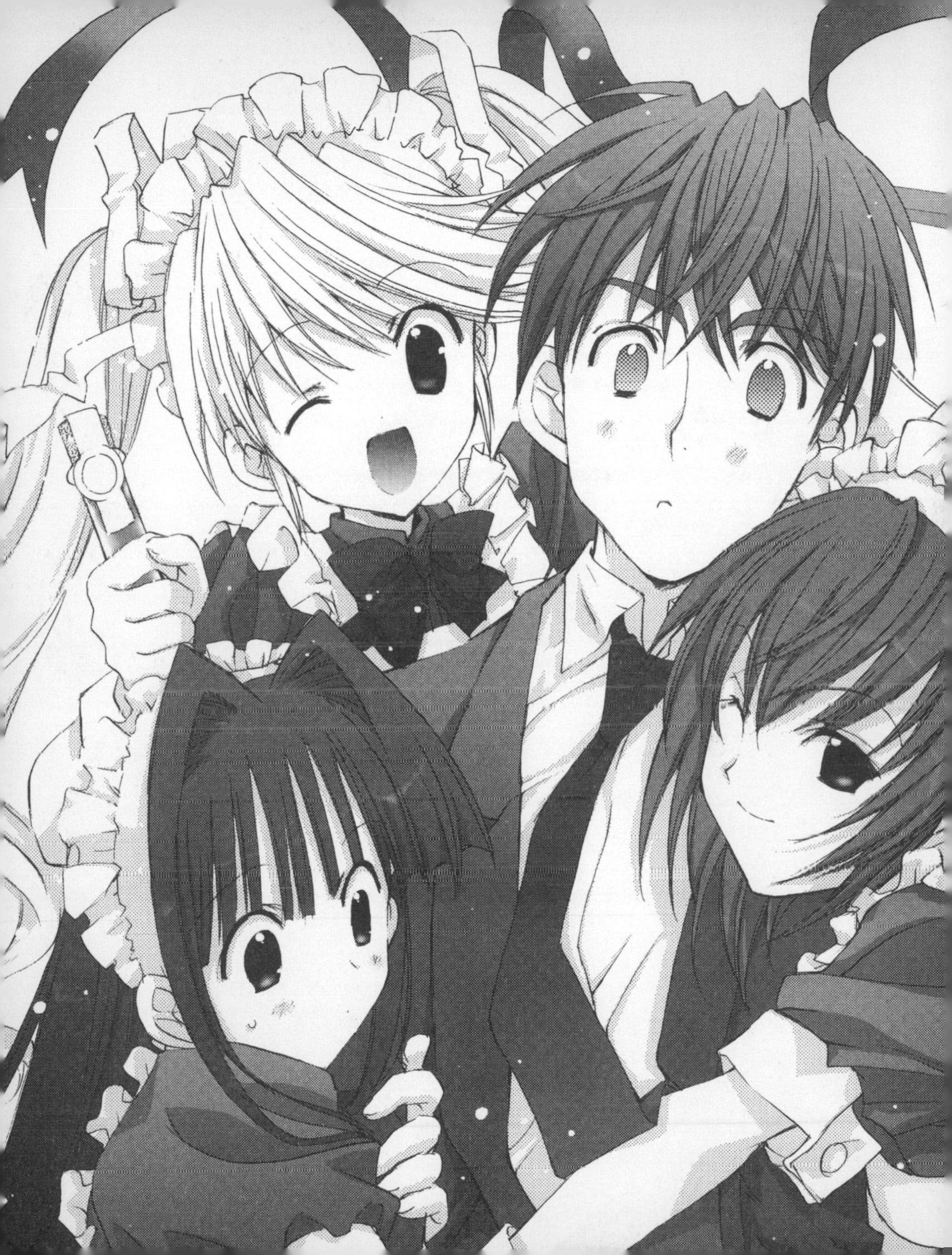

ANGEL / DUST NEO

© AOI NANASE 2003
ORIGINALLY PUBLISHED IN JAPAN IN 2003 BY KADOKAWA SHOTEN PUBLISHING CO., LTD., TOKYO.
ENGLISH TRANSLATION RIGHTS ARRANGED WITH KADOKAWA SHOTEN PUBLISHING CO., LTD., TOKYO.

Produced by the staff of *Newtype USA*

Lead Translator **JACK WIEDRICK**
Translators **HIROAKI FUKUDA, GINA KOERNER and TOMOE SPENCER**
Editors **PAIGE RECORD and CHRIS JOHNSTON**
Graphic Artists **SCOTT HOWARD and HEATHER GARY**

Editor in Chief **GARY STEINMAN**
Print Production Manager **BRIDGETT JANOTA**
Production Coordinator **MARISA KREITZ**

International Coordinators **MIYUKI KAMIYA and TORU IWAKAMI**

Publisher **JOHN LEDFORD**

Email: editor@adv-manga.com
www.adv-manga.com
www.advfilms.com

For sales and distribution inquiries please call 1.800.282.7202

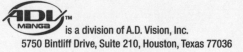

is a division of A.D. Vision, Inc.
5750 Bintliff Drive, Suite 210, Houston, Texas 77036

English text © 2005 published by A.D. Vision, Inc. under exclusive license.
ADV MANGA is a trademark of A.D. Vision, Inc.

ISBN: 978-1-4139-0353-9
First printing, January 2007
10 9 8 7 6 5 4 3 2 1
Printed in Canada

THE HIT MANGA FROM
NEWTYPE USA!

ANGEL/DUST

A SHY SOPHOMORE GETS CAUGHT UP
IN THE STRUGGLE BETWEEN GOOD AND EVIL

ADV
MANGA™
www.adv-manga.com

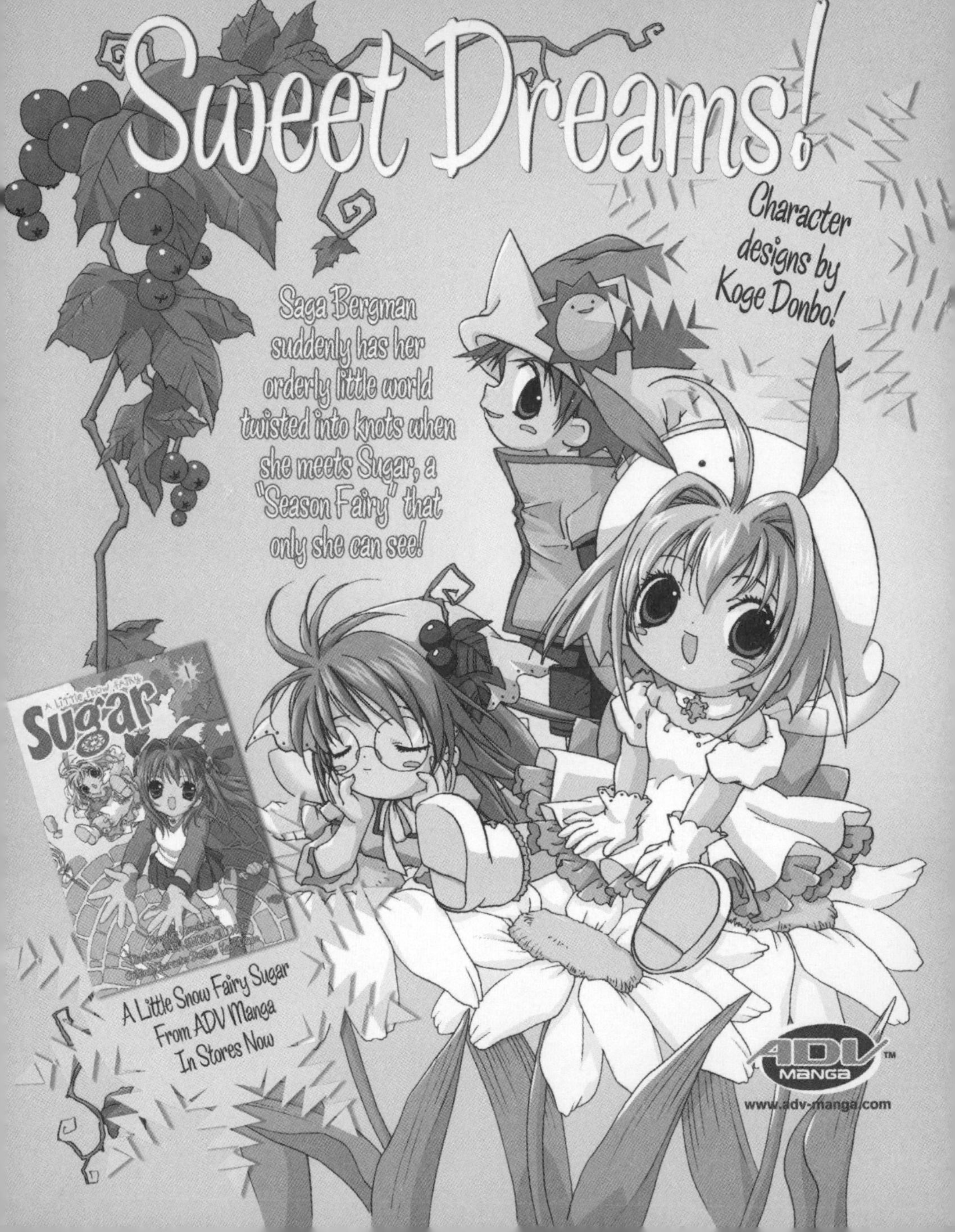
Sweet Dreams!
Character designs by Koge Donbo!
Saga Bergman suddenly has her orderly little world twisted into knots when she meets Sugar, a "Season Fairy" that only she can see!
A Little Snow Fairy
Sugar
1
A Little Snow Fairy Sugar From ADV Manga In Stores Now
ADV MANGA™
www.adv-manga.com

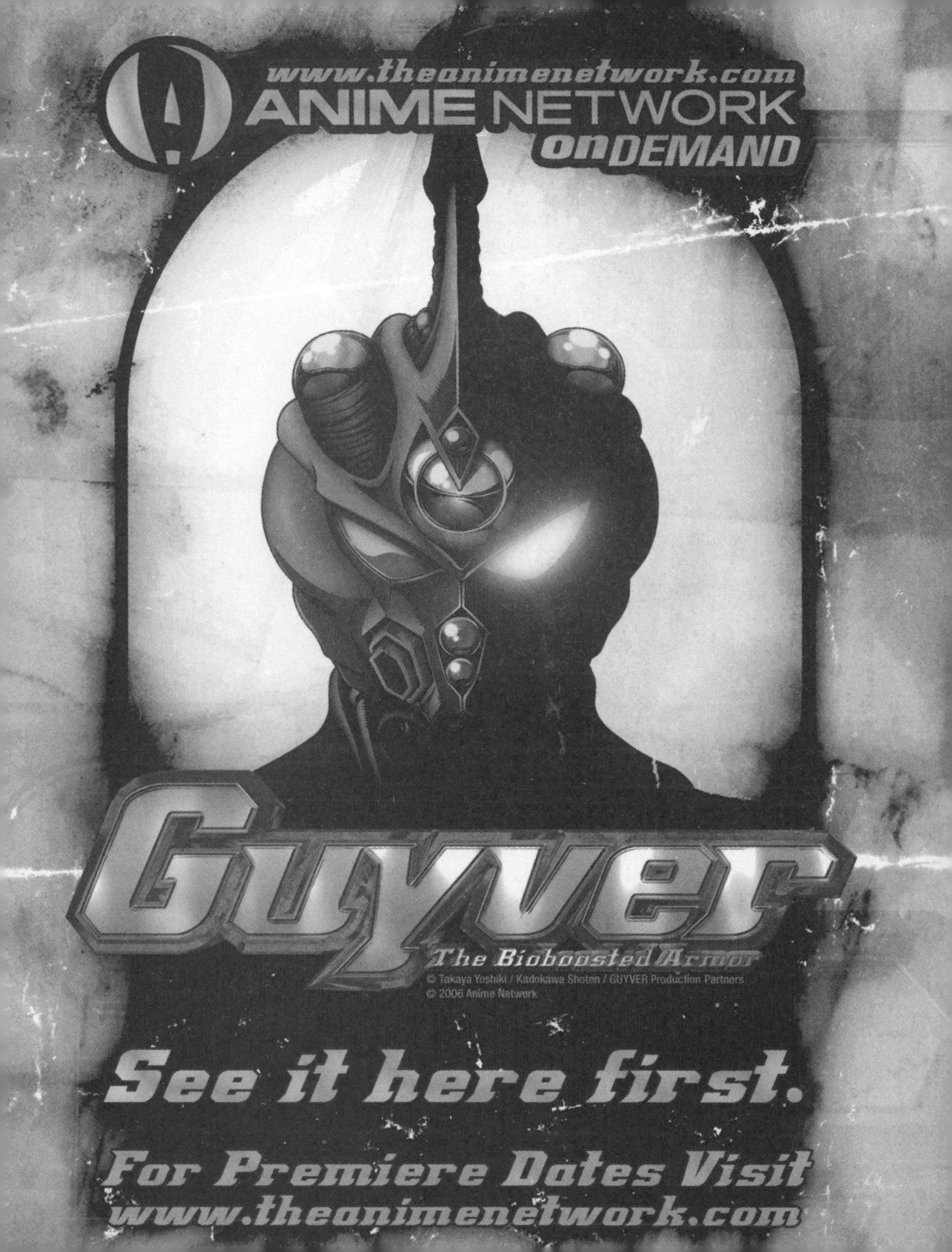

www.theanimenetwork.com
ANIME NETWORK
onDEMAND
Guyver
The Bioboosted Armor
© Takaya Yoshiki / Kadokawa Shoten / GUYVER Production Partners
© 2006 Anime Network
See it here first.
For Premiere Dates Visit
www.theanimenetwork.com

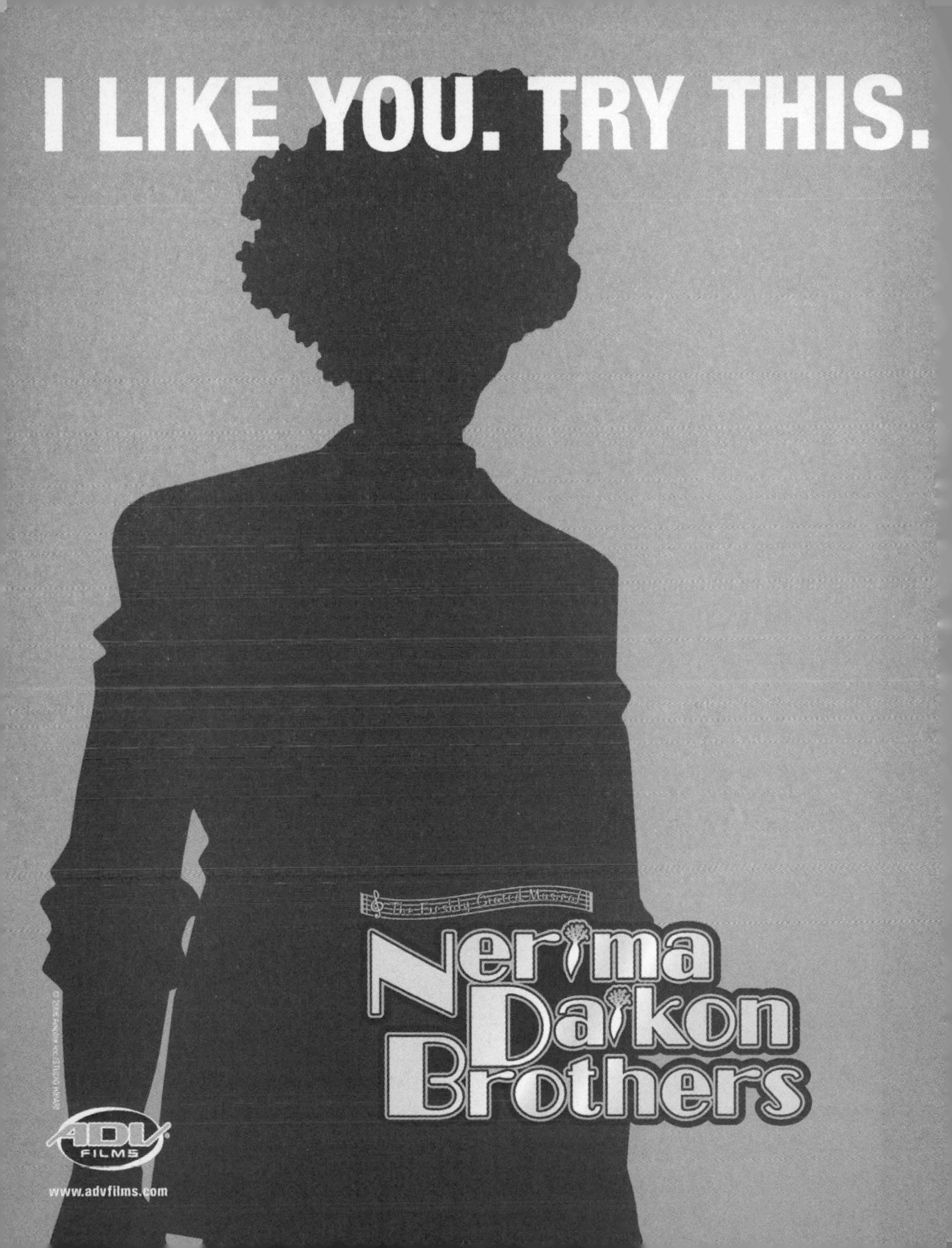

I LIKE YOU. TRY THIS.
The Freshly Grated Musical
Nerima Daikon Brothers
ADV FILMS
www.advfilms.com

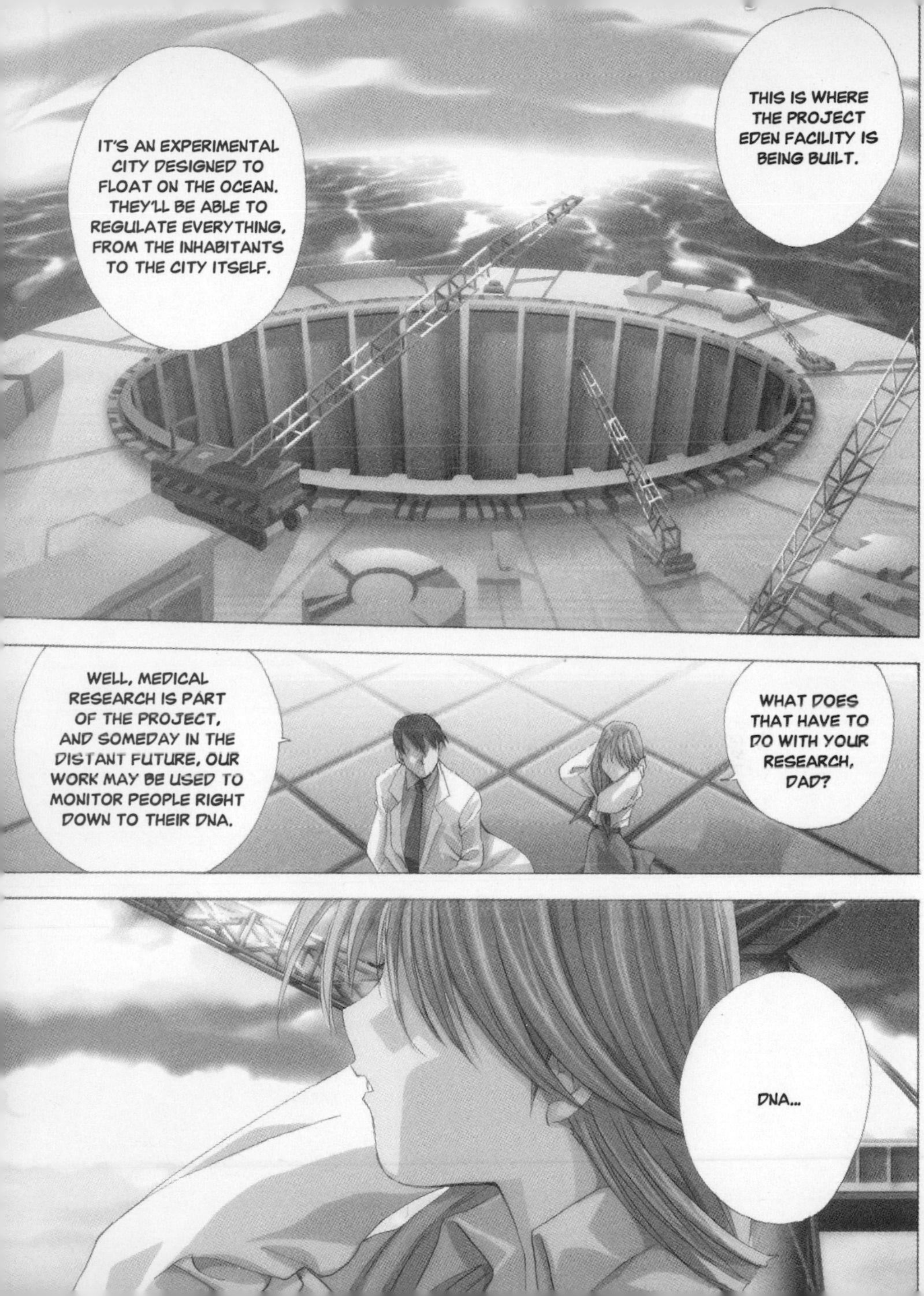
THIS IS WHERE THE PROJECT EDEN FACILITY IS BEING BUILT.
IT'S AN EXPERIMENTAL CITY DESIGNED TO FLOAT ON THE OCEAN. THEY'LL BE ABLE TO REGULATE EVERYTHING, FROM THE INHABITANTS TO THE CITY ITSELF.
WHAT DOES THAT HAVE TO DO WITH YOUR RESEARCH, DAD?
WELL, MEDICAL RESEARCH IS PART OF THE PROJECT, AND SOMEDAY IN THE DISTANT FUTURE, OUR WORK MAY BE USED TO MONITOR PEOPLE RIGHT DOWN TO THEIR DNA.
DNA...

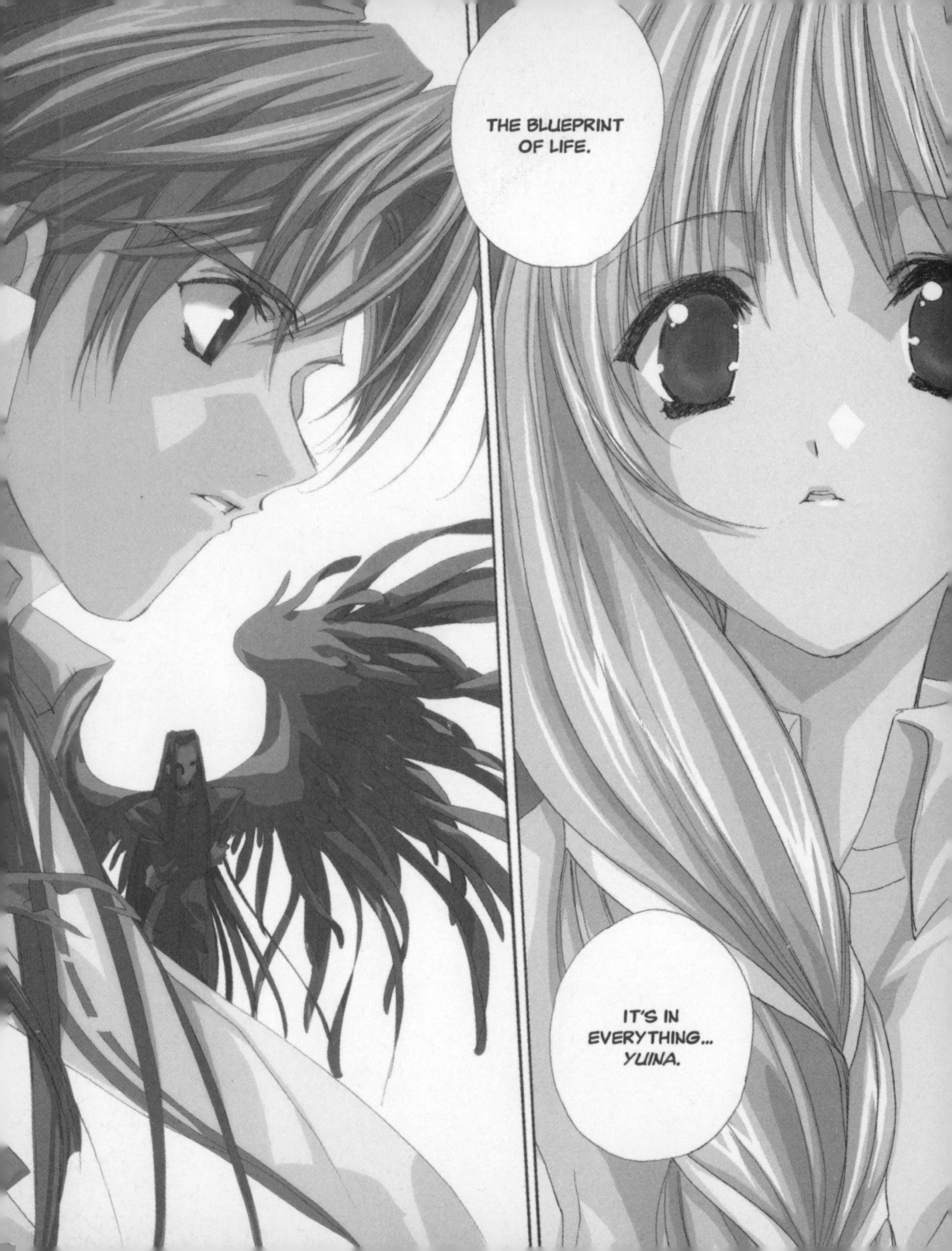
THE BLUEPRINT OF LIFE.
IT'S IN EVERYTHING... YUINA.